Woe to those who decree iniquitous decrees,
and the writers who keep writing oppression,
to turn aside the needy from justice,
and to rob the poor of my people of their right,
that widows may be their spoil,
and that they may make the fatherless their prey!
What will you do on the day of punishment,
In the storm which will come from afar?
To whom will you flee for help,
And where will you leave your wealth?

Isaiah 10:1-3, Revised Standard Version, Holy Bible

Ideas, both when they are right and when they are wrong, are more
powerful than is commonly understood. Indeed, the world is ruled by
little else.

John Maynard Keynes, quoted by Nicholas D. Kristof,
New York Times, 9 April 2009

Our default reflex is that the world knows what it is doing, and this is
extravagant nonsense.

Jeremy Grantham, *New York Times,* 6 June 2009

Economic injustice erodes human capital.
Challenged households blight human lives.

The recent global crisis of political economies, whose consequences
continue, shows how the impulses of the human spirit can go wrong,
causing catastrophes to many households and misery to even more. The
recession is not just a crisis of economies. It's a crisis of the human spirit.

Lewis Mudge, notes for this book, early September 2009

We Can Make the World Economy a Sustainable Global Home

Lewis S. Mudge

Edited by
Jean McClure Mudge

WILLIAM B. EERDMANS PUBLISHING COMPANY
GRAND RAPIDS, MICHIGAN / CAMBRIDGE, U.K.

Published 2014 by
Wm. B. Eerdmans Publishing Co.
2140 Oak Industrial Drive N.E., Grand Rapids, Michigan 49505 /
P.O. Box 163, Cambridge CB3 9PU U.K.

Printed in the United States of America

20 19 18 17 16 15 14   7 6 5 4 3 2

Library of Congress Cataloging-in-Publication Data

Mudge, Lewis Seymour, 1929-2009.
    We can make the world economy a sustainable global home /
    Lewis S. Mudge; edited by Jean McClure Mudge.
        pages   cm
    Includes bibliographical references and index.
    ISBN 978-0-8028-6987-6 (pbk.: alk. paper)
    1. Economics — Religious aspects — Christianity. 2. Economics — Religious aspects.
    3. Sustainability. 4. Christianity and other religions. 5. Abrahamic religions.
    I. Mudge, Jean McClure, 1933-   II. Title.

BR115.E3M74   2014
261.8′5 — dc23

                                                    2013044459

www.eerdmans.com

Contents

Foreword

Lew Mudge and I, as the saying goes, "go back a long way." In a sense, we began at the same time and place, as members of the entering freshman Class of 1951 at Princeton University in 1947. But during and after those college days, our paths diverged widely, only to converge in a remarkable way some four decades later. We would remain on strikingly parallel paths in the years that followed. In this foreword, I tell that story.

Different Educational Experiences

In college, I recall (through the mists of time) Lew as one of the shining stars of our class. He was a serious but friendly young man, with little time (and likely little patience) for the high-jinks of our still less-than-mature classmates. (We were all males. Coeducation didn't arrive until 1969.) Lew majored in religion, graduated with High Honors, earned a Rhodes Scholarship, and attended Oxford. When he returned from England to the United States, he entered Princeton Theological Seminary and was awarded a Master of Divinity degree, and later, a Ph.D. from the Department of Religion, Princeton University.

In my four years at Princeton, I also recall being, well, serious and friendly. But early on, I struggled with academic challenges, nearly losing my scholarship, which would have ended my college years. I was also struggling financially, spending much time and effort first as a waiter in Commons and then as manager of the Athletic Association's student ticket office. Over the years, my grades improved. An economics major, I wrote my senior thesis on the "tiny but contentious" mutual fund industry. Against all odds, the thesis earned High Honors. But I never even considered graduate school, and within a month of commencement, I was hard at work in my first full-time job.

Different Careers

In the years that followed, Lew's career marked him as a true "pillar of the church." He became the first theological secretary for what is now the World Communion of Reformed Churches in Geneva; then professor of philosophy and religion as well as chaplain to the college at Amherst College; then Dean at two major theological seminaries, earning high positions in the Presbyterian Church hierarchy along the way. In addition to innumerable essays, papers, and tracts, Lew wrote several books, including his last, *The Gift of Responsibility*. Before his death in 2009, he had drafted much of *We Can Make the World Economy a Sustainable Global Home*. It's fair to say that Lew Mudge lived as he died — doing the Lord's work, with honor, excellence, and integrity.

In its skeletal outline, my own career could hardly have been more different. I was a mere layman, focused on business and finance, spending my entire sixty-two-year career (and counting!) in that very mutual fund industry on which I had penned my Princeton thesis. When I started that career, the industry — pretty much bereft of young college graduates — would soon be on the way to become one of the fastest-growing businesses in America (fund assets under management in 1951, $2.5 billion; in 2013, $12 trillion).

My career, dare I say, had its ups and downs. First, a meteoric rise at Wellington Management Company (where founder Walter L. Morgan had hired me, largely because of that thesis). In 1965 he asked me to take charge of the firm. A year later, I made an incredibly stupid decision: to merge the traditionally conservative firm with a far smaller firm led by aggressive, risk-oriented managers. Our fall from grace in the great bear market in stocks (down 50 percent in 1973-74) struck me down. In January 1974, I was fired for my failure and the near-collapse of the mutual funds that we managed. But in September 1974, out of the ashes of that defeat, I created a new mutual fund firm. I named it Vanguard. It would have a new vision, a unique structure designed to serve investors, and an investment strategy that would, decades later, make it by far the largest firm in our industry. We were on our way.

A Similar Passion for Reform

And it is at that very point, almost thirty-nine years ago, that the then-utterly-disparate career paths began to converge for the churchman and the businessman from Princeton's Class of 1951. In the years that followed, we would both become reformers, energetically challenging the status quo in our respective fields.

As he climbed to the upper ranks in Presbyterian clergy, Lew's career was diverse. His role in the academy — as a teacher, leader, and inspirer of collegians and seminarians alike — was accompanied by a prodigious output of essays and numerous books with new ideas for reform in the church. He also personally leaped into controversy, most notably leading student activists to the South during the civil rights struggles of the 1960s.

Perhaps unusual among our nation's clergy, Lew had a longstanding concern for our nation's economic life and values, especially after the September 11, 2001, attack culminating in the destruction of New York's World Trade Center towers. His concern was further sparked by the near-meltdown of the global financial system during 2007-9. Lew focused on comity among the three Abrahamic faiths and urged Christians, Muslims, and Jews to join in seeking a fundamental change in the way we define ourselves in our world political economy. He was hard at work on this project of reconciliation and reform until the day of his death late in 2009.

My own career in the money business through the mid-1980s displayed few, if any, similarities with Lew's career in religion and faith. Yet the creation of a new mutual fund model was also a fundamental reform. Vanguard, uniquely, was designed to serve the interest of fund shareholders rather than fund managers. We focused on simple investment strategies (notably creating the world's first index mutual fund, designed to match the returns of the stock market at rock-bottom costs), and established "Golden Rule" human values aimed at serving our clients and crew alike (we sought neither "customers" nor "employees"). From a slow start, we gradually gained huge (and ultimately virtually unstoppable) momentum in the marketplace. I developed a passion for extending those reforms beyond Vanguard to the broader mutual fund industry, and, later to the U.S. financial system as a whole. A large challenge? Of course! Indeed, a task nearly as overwhelming as Lew Mudge's efforts for religious reform and global comity.

Two Different Paths Converge

Lew Mudge sought a new global political economy. He articulately describes our societal weakness, and tells us what needs to be done:

> In traditional theological terms, this crisis has taught us very little, if anything, new about ourselves, about human nature. We are full of avarice. We cheat our fellow human beings. It is hard to think or act in terms of the public good. Reinhold Niebuhr had it about right in *The Nature and Destiny of Man* (1941): humanity creates evil through its deep-seated pride; even the "good" among us are quite corruptible, and perfectibility is beyond our grasp. We will resist regulation, and if it is enacted, we will try to evade it. Our fundamental self-interest is only expanded when, for the most part, economic science is taught and business practices are constructed to place second, marginalize, or even omit questions of the public good. . . . Economics needs to be reconnected and integrated with its humanistic roots, especially with the principal Abrahamic faith traditions — Judaism, Christianity, and Islam — with their rich interreligious histories, their numerical majority among the world's religions, and their global presence.

> Perhaps humanists, including believers, could start the process by seeing themselves as "economic actors" or *"economes,"* who invite secularists and economists as fellow actors to enter into a "tactical collaboration." On their side, humanists could reevaluate money as not merely hard coin, but rather, an expression of our spirit: both a token of exchanging our capabilities and also a form of portable energy to be applied imaginatively wherever and however we may wish. As the "substance" of life-together, money could then be seen as a transparent tool of our evolution and culture. (Of course, when misused, distorted, or corrupted — gone bad — money becomes mere "mammon," gains from sheer greed.) In return, secularists and economists might be led to respect a realm of meaning beyond mathematical reasoning and acknowledge money's spiritual force.

> . . . I envision a political economy organized to bring blessing to earth's households: a way of doing things at the whole-earth level that makes for all human beings to be known, nurtured, and cared for; and that brings goodness and blessing into the world rather than curse. The kinds of political economies we create tell much about who we are and who we might become as a species.

I came to seek similar reforms in my field. In *The Battle for the Soul of Capitalism* (Yale University Press, 2005), I excoriated the change from owners capitalism to managers capitalism. In *Enough.* (John Wiley, 2007), I quoted T. S. Eliot's "Choruses from 'The Rock'": "Where is the Life we have lost in living? . . . / The cycles of Heaven in twenty centuries / Bring us farther from God and nearer to the Dust." In the same book, I quoted from the sermon given by the Right Rev. Richard Chartres, Bishop of London, in St. Paul's Cathedral on October 23, 2005, the 200th anniversary of the Battle of Trafalgar:

> . . . at times of decision, leaders need to make contact with foundational convictions and with a sense of calling which comes from going deep within oneself. . . . Yet we live at a strange time when the periodic table and anything that can be quantified and reduced to a mathematical truth is regarded as an accurate description of reality, but the Beatitudes and the teachings of the world's wisdom traditions are seen as little more than the debatable opinions of dead sages.

"A Crisis of Ethic Proportions"

The ultimate convergence of our missions was perhaps best reflected in my op-ed essay published in *The Wall Street Journal* in April 2009, as the global economic meltdown was beginning to abate. It was titled "A Crisis of Ethic Proportions." Some excerpts:

> The fields of commerce, business, and finance have hardly been exempt from this trend. Relying on Adam Smith's "invisible hand," through which our own self-interest advances the interests of our communities, our society had come to rely on the marketplace and open competition to create prosperity and well-being.

> But that self-interest developed into a "bottom line" society in which success is largely measured in monetary terms. Dollars became the coin of the new realm. Unchecked market forces totally overwhelmed traditional standards of professional conduct, developed over centuries.

> The result has been a change in our society, from one in which "there are some things that one simply does not do," to one in which "if everyone else is doing it, I can do it too" — a shift from moral absolutism to moral

relativism. Business ethics has been a major casualty of that shift in our traditional societal values, and the idea of professional standards has been lost in the shuffle.

We seem to forget that the driving force of any profession includes . . . the duty to serve responsibly, selflessly, and wisely, and to establish an inherently ethical relationship between professionals and the society they serve. The old notion of trusting and being trusted — which once was not only the accepted standard of business conduct but the key to success in the marketplace — came to be seen as a quaint anachronism, a relic of an era long gone.

The malfeasance and misjudgments by our corporate, financial, and government leaders, declining ethical standards, and the failure of our new agency society reflect a failure of capitalism. . . . We must set about establishing a "fiduciary society," one in which our manager/agents who are entrusted with the responsibility for other people's money are required — by federal statute — to place front and center the interests of the owner/ principals whom they are duty-bound to serve. . . . It will be no easy task.

I'm confident that Lew Mudge, my Princeton classmate of all those years earlier, would enthusiastically endorse those values.

A Wonderful Book

We Can Make the World Economy a Sustainable Global Home offers a fine perspective on where we've been, where we stand today, and where we must now aim in the eternal search for peace. As Lew suggests, prosperity is an important part of that search. Today's disparities of wealth among the world's nations — and within those nations — have always existed and will never vanish from this earth. But the egregious inequality we have today threatens the very social fabric that holds us together, and if we are not conscious of the need for greater equity among our peoples — and work diligently toward that end — surely trouble lies ahead.

For the reader with strong religious convictions, the reader who seeks restoration of faith, the reader who has been a successful entrepreneur, the reader whose financial wealth places him or her in the upper echelons of our society, and perhaps most of all the reader who has prospered on Wall Street, it is fair to place Lew's book on the "must-read" list. We must do our best to keep an open mind to new ideas, particularly those outside our own parochial careers.

Yet I fear that *introspection* is becoming one of the vanishing values of our society. Reflection about the larger purposes of economic wealth surely has played a major role in my own career and in the financial reform it embodies. This introspection has played an important role in serving our society at large, and reform will play an ever-larger role in the years ahead. Yes, now is the time for "resetting who we are," and Lew Mudge's sound ideas will help us achieve that goal.

JOHN C. BOGLE
Valley Forge, PA
January 2013

Introduction

Approaching his eightieth birthday on 11 September 2009, Lew Mudge died peacefully and at home. That day was the eighth anniversary of the surprise attack on the World Trade Center's twin towers, icons of wealth and power. It also coincided with the second year of global economic instability now known as the "Great Recession."[1] These two interconnected and far-reaching events at the century's start, one shortly after the other, were the principal motivations for Mudge's last two books: *The Gift of Responsibility* (2008),[2] and now this one, *We Can Make the World Economy a Sustainable Global Home*. They are, in fact, companion studies. This current book builds on *Gift*'s vision of an interfaith covenantal humanism as a platform for international peace, and applies that concept, with important additions, to global political economic theory.

As the 2007 downturn became a full-fledged recession, Mudge recognized that this financial crisis would have lasting and widespread consequences for those who were its most predictable victims. His search for an explanation of its root causes and his in-depth analysis of humanity in its present economic and spiritual state assure the continuing timeliness of this book. In fact, a plea from two scholars (one in public policy and the other in law) for the sort of moral voice and humanistic language that Mudge offers appeared in September 2011 in a *New York Times* article, titled "How Do You

---

1. Chris Isidore, senior writer CNNMoney.com, "It's Official: Recession since December '07," money.cnn.com/2008/12/01/news/economy/recession/index.htm. Paul Krugman has even labeled the crisis a depression, as in his latest book *End This Depression Now!* (New York: W. W. Norton, 2012).

2. *The Gift of Responsibility: The Promise of Dialogue Among Christians, Jews, and Muslims* (New York: Continuum, 2008).

Say 'Economic Security'?"[3] In these pages, Mudge lays out an exploration of this and other penetrating questions about the ethical roots of economic thinking.

An even larger framework for Mudge — because a vital part of his life perspective — was evident in his reaction to the widely noted joint birthday of Charles Darwin and Abraham Lincoln on 12 February 2009. For Mudge, Darwin and Lincoln exemplified his longstanding belief in the Hegelian idea of an ongoing evolution and refinement of human consciousness. Their accomplishments stood as earthly expressions of *Geist,* or Objective Spirit, working itself out in history — of Consciousness becoming more explicitly conscious of itself through humanity. Mudge had a favorite term for gifted persons who represented this Spirit: "carriers" he called them. Carriers made Spirit explicit while also exemplifying enlarged human capabilities. Put another way: both Darwin and Lincoln enhanced civilization, thereby advancing *Geist*'s concrete presence in the world. Directly or indirectly, this assumption appears everywhere in these pages.

Although the economy has somewhat improved, higher income earners have been the chief beneficiaries.[4] In other sectors of society, the recession's penetrating effects that Mudge observed in 2009 are still with us. The rescue programs designed to keep the middle class afloat that began soon after the collapse were unfulfilled in late summer 2011. Business journalist Gretchen Morgenson observed, "Main Street is in a world of hurt, facing high unemployment, rampant foreclosures and ravaged retirement accounts."[5] In late

---

3. Theodore R. Marmor and Jerry L. Mashaw, "How Do You Say 'Economic Security'?" Op-Ed, *New York Times,* 24 September 2011, p. A19. Commenting on this article, Martha Holstein, professor of healthcare ethics at Loyola University, wrote, "Richly evocative moral ideals as reflected in language matter; they are powerful indicators of what we as a nation value and what we will fight for." Letter to the Editor, *New York Times,* 1 October 2011, p. A18. Writing more generally, Adam Gopnik comments, "[T]he horizon of the good life that is included in what we have called, since the Renaissance, humanism [is] the belief that, while our lives should be devoted to happiness, they're impoverished without an idea of happiness deeper than mere property-bound prosperity." Adam Gopnik, "Decline, Fall, Rinse, Repeat," *The New Yorker,* 12 September 2011, p. 47.

4. A June 2013 survey showed higher-income households, the top third of all consumers, more optimistic about their incomes and wealth than lower-income households, or 66 percent of all buyers. Reuters, "Consumer Sentiment Ended June Near a Six-Year High," *New York Times,* 28 June 2013, http://www.nytimes.com/2013/06/29/business/economy/consumer-sentiment-ended-june-near-a-six-year-high.html?_r=0.

5. Gretchen Morgenson, "The Rescue That Missed Main Street," *New York Times,* 28 August 2011, Sunday Business, p. BU1.

2012, improvements were reported in housing, consumer confidence, and selected investment in machinery and equipment. But the U.S. growth rate deceased from 2.7 percent in the third quarter of 2012 to a near-stall rate of 0.4 percent in the fourth. And the first-quarter estimate of higher growth in 2013 had to be adjusted downward by 25 percent.[6] The danger of sliding back into recession is far from over. By early summer 2013, the unemployment rate was up to 7.6 percent, from 7.5 percent in April, and income was flat.[7] A positive housing outlook also looked premature to Robert J. Shiller, an eminent Yale economist.[8] And a new threat heightens this caution: certain Wall Street investment houses (e.g., the Blackstone Group, Colony Capital, Carrington Holding Company) have been buying quantities of depressed housing to renovate as rentals, quickly pushing up prices, and encouraging sell-offs. If they should snowball, another downturn could result. Meanwhile, these absentee landlords cut out average buyers seeking single-family homes as fixer-uppers.[9]

Another expert's 2011 list of worst-case scenarios still looms in 2013 with this uncertainty: "whether the international financial system will survive the next six months in the form we now know it."[10] In Europe, unprecedented problems face the euro zone in covering the debts of its poorer nations — Greece, Ireland, and Portugal — and the internal finances of its leading ones — Britain, France, and Germany. Fixing Europe's woes is predicted to be a long process.[11] Paul Krugman declares that the international policy of aus-

6. Lucia Mutikani, "U.S. First-Quarter Growth Is Cut," *New York Times*, 26 June 2013, http://www.nytimes.com/reuters/2013/06/26/business/26reuters-usa-economy.html?_r=0.

7. Catherine Rampell, "Middling Jobs Numbers Signal a Long Path to Healthy Payrolls," *New York Times*, 7 June 2013, http://www.nytimes.com/2013/06/08/business/economy/us -added-175000-jobs-in-may-jobless-rate-rises-to-7-6.html?_r=0.

8. Nelson D. Schwartz, "U.S. Growth Revised Up, but Year-End Slowdown Is Feared," *New York Times*, Business, 30 November 2012, http://www.nytimes.com/2012/11/30/business/economy/ third-quarter-gdp-growth-is-revised-up-to-2-7.html?_r=0; Nelson D. Schwartz, "Economy Contracted Unexpectedly in Fourth Quarter," http://www.nytimes.com/2013/01/31/business/ economy/us-economy-unexpectedly-contracted-in-fourth-quarter.html?_r=0. Robert J. Shiller, "A New Housing Boom? Don't Count on It," *New York Times*, 26 January 2013, http://www.nytimes .com/2013/01/27/business/housing-markets-future-still-has-many-clouds.html?_r=0.

9. Nathaniel Popper, "Behind the Rise in House Prices, Wall Street Buyers," 3 June 2013, *New York Times*, http://dealbook.nytimes.com/2013/06/03/behind-the-rise-in -house-prices-wall-street-buyers/.

10. David Brooks quoting foreign policy expert Walter Russell Mead, "The Lost Decade?" Op-Ed, *New York Times*, 26 September 2011, p. A27.

11. "Be afraid," *The Economist*, 1 October 2011, p. 13; Graham Bowley and Liz Alderman, "In European Crisis, Little Hope for a Quick Fix," *New York Times*, 30 September 2011, p. A1; see

terity rather than stimulus has amounted to "A Big Fail," with little evidence of change.[12] Simultaneously, the U.S. poverty level has reached its highest level (46.2 million people or 15.1 percent of the population) in the fifty-two years since the Census Bureau has kept such records.[13] Consumer spending is up on certain luxuries, but down on practical products, thus stalling business investment. The poor, of course, suffer even more than the middle class, and their ranks are increasing. Although extreme poverty (less than $1.25/day income) appears to be fast diminishing, especially in developing countries, the worldwide problem of everyday poverty remains.[14]

A spate of book-length studies focusing on the economic crisis alone has appeared in the last few years. But the ethical dimension of the problem has been noted by only a handful, and then, not with any sustained focus.

---

also editorial, "More of the Same Won't Save Europe," same issue, p. A20; Jack Ewing, "Lowering Forecast, European Central Bank Keeps Rate Steady," *New York Times*, 6 June 2013, http://www .nytimes.com/2013/06/07/business/global/ecb-keeps-interest-rates-unchanged-in-hopes-for -recovery.html?_r=0. See also Landon Thomas Jr., "Financial Fears Gain Credence as Unrest Shakes Turkey," *New York Times*, 5 June 2013, http://www.nytimes.com/2013/06/06/world/ europe/financial-fears-as-street-unrest-shakes-turkey.html?pagewanted=1.

12. And this despite the International Monetary Fund's admission in January 2013 that practicing austerity was a mistake; the European Central Bank, the British government, and other nations are still advocating austerity. Paul Krugman, "The Big Fail," *New York Times*, 7 January 2013, http://www.nytimes.com/2013/01/07/opinion/krugman-the-big-fail.html?_r =0. See also Anne Lowrey, "I.M.F. Concedes Major Missteps in Bailout of Greece," *New York Times*, 5 June 2013, http://www.nytimes.com/2013/06/06/business/global/imf-concedes-major -missteps-in-bailout-of-greece.html. Martin Wolf, chief economic commentator for the *Financial Times*, flatly states that austerity in the euro zone has failed, freezing the start of recovery and causing stagnation, but he also notes, "It is not too late to change course." "How Austerity Has Failed," *The New York Review of Books*, 11 July 2013, pp. 20-21.

13. Sabrina Tavernise, "Soaring Poverty Casts Spotlight on 'Lost Decade,'" *New York Times*, 14 September 2011, http://www.nytimes.com/2011/09/14/us/14census.htm. Adam Gopnik, "Decline, Fall, Rinse, Repeat," *The New Yorker*, 12 September 2011, p. 47. Fortunately, safety-net features in the economy proved their worth by keeping poverty from escalating even more than it might have. Jared Bernstein, "Lessons of the Great Recession: How the Safety Net Performed," *New York Times*, 24 June 2013, http://economix.blogs.nytimes.com/2013/06/24/ lessons-of-the-great-recession-how-the-safety-net-performed/?_r=0. In late 2013, poverty in America — occurring in both urban and rural settings — averaged over 50%. However, in any one case, it was normally short-lived. Mark R. Rank, "Poverty in America Is Mainstream," *New York Times*, 2 November 2013, http://opinionator.blogs.nytimes.com/2013/11/02/ poverty-in-america-is-mainstream/?_r=0.

14. Jim Wallis, "Who Didn't Win the Presidential Debate?" Hearts and Minds, Sojomail, 4 October 2012, SojoMail@sojo.net. In the past twenty years, the extreme poverty rate has been reduced globally by 50 percent. "Poverty: Not Always with Us," *The Economist*, 1-7 June 2013, pp. 22-24.

Apart from Jim Wallis's *Rediscovering Values: A Guide for Economic and Moral Recovery* (2011), a solid evangelical Christian guidebook to more ethical and egalitarian economic practices, these books have not done much more than ask us to pull up our moral socks. Former UK prime minister Gordon Brown's *Beyond the Crash: Overcoming the First Crisis of Globalization* and Stephen Green's *Good Value: Reflections on Money, Morality, and an Uncertain World*, both of 2010, were followed by Tomas Sedlacek's *Economics of Good and Evil: The Quest for Economic Meaning from Gilgamesh to Wall Street* in 2011. Other recent books on the sociology of this "second depression" emphasize America's loss of faith in both business and government. According to George Packer's review, they reveal a desperate return to an Emersonian individualism "by way of Napoleon Hill to Oprah Winfrey." For many, gone are any workmen heroes, while the middle class has solidly slipped into the lower class. Packer plays down the efforts of Occupy Wall Street as a vision without adequate numerical support in this "age of individuals."[15]

Mudge's book is different. Not only does he see the recent crisis as arising from a great moral meltdown, but to reverse course and move toward a lasting recovery, he suggests a new definition of humanity: *Homo oeconomicus* with deeply spiritual and social dimensions. From this "reset" of our fundamental identity, everyone's voice may be universally heard and valued. To give context and concrete historical models, he asks for the pooling of common energies, insights, and wisdom about economic matters that the Abrahamic religions may share, compare, refine, and offer to the world. Like everyone, Mudge sees the crisis and its ramifications as a clear disaster. But noting that it told us "some old truths in new ways," he reads it as an "opportunity."[16] He likens the recession to an earthquake whose fissures opened to wider view previously known, but tolerated, problems: social and economic inequities embedded throughout our society, especially in financial institutions — from banks, mortgage companies, and hedge funds — to certain common business practices and beyond. Since these institutions are reflections of our values, he calls for the reexamination of such fundamental matters. In short, he finds the recession a great "springboard for redirecting the human spirit."

15. George Packer, "Don't Look Down: The New Depression Journalism," *The New Yorker*, 29 April 2013, pp. 70-75. See Chapter 2, notes 15 and 107 for a more positive estimate of the OWS movement.

16. Gary Dorrien has also called the recession "a crisis not to be wasted." Writing after Mudge's death, he notes that it could set the stage for building a "better social order" (*Tikkun*, September 2010).

That job is so important and so vast as to require the infusion of the best ancient and modern wisdom. Such old-new sources may be found, Mudge argues, by starting an ongoing dialogue among and between the "religions of the book" — Judaism, Christianity, and Islam — and contemporary writers in each tradition. Why there? Because he sees that the Abrahamic texts, and their following commentaries, contain advice that takes "the nature of the human as a species that values and is valued." Equally important, he notes that these texts invariably deal with concrete economic relationships, potentially helpful parallels for today. For Mudge, now is the time for these faiths to separately and together make known their contributions in both word and practice, hoping they might effectively influence present financial and political forums. (As an American, he assumes the continuation of a separation of power between any religious body or bodies and the state.) This interfaith collaboration is a vital part of his starting point toward a new global political economy.

Toward such goals, Mudge was coalescing ideas from an impressive array of sources. As a wide-framed synthesizer, he naturally questioned modernity's long-accepted compartmentalization of fields of study that often separate them from larger moral concerns and responsible action. For him, all inquiry undertaken by humans is by definition humanistic. After this crisis, Mudge particularly wanted to bring economics back from its predominant isolation within mathematical science to its humanistic roots in eighteenth-century political economics. He believed such a reunification would help close the gap between "human misery and abstract critical thought." This was an important part of his more general desire to break down the contemporary separation dividing secular and spiritual worlds. Further, he argued that values are, and must be, embedded in a sense of well-being for all. To both reach and connect everyone, he naturally rejoiced in the powerful role of electronic communication via the Internet.

The genesis of this book began after 9/11, when that event sparked Mudge's concern about the role of faith traditions in forestalling international violence and building peace. He began to explore the historic connection of a responsibility ethic shared between Jews, Christians, and Muslims. At a meeting of the National Council of Churches in 2007, he presented his original idea of "covenantal humanism."[17] By the next year it had become the backbone of his book *The Gift of Responsibility*. The book's last chapter

---

17. "Christian Ecumenicism and the Abrahamic Faiths," National Council of Churches, Oberlin, Ohio, 2007.

calls for "a humanity that gives reasons to one another," and Mudge's covenantal humanism provides a lasting touchstone for the health of such an exchange.

That study does much more, according to Edward L. Long, who commented on its historical context. "Lew's *Gift* announces the major agenda for the theological enterprise in the next quarter century. In recent history, we've had Christian realism, a temporary enthusiasm for the secular, and liberation theology — clearer about what it was against rather than for. Now we have an interfaith emphasis. *Gift* shows Lew going far beyond Reinhold Niebuhr on the subject of violence. Niebuhr's thought was inadequate. He left no room for forgiveness, solidarity, trust." Long also added, "Lew helps us to hope. A new and deeper theological understanding may emerge from this intercultural contact. Going along with it is a much more sophisticated form of peacemaking."[18]

While Mudge was thinking about *Gift*'s successor in the first eight months of 2009, he was also serving as an elected member of the Presbyterian Church's Advisory Committee on Social Witness Policy (ACSWP). He suggested that the committee prepare a report on the global meltdown and what might be done about it. Not surprisingly, his ideas from *Gift* fed both projects. In addition, he drew upon an earlier ACSWP report that he had drafted, *The Nature and Value of Human Life* (December 2008). There, he explicitly attributes the economy's malfunction to "usurious exploitation of the poor, and now the middle class." In addition, this report's final section begins with an issue study focused on economics and human rights. Mudge sought input and criticism from members of ACSWP, and in addition, a larger group of domestic and international friends and acquaintances in academe, the ministry, social work, and business.

This activity can only be described as impressively focused and energetic, entailing ideas for meetings, research in a variety of print and online media, and intensive study examining connections between scriptural ethics, interfaith dialogue, and the quest for economic justice. From his array of correspondents, Mudge was developing a substantive exchange that he hoped would track developments in the domestic and world economy. Meanwhile, he closely followed the January 2009 meetings of the World Economic Forum at Davos and the World Social Forum at Belem, whose results disheart-

---

18. Edward L. Long (professor emeritus, Drew University), convener of a breakfast-table discussion of Mudge's *Gift*, annual meeting of the Society for Christian Ethics, San Jose, California, January 2010.

ened him. He submitted comments on the current scene to both the Op-Ed section of the *New York Times* and to *The Christian Century.*

These critiques borrowed from Mudge's starter report, initially titled "A Modest Proposal," which he had begun to circulate among his colleagues as early as January 2009. By July, it had grown into a much longer document, "Global Meltdown: Can Any Good Come Out of It?" Using a number of responses he'd received to this paper, he was planning a second draft before a meeting of ACSWP in October. After that, he envisioned as one possible future for the two drafts "a group of three or so commentator-editors" to which he'd serve as a consultant. By late summer in writing to his circle, Mudge repeated the report's purpose: "The point is to have a conversation on what our church should do or say on the topic — merely to launch the dialogue."

This book carries on that same purpose with "church" now enlarged to include the Abrahamic faiths, which had been his intent. But also, as planned, it allowed him to speak in his own voice more fully and completely than he might as the committee's drafter. Therefore, the book is a composite text. To his "Global Meltdown" draft have been added and incorporated his shorter papers on related issues, the most helpful criticism that he received, and key passages from his large collection of general and particular notes. Also, updates from the current press have been added as footnotes to keep his argument current.[19] These updates only heighten the relevance of what Mudge recommended: a fundamental change to both the way we define ourselves and foresee a future world political economy in which the joint lenses of the Abrahamic faiths would play a vital part. The result is Chapter 2, the heart of this book, "An Interfaith Challenge to the Global Economic Crisis."

As a necessary prelude to these hundred odd pages, Chapter 1, "A New Humanity in a Universal Household," Mudge succinctly states his key ideas and terminology. Sources for this text are his notes. These include lengthy musings for his introduction to the book that were simultaneously developing with the ACSWP report. Three ideas stand out as essential to his thought. First, he restates his foundational notion of "covenantal humanism" as a basis for interfaith economic collaboration. Second, he presents a new view of human identity as *Homo oeconomicus* with a spiritual dimension, what he called a "revisionist theological anthropology." Finally, he redefines "stake-

---

19. Additions include Mudge's substantial paper, "After the Financial Crisis: Fostering Stakeholder Responsibility as Practical Theology," read at the International Academy of Practical Theology, held at the Catholic Theological Union, Chicago, 3 August 2009.

holdership" as a pivotal practical step, although it envisioned all humanity, toward implementing a new world economy.

Chapter 3, "Outline for My Unfinished Book," is something of a summary of the preceding two chapters, while it also points beyond them to what Lew envisioned doing in a finished manuscript. Given the simultaneous history of the ACSWP report and this prospectus, the two naturally overlap. But the outline includes additional important ideas that he hoped to develop. Begun in July 2009, it was far along, but incomplete. He was working on it the morning of his death. Nevertheless, its three-part, eight-chapter structure is clear, and its strong through-line points forward. As presented here, this chapter is only slightly edited to finish incomplete sentences, to link others, and also to include apt passages from his notes. Its hopeful ending is inspired by a favorite piece of music among classics that he often listened to as he worked: Beethoven's "Consecration of the House," Opus 124.

Chapter 4 collects three responses to Mudge's ideas from representatives of the three Abrahamic faiths: Elliot N. Dorff for Judaism, John C. Knapp for Christianity, and Djamel Eddine Laouisset for Islam (see Contributors). This section follows Mudge's purpose: to "launch the dialogue," and these three writers formally start that process with insight and spirit. I very much appreciate their participation.

Additional thanks are my pleasure to give others, two in particular. John C. Bogle, Lew's friend and Princeton classmate, has written a stirring foreword of how his lifelong study of economics coalesced with Lew's ecumenical ethics. Lew's former colleague, Clare Benedicks Fischer, emeritus professor of the sociology of religion at the Starr King School for the Ministry, Graduate Theological Union (GTU), Berkeley, helped me review a quantity of manuscripts — from finished papers to emails and random musings. She critiqued my working outline for the book. I then integrated Lew's words into a readable whole. Clare and I also researched certain footnotes beyond ones he had already made. In September 2011, I became sole editor, adding more references to update the text. These additions are now separated from Lew's original notes by parentheses.

Still other friends due warm thanks are members of the above-mentioned ACSWP Committee of the Presbyterian Church (USA), in particular Christine Darden, Marsha Fowler, John C. Knapp, William Saint, and the committee's coordinator, Christian T. Iosso. Mudge's wider circle of correspondents included a number of GTU colleagues, especially Judith A. Berling, James A. Donahue, Arthur Holder, William O'Neill, and Carol Robb. Besides these respondents, others were Don Browning, John M.

Buchanan, John R. Buchanan, Martin Conway, Alain C. Enthoven, Adam Fronczek, Clifford Kirkpatrick, Walter Owensby, Julio de Santa Ana, William Maxwell Scott III, Joyce Shin, Donald and Peggy Shriver, Chandler Stokes, John Vest, and Philip L. Wickeri. Another commentator is Edward L. Long. If I have inadvertently missed anyone, I hope that their private knowledge of participation will be enough reward.

Heidi Hadsell and Norman Hjelm kindly assisted in my lengthy search for an editor. Heidi introduced me to Yahya Michot, professor of Islamic Studies and Christian-Muslim Relations at Hartford Theological Seminary, who suggested I find a co-editor to work with me. I pursued this idea until the responsibility became mine alone. Norman, a book editor and Lew's longtime friend, deserves additional thanks. Even before Lew's death, Norman brought the idea of the book to the publisher William Eerdmans. I am also indebted to John Knapp, a contributor, who kindly introduced me to the Islamic responder, Djamel Eddine Laouisset. Both Norman and John have reviewed this text and made helpful suggestions.

Working to shape Lew's materials for publication has been a great privilege and pleasure. Although I followed his enthusiasm for light plane flying only so far (I could land the craft in an emergency), I was more intrigued by his many intellectual projects about which we had long and searching discussions. As I edited his words, he clearly wasn't dictating to me, but almost. It was good to hear his imagined voice again. Of course, the errors that may remain belong to both of us.

JEAN McCLURE MUDGE,
writer/documentary filmmaker
Berkeley, California, 2013

CHAPTER 1

A New Humanity in a Universal Household

The Recession as a Material and Spiritual Crisis

Major economic crises give us an opportunity to challenge what we've previously understood about ourselves and to reach a "reset" by asking, who
do we think we really are? At such a moment of crisis, the question becomes
how deep into the human *Geist* — Spirit or collective meaning — can this
reset be made to go? Quite far, it seems, because the roots of our distress
lie not merely in malfunctioning financial systems that only specialists can
understand, but in a kind of spiritual disorder that can be described as a
single-minded idolatry of profit. We've lost our souls in a Faustian bargain
for imaginary, purely paper gains. Someone has said that economic values
are our *Geist* or spiritual substance in common today, that the cash nexus is
the expression of what we take to be the human.

We value one another in terms of our economic power, the one thing on
earth everyone understands.[1] Spiritual disorders call for spiritual remedies.
Where and to what extent are such remedies on offer? And why should
humanists have a say about economics anyway?

In January 2009, *New York Times* Op-Ed columnist David Brooks explored where economic theory went wrong in a piece titled "An Economy of

---

1. After the 9/11 collapse of the World Trade Center towers, the state of New York appointed a referee to calculate the economic worth of each of the persons who died, for insurance and other purposes. The idea was widely criticized as crass, yet no one came up with
anything better. It's a clear example that the most basic way we define being human today is to
have a recognized, valued role in the human household. Yet each person is, by his/her inherent
nature, of "supreme worth" *(Bhagavad Gita).* So we live with the paradox of immeasurable
human life being assessed in monetary terms.

Faith and Trust."[2] He blamed both political parties for following a "mechanical, dehumanized view of the economy," and argued that ideally "an economy is a society of trust and faith." The gist of his analysis came to this: economists of the right and left are "rigorous empiricists" who did not, and still do not, grasp the nature of human nature or effectively honor basic human values. In this dire situation, it's not just economists or columnists who have standing to critique economics. It's a job for everyone, if we do our homework.

That's all the more true if one equates the term "public economy" with "political economy," as I am doing. Political economy is the public discussion and action in which I have a right to participate as a citizen affected by political decisions made by representatives I have voted for or against. It also means the economics of the *polis* — the realm of public finance and the economics of government operations. Political economy used to be applied to nations, but I am now extending it to include the management of the world's resources for the well-being of the entire human household (Greek, *oikonomia*), or the whole inhabited earth *(oikoumene)*. It is not a technical discipline learned only from university textbooks and monographs on economics, but is broadly available in publications like *The Economist,* the financial pages of the *New York Times, Newsweek,* and on the Internet. In short, it's economics as a matter for public discussion in a readily accessible form about which citizens should be knowledgeable and concerned. I need to claim no knowledge beyond this. The fact that I am not in business makes no difference. I am impacted by what business decides.[3]

Ethicists, philosophers, and theologians — carriers of traditions who explore human nature and values — should naturally be among those informed citizens with a say in the economy. As both a citizen and an ecumenical ethicist, I know that the notion of a political economy for human well-being has eighteenth-century roots, and is therefore not new. I also know that it is not customary to read the histories of biblical Israel, of Christianity in the Roman Empire, and of Islam in Arab civilization, as a series of attempts to devise political economies capable of embodying the ideals of their founding documents: the Torah, Bible, and Qur'an. And yet indeed they were. If we stand in continuity with such traditions, then major terms generated by them in the past may also apply to us in our own economic travail, such as "sin,"

2. David Brooks, Op-Ed, *New York Times,* 15 January 2009, p. A29.

3. A review of the latest books of Paul Krugman and Joseph Stiglitz reemphasizes the intimate connection between politics and economics. Its two authors make the political economy a crucial subject matter for all voting citizens. Jacob S. Hacker and Paul Pierson, "What Krugman & Stiglitz Can Tell Us," *New York Review of Books* 59, no. 14 (September 27, 2012): 55-58. — *Ed.*

"pride," and "greed," as well as certain regenerating ideas such as "renewal," "hope," and "household." So my project for a new global political economy is a scriptural, and therefore ethical, analysis of what has recently befallen our economy and its value system.

Human Identity: *Homo oeconomicus* with a Spiritual Dimension

In traditional theological terms, this crisis has taught us very little, if anything, new about ourselves, about human nature. We are full of avarice. We cheat our fellow human beings. It is hard to think or act in terms of the public good. Reinhold Niebuhr had it about right in *The Nature and Destiny of Man* (1941): humanity creates evil through its deep-seated pride; even the "good" among us are quite corruptible, and perfectibility is beyond our grasp. We will resist regulation, and if it is enacted, we will try to evade it. Our fundamental self-interest is only expanded when, for the most part, economic science is taught and business practices are constructed to place second, marginalize, or even omit questions of the public good.

The current recession has taught us that economic rationality, single-mindedly pursued for profit, collapses under its own weight, or does great damage that cannot be easily ignored. In its wake, we have a great opportunity not only to expose the areas of venality, corruption, greed, and emptiness in the global economic system, but at the same time, to call on faith communities that have kept ancient meanings alive to reaffirm them, meeting this crisis at its most basic level. As human beings we are the institutions we devise and the meanings we give them; therefore, we have a momentous job to do.

The odyssey of human self-understanding that we've now reached is predominantly described in economic terms. Who we are has, for the moment, become an economic question. To be persuasive, then, a new perspective needs to make use of a language that draws from both economics and historical ethics. Interestingly, they come together in the very definition of the term "economics," derived from the Greek words *oikos* or "household" and *nomos* or "law" (regulation, statutory system). To emphasize our natures as *Homo oeconomicus* rather than *Homo sapiens* is to analyze human beings as basically homemakers who are following assumed or agreed-upon household rules. As *Homo sapiens,* we may be able to think. But first, we make homes and constitute our identities in terms of our primary relationships in families and in circles of persons closest to us or with whom we have special contact.

Human spirit — our presence and imagination linked with power — is

13

most fully expressed through our household relationships. They generate the mores that determine each home's peace and prosperity. Therefore, *Homo oeconomicus* has a spiritual dimension. I am not referring to what has come to be called "spirituality" as devotional practice. Spirit is the "atmosphere" of the home or *polis*, what is in the private and public air. It's in the stories that lie behind the arguments we use. And following Niebuhr, we cannot forget that "human spirit" may be a wild thing, liable to promote evil, as in actual and virtual slave cultures. Although it is our highest expression of self, human spirit is also capable of infinitely destructive distortion. The question is: *What story do we attach ourselves to as our formula for the expression of objective spirit in our lives and culture?* If this spirit is not holy (pure, or morally perfect), how does it get restrained and converted for the broader good? In particular, in a whole range of efforts, what is the role of religious communities toward this goal?

I am here describing a "theological anthropology," a material and spiritual understanding of humanity, whose basis in household relationships makes it a major kind of anthropology, one to be taken seriously for its individual, communal, and global implications. The Abrahamic faiths as self-named "households of God" are prime candidates to carry this anthropology to "all God's peoples," meaning every human family. No strings would be attached; no matters of apologetics or conversion raised. Rather, these faiths — joined by nonbelievers of good will — would be passing on God's gift of "blessing," the theological term for conferring well-being, that they long ago had understood themselves to be receiving (see "Covenantal Humanism," pp. 16-17 below).

The Centrality of Economics and the Hope for a New Political Economy

The wide negative effects of the recession on our world household has highlighted a given: economic activity is necessary for the creation, support, and maintenance of culture. It's the engine that allows us to express our many ways of being human as well as our potential for responsibility. In short, economics is central to the organic and cultural evolution that has produced us as we now are.[4] Functioning at its best, an economy does indeed deserve our trust and faith.

4. The economy of exchanging, borrowing, and lending is the means by which we par-

But global economics has gone radically awry, primarily by having been narrowed to a mere mathematical discipline. The public discussion of economics is carried on in highly technical language of algorithms and derivatives, little understood even by professionals in economics and business, but with a much larger penumbra of effects on human society. The technical core and the human wrapping are not clearly related, or not related at all. Economists think that their math determines what *must* be, when humanists, including economists-as-humanists, really need to decide it.

Economics needs to be reconnected and integrated with its humanistic roots, especially with the principal Abrahamic faith traditions — Judaism, Christianity, and Islam — with their rich interreligious histories, their numerical majority among the world's religions, and their global presence. Yet how may these traditions of valuation and meaning offer their insights to secular economic culture without proselytizing? How may their deeper stories — and the generations of moral reasoning seeking to explain them — be broadly circulated so that together they might produce commonly held ideas of economic justice? These ideas could then take form as the "laws of the human household." That is both the problem and the hope.

Perhaps humanists, including believers, could start the process by seeing themselves as "economic actors" or *"economes,"* who invite secularists and economists as fellow actors to enter into a "tactical collaboration." On their side, humanists could reevaluate money as not merely hard coin, but rather, an expression of our spirit: both a token of exchanging our capabilities and also a form of portable energy to be applied imaginatively wherever and however we may wish. As the "substance" of life-together, money could then be seen as a transparent tool of our evolution and culture. (Of course, when misused, distorted, or corrupted — gone bad — money becomes mere "mammon," gains from sheer greed.) In return, secularists and economists might be led to respect a realm of meaning beyond mathematical reasoning and acknowledge money's spiritual force. But big questions would still hover over such collaboration. Where among humanists, especially theologians, is the economic conviction? Where among economists is the depth-conviction, the compassion?

Nevertheless, we may begin by seeing that the Abrahamic scriptures are accounts of organizing a just commonwealth under God, however mixed

---

ticipate in the entire being of life, the master genome of the whole. Or put another way, how we conceive and manage the economy, as with how we produce art and literature, expresses our fundamental identity, our spiritual DNA.

their success and failure. This sort of community is what the "rule" or "kingdom" of God means, and what the Torah, Bible, and Qur'an are about. Now we see that this rule might be the goal of the whole human race. The challenge is to enlist these different religious traditions in the universal household project by bringing their best insights and values to bear upon it. As a start, their materials may be used, whether true believers are aware of the raid or not. The important thing is to insert the global humanity effort into the heart of these traditions so as to transform the ways their own believers understand them.

As a reminder, I am talking not about economics as an academic science but about political economy, which I see as one of the most important expressions of the human spirit. Again, political economy here means ensembles of institutions that manage our shared capacities and resources as matters of both familial and public concern. I envision a political economy organized to bring blessing to earth's households: a way of doing things at the whole-earth level that makes for all human beings to be known, nurtured, and cared for; and that brings goodness and blessing into the world rather than curse. The kinds of political economies we create tell much about who we are and who we might become as a species.

Covenantal Humanism: Abrahamic Engagement

In my book *The Gift of Responsibility* (2008), I introduced the concept of covenantal humanism as a common symbol for followers of the Abrahamic faiths. It unites them as a people responsible to live so as to bless the whole world. I now build on this symbol by inviting a dialogue about how persons of faith, and secularists, may use covenantal humanism to contribute ideas and practices for a new political economy. For the Abrahamic faiths, this means living up to God's promise to Abraham as described in Genesis 12:1-3, to benefit (bless) rather than diminish (curse) humanity, with its scriptural parallels and echoes. Adherents of Judaism, Christianity, and Islam, sharing both this understanding with Abraham and key passages in their sacred books, have already inherited an implicit gift of responsibility to covenant together. They are natural points of entry to, and spheres of nurture for, the extension of covenantal humanism into the world household.

Clearly, covenantal humanism is neither godlessness nor a new organization. Rather, it's a meta-ethic helpful, among other things, for meeting our serious recession, based upon Abraham's acceptance of God's call. Humanity or "all the families of the earth" — members of the same household, or "home of meaning" — could, like Abraham, similarly covenant before God. Before such a day ever approached, the historically linked Abrahamic faiths might hold up a mirror of responsibility to the rest of humanity. Concretely, a common basis could be found in the sets of rules, or *nomoi,* inspired by their sacred texts as worked out with the needs and tools of the modern world. In this deep economic crisis, it's vital that we at least explore covenantal humanism anew with an eye to applying it on a world scale via local, culturally differing discussions of it.

Curse, in contrast to blessing, occurs when human striving after purpose becomes corrupted, narrowing to the purely personal or purely acquisitive, and focusing almost exclusively on the profit motive. Scripture, particularly Genesis 1–3, provides a moral narrative to deal with the failure of many generations of Israelites to forge a just politico-economic system out of the Abrahamic covenant idea. They already knew from Abraham's history what moral failure was. Not without fault, he was nevertheless unique among preceding nomad leaders of the ancient Middle East in seeing that God's earlier promise required more than blind acceptance of divine gifts, more than the uncritical giving of traditional tokens of thanks (Genesis 22). Abraham's appropriate response, he discerned, was not to sacrifice his son Isaac as a symbol of his gratitude. Rather, it was a radically different, life-affirming one: to take on the responsibility of extending God's gifts by blessings to his own and later generations. Following Abraham, we may take on a similar gift of responsibility by restructuring our economy away from "curse" — excessive profit — toward a system assuring everyone of basic material and spiritual well-being.

Stakeholdership: Just Institutions and the Common Good

If the notion of covenantal humanism is a type of meta-ethic, stakeholdership is its concrete application. Stakeholdership as a structural plan is a practical alternative to the world's present economic oligarchy with its widely uneven distribution of wealth. Using the term, I am adopting and enlarging the present meaning of stakeholder analysis by business managers who try to identify all those persons or organizations likely to be impacted by their companies, largely to forestall complaints. Stockholders, or traditional owners of companies, have been the only persons to whom managers were thought to have responsibility. However, stakeholders constitute a wider and more varied circle with broader interests and concerns. Who stakeholders are depends upon the nature of the enterprise, but the title gives them an interest in it. This interest is an attribute of their personhood.

Why not agree that the definition of stakeholder be extended beyond those immediately impacted by a business to include those more distantly affected, in short, all human beings? As such, they have a broadly recognized right to be a stakeholder in the earth's resources. Everyone would then have a stake in the totality of the world's businesses in developing these resources. And most importantly, businesses would conceive and carry out their enterprises with the purpose of serving these vast but now digitally identifiable and named persons. Designing their policies and procedures, companies would then personalize their objectives, not only for targeted groups but for the enhancement of households worldwide. Both groups would stand to generate reasonable profits, adding value all around to entrepreneurs and every home alike.

Such universal stakeholdership would also help assure that earth's finite treasures were monitored to prevent over-use at the same time as the products produced contributed to the common good. Stakeholders' capital could be figured on their human "capabilities," as economist Amartya Sen and philosopher Martha Nussbaum have described.[5] With these encompassing duties, stakeholders' commitment to using money for all humanity and to sustain resources might be called Enterprise Earth. If stakeholdership became the standard principle for business operations everywhere, it would also reinsert the idea of legal contract governing the rights of ownership into a larger area of trust, promise keeping, and solidarity. In essence, this new global political economy would be practicing covenantal humanism.

Each citizen's voice would need to be heard because of the given stake s/he has in the whole. But there's something more. My inviolate personhood would be recognized, yes, but also my stake in the honor of the company with which I am dealing would need to be acknowledged. I require that the institution recognize me as a stakeholder, and as a corollary, I would require it not to deal with me in a way that corrupts its purpose. Otherwise, my association with the company would also corrupt me by association with such dealing. This double understanding of stakeholdership would be a full covenantal form of participatory economic justice.

A planetary political economy means an economy of just participation

---

5. Amartya Sen, *Development as Freedom* (New York: A. Knopf, 2001). [Martha Nussbaum, *Women and Human Development: The Capabilities Approach* (Cambridge: Cambridge University Press, 2011). — *Ed.*]

in the stakeholder scheme just outlined. Our sense of justice — above all in the production and distribution of resources, the *nomos* of *oikos* (household rules) — is rooted in the sense of fairness, or the lack of it. Paul Ricoeur observes that love is not possible without justice and justice is impossible without love.[6] Mutuality, love, relationships, and listening thrive in households as just institutions. Our goal is to reform companies or institutions, particularly those that protect and advance society's well-being. We must make them just and fair in the first place and bring people back into the household. This requires engaged citizens active in the political process at every level.

The Christian Tradition and Economics in an Abrahamic Context

The present recession has happened at a time when the church is trying to find its voice and effective role in the context of fundamental social change affecting all the Abrahamic faiths. As one among other Christians reacting to the crisis, I identify specifically with the Reformed Protestant tradition. Among Christians, is that tradition best positioned to do this reaching out? I am not arguing that this is so. It's only where I happen by historical-genetic accident to stand. In all this, I am a philosophical pragmatist, attempting to say what something means and how it affects the world.

In the Reformed tradition, I've been associated with the World Council of Churches, or the ecumenical Christian movement. Founded in 1948, this movement took its name from the Greek *oikoumene,* or "the whole inhabited world." But not until recently have I seen how the concept of covenantal humanism may apply to lift the present stress on this household. From this double position of one wing of Christianity allied with its contemporary ecumenical arm, I hope to open the door for a wide range of responders from their own perspectives, especially those from Judaism and Islam, but from other religions and the secular world as well.

To be quite clear, I should specify my position within the Reformed Christian tradition. In modern times, Christians have been divided on the economy between right and left. Few opt for a middle position. Either a conservative view shapes what I term social noninvolvement but puts a "right"

---

6. Paul Ricoeur, "Love and Justice," in *Figuring the Sacred: Religion, Narrative and Imagination,* trans. David Pellauer, ed. Mark I. Wallace (Minneapolis: Augsburg Fortress, 1995), pp. 315-30.

orientation into practice, or a radical "left" vision prevails that is borrowed from certain forces in the global South. I stand in the church's center-left, and am trying to move the center forward. I do so not only with the fundamentally Christian idea of *oikoumene*, but with other multiple insights drawn from major Christian movements important to my background. In historical order as they appeared in the twentieth century, they are the social gospel, neo-orthodoxy, and liberation theologies.

Now I am asking how such standpoints look when they are in dialogue with scholars studying Torah and Qur'an. Together we need to ask what all our faiths have to say about a new political economy. I take seriously Jesus' parable of the sheep and the goats (Matt. 25:31-46); those words apply to theological communities as well as individuals. At the last day, our religious bodies will not be judged by their size, influence, or orthodoxy but by what they have contributed to the well-being or blessing of humankind. Faith communities, then, are not only places of particular sensitivity to the failure of the world's economies in supporting every household, but they have a responsibility to do something about it.

Traditionally, Christians have held two broad views. One affirms that Jesus' preaching and teaching provide the basis for ethics with strong economic implications. One example is the Jubilee proclamation that goes back to Hebrew scripture (Leviticus 25). It mandates that debts are canceled and slaves are liberated every forty-nine years. In essence, the system of debt is disrupted — a situation resembling our current economic crisis, but for the Israelites, brought about by community consent. Building on his Jewish heritage, Jesus' economic teachings treat at least four major areas: (1) He proclaims an "acceptable year of the Lord" — the Jubilee has come (Luke 4:18). (2) His words in Matthew 5, familiarly known as "The Sermon on the Mount," include the Beatitudes, announcing that "blessed are the poor" and "blessed are those who thirst after justice." (3) The Lord's Prayer appeals for the forgiveness of our debts "as we forgive our debtors" (Matt. 6:9-13). Finally, Jesus speaks in parables to raise issues in agricultural economics (Matthew 24 and 25).

The second approach asserts that Jesus' teachings are too radical to be practical. In this case, "situational ethics" comes into play: one looks to particular personal circumstances and applies the love commandment and its implications for justice in that time and place. We can learn from both positions, but different Christians tend to foreground one or the other. If Jesus' reputed words are read literally, the standard is an exemplary community of righteous works over against most of society. But if the primary guide is justification by faith (that is, being acceptable in God's sight not by one's actions but by the sincerity of one's belief), adjusting to the world is more easily negotiated. We need both positions: the sense of demand that we never can fulfill and a sense of forgiveness that lets us keep on keeping on. In justification by faith, we understand that the world is still with us. It is not a Jubilee world. We either construct a community apart where we try to live differently, or we make an effort to impart the values of the Jubilee within the world we know. This invariably leads to a conversation about perfected love and imperfect justice.

To these general guidelines — with no attempt to exhaust examples — more specific Christian economic practices are found in the New Testament's passages about lending and borrowing. These issues, of course, dominate in today's recession. In these situations, what is required of justice, of love? Both Torah and New Testament provide unqualified instructions governing loans and interest. Exodus 22:25 exhorts the believer not to lend money with interest to the needy. Luke 6:34-35 resonates with, as it repeats, this teaching. Jesus instructs his disciples that sinners expect repayment in full, but love of enemies and doing good require that loans be made "expecting nothing in return." Indeed, a far richer reward is promised: to be blessed as God's children.

We clearly need a new stage in the development of religious teachings on borrowing and lending that can give ethical underpinnings to secular regulation. What might it look like? There is much to discuss, but it could include this fugitive thought: that recessions in the present economy might be seen as blessings in disguise, interrupting the usual system and forcing the periodic remission of debt, lest the whole system collapse because debts cannot be paid. *Maybe what we are going through is a form of Jubilee in which unpayable debts are canceled, or at least, mitigated.*[7] The problem, then, is

7. Practical suggestions for the mitigation of debts are in Daniel Alpert, Robert Hockett, and Nouriel Roubini, "The Way Forward: Moving from the Post-Bubble, Post-Bust Economy to Renewed Growth and Competitiveness," New America Foundation Policy Paper, 10 October 2011, http://newamerica.net/publications/policy/the_way_forward. [See also Martin S. Feldstein, "How to Stop the Drop in Home Values," Op-Ed, *New York Times*, 13 October 2011, p. A25. In addition, Robert Kuttner's "The Debt We Shouldn't Pay," a review of David Graeber's book, *Debt: The First 5,000 Years*, emphasizes the difference between public and private debt; points to the unequal debt treatment of banks and corporations versus homeowners, students, and nations; and then suggests reforms. But Kuttner ends by lamenting the "sheer political power of creditors and the momentum of the austerity campaign" — in which the U.S. participates as sequester measures are implemented — an assurance that these reforms will have little hope of happening soon. *The New York Review of Books*, 9 May 2013, pp. 16-18. — Ed.]

first to minister to those who are hurt, and then to make the outcome of this crisis a more just economic system overall. In the pages to follow, I will add more to these summarized suggestions for faith communities and others in helping to do just that.

CHAPTER 2

An Interfaith Challenge to the Global Economic Crisis

No one knows what will come of our present economic travail. Even as certain banks and investment houses report surprising profits, unemployment levels continue to grow. With that situation come nonpayable medical bills, home foreclosures, increased domestic violence, bankruptcies, the disintegration of families, and general human misery.[1] Let us hope that the reces-

1. The September 2013 unemployment rate fell to 7.2%, but excluded those no longer looking for work and is well above its pre-recession levels of 4 to 5%. Also, the monthly increase in those employed was below average for the previous year. Jobs were virtually static at levels not seen since 1978, and economic growth remained anemic at 2%. Catherine Rampell, "Weak Job Gains May Cause Delay in Action by Fed," http://www.nytimes.com/2013/10/23/business/economy/us-economy-added-148000-jobs-in-september.html?_r=0. Reuters reported that October 2013 employment in the private sector was at its lowest level in six months, the strongest evidence yet that the 16-day federal government shutdown dragged down the economy. Reuters, "Private Hiring Slows: Consumer Inflation Stays Muted," *New York Times,* 30 October 2013. "Databases, Tables & Calculators by Subject," Bureau of Labor Statistics, 26 June 2013, http://data.bls.gov/timeseries/LNS14000000; http://www.nytimes.com/reuters/2013/10/30/business/30reuters-usa-economy-employment-adp.html. In another sign of a static economy at the end of October 2013, the Federal Reserve Board decided to continue its stimulus plan, a policy that may hold well into 2015. Binyamin Appelbaum, "Fed Extends Stimulus as Growth Fails," *New York Times,* 31 October 2013, http://www.nytimes.com/2013/10/31/business/economy/fed-maintains-stimulus-awaiting-sustainable-growth.html?pagewanted=1&_r=0. The continuing recessions throughout the euro zone have produced over 25 percent unemployment in Greece and Spain, with Portugal, Ireland, and Italy well above 10 percent. Martin Wolf, "How Austerity Has Failed," *The New York Review of Books,* 11 July 2013, pp. 20-21.

From late 2012 into 2014, the IMF has forecast slower growth with an 80 percent chance of a continuing recession in Europe (25 percent in Japan and 15 percent in the U.S.). In late 2012, a World Bank report noted that "more than half a billion young people are neither working

sion will not be declared "over" until these evils are effectively addressed. Let us also hope that the eventual resolution of the downturn will include a basic shakeup in our thinking. How might our "political economy" be made to embody a transformed human spirit[2] rising from these challenges? *We need some new social-financial-legal-theological paradigm for envisioning a different kind of economic world.*[3]

With every crisis in human affairs there are those who seek quick fixes and those who think long thoughts. Politicians and managers wrestle with challenges like those of the long-term effects of the global economic meltdown. Visionaries seek to glimpse the future to which such challenges could give birth. Today, the three Abrahamic faiths and other religious institutions need to ask if they can help make possible both sorts of effort, immediately, for the short-term, as well as for a future vision. Can they assist policymakers of the North and radical economic revisionists of the South in working through their enmities, differences, and mutual distrust to find more just and inclusive global economic institutions than those we now have? Above all, can they help generate a moral culture in which financial institutions at last have their proper place as servants rather than masters of humanity's economic well-being?

---

nor studying, and estimated that the world would need to create about 600 million new jobs in the next 15 years just to keep the unemployment rate constant." Global peace, prosperity, and stability all depend upon jobs, according to the World Bank's president, Jim Yong Kim. Annie Lowrey, "I.M.F. Lowers Its Forecast for Global Growth," *New York Times,* 9 October 2012, p. B1. Low expectations for global growth have continued into 2013, not on a par with pre-recession percentages. Annie Lowrey, "I.M.F. Forecasts Modest Global Economic Growth, at Best," 23 January 2013, http://www.nytimes.com/2013/01/24/business/economy/imf-fore cast-global-economic-growth-modest-at-best.html. For every evidence of world improvement, a counterbalancing factor meets it. "The World Economy: Semi-Rational Exuberance," *The Economist,* 26 January–1 February 2013, p. 13. — Ed.

2. Behind my use of this expression is Hegel's idea of "objective spirit." Not only are art, music, literature, and architecture manifestations of *Geist,* but also economic and political structures.

3. Italics added. Princeton economist Paul Krugman invoked ethics in observing the country's deep division of values clearly evident in our preelection political debate: ". . . at this point, American politics is fundamentally about different moral visions." "Free to Die," Op-Ed, *New York Times,* 16 September 2011, p. A23. On the same page, in "The Planning Fallacy," David Brooks alluded to the need for deeper and broader thinking about the economy than putting forth mere practical plans. — Ed.

A Continuing Crisis: Where Might It Lead?

These questions are asked in the midst of an ongoing crisis. It is difficult to keep up. Each day brings new news: sometimes dispiriting, sometimes hopeful. As early as fall 2008, Gary Dorrien, Reinhold Niebuhr Professor of Social Ethics at Union Theological Seminary, New York, was analyzing the downturn in terms not only of its severity but also of its potential to resurrect basic social issues.

> [T]his crisis . . . puts into play questions of national purpose and vision that have been off the table politically for decades. Instead of the usual Pepsi or Coke options and the usual fixation with trivia, there is now an opening for larger concerns. What would a good society look like? What kind of country should we want to be?[4]

These topics will be recast from an interfaith perspective and dealt with in pages to come. But first, a brief overview of the downturn's deep and far-reaching effects brings them home, even literally, in the collapse of the housing market.

In the years leading up to this continuing blight, many banks writing "subprime" mortgage contracts for minority borrowers knew exactly what they were doing. In 2008, Baltimore City officials alleged in a lawsuit that deliberate, discriminatory, and lucrative lending practices, aimed mainly at African Americans — "hungry to be part of the nation's home-owning mania" — were consciously plotted by Wells Fargo (the "Stagecoach from Hell"). Beth Jacobson, then a loan officer at Wells Fargo, has said that the bank, seeking greater profits, pushed customers who might have qualified for prime loans into the subprime category. Another loan officer stated in an affidavit that employees had referred to blacks as "mud people" and to subprime contracts as "ghetto loans."

Ms. Jacobson, who is white, said she was once the bank's top-producing subprime loan officer nationally. She added, "Wells Fargo mortgage had an emerging markets unit that specifically targeted black churches, because it figured church leaders had a lot of influence and could convince congregants to take out sub-prime loans." In addition, as the *Times* further reported, "The toll taken by such policies, Baltimore officials argue, is terrible. Data released by the city as part of the suit show that more than half the properties subject

---

4. Gary Dorrien, "Financial Collapse: Lessons from the Social Gospel," *The Christian Century*, 30 December 2008.

to foreclosure on a Wells Fargo loan from 2005 to 2008 now stand vacant. And 71 percent of these are in predominantly black neighborhoods."[5]

Large banks and other corporations have received enormous government bailouts while showing every sign that they intend to continue in their old ways. They have scrambled to quickly return their Troubled Asset Relief Program (TARP) funds in order to escape much-needed regulation.[6] There is

5. [The then] New York State's Attorney General [now Governor] Andrew Cuomo raised similar questions about practices at Wells Fargo, JP Morgan-Chase, and Citi-Group, among other banks. Michael Powell, "Bank Accused of Pushing Mortgage Deals on Blacks," *New York Times,* 7 June 2009, p. A16. [In January 2010, the presiding judge of the Federal District Court ruled against the City of Baltimore, holding that lending practices could not be proven to have "resulted in broad damage to poor neighborhoods." However, similar cases are pending against Wells Fargo in several other jurisdictions, including Memphis. Michael Powell, "Federal Judge Rejects Suit by Baltimore Against Bank," *New York Times,* 8 January 2010, p. A11. As this Baltimore case illustrates, the negative effect of the crisis on blacks and Hispanics has been double that of whites. In 2009, 35 percent of black households and 31 percent of Latino households had zero or negative wealth, compared to 15 percent of white households. Desmond S. King and Rogers M. Smith, "On Race, the Silence Is Bipartisan," Op-Ed, *New York Times,* 3 September 2011, p. A15. Two years passed after the recession began before banks were being sued for their misdeeds during the housing boom. Nelson D. Schwartz and Kevin Roose, "U.S. Sues 17 Mortgage Institutions," *New York Times,* 3 September 2011, p. B1. And it was not until a year later that the Justice Department brought Wells Fargo to a $175 million settlement for its independent brokers' discrimination of over 30,000 black and Hispanic borrowers in the period 2004-5. Charlie Savage, "Wells Fargo Will Settle Mortgage Bias Charges," *New York Times,* 12 July 2012, p. B3. At the same time, Wells Fargo reported its tenth consecutive profitable quarter, largely due to its mortgage lending division. Nathaniel Popper, "Wells Fargo Posts $4.6 Billion Profit, Up 17%," *New York Times,* Investment Banking, Wall Street Earnings, 13 July 2012. In early October 2012, the government pursued Wells Fargo's alleged illegal mortgage lending history, having already settled such matters out of court with a number of other leading banks, including Bank of America. Peter Lattman, "U.S. Sues Wells Fargo, Alleging Mortgage Deceit," *New York Times,* DealBook, 9 October 2012. In January 2013, the government reached two huge agreements with U.S. banks, a total of $20.15 billion, highlighting the extent of the banks' role in the excesses of the credit boom, from the making of loans to the seizure of homes. Jessica Silver-Greenberg and Peter Eavis, "In Deal, Bank of America Extends Retreat from Mortgages," http://dealbook.nytimes.com/2013/01/07/bank-of-america-extends-retreat-from-mortgages/. But as of the summer of 2013, no bankers have been sent to prison, despite inside testimony and detailed documentation of fraud at banking's highest levels by due diligence underwriters and other whistleblowers. Martin Smith, producer and writer, "The Untouchables," Frontline, PBS, 23 January 2013; rebroadcast 21 May 2013. In an interview with Bill Moyers, Gretchen Morgenson referred to Jamie Dimon's winning stockholder support to remain both CEO and board chair of J. P. Morgan Chase, overlooking any possible conflict of interest, as good evidence that Wall Street's system is unchanged. "Moyers and Company," PBS, 26 May 2013. — *Ed.*]

6. TARP was created in October 2008 to relieve market instability and to enhance market liquidity through the government's purchase of assets and equity. Yet its leniency in settling

every reason to fear that financial markets will recover and return to former patterns long before foreclosures, unemployment, and consequent human suffering are over. Sky-high salaries and bonuses are reappearing in corporate suites and on Wall Street.[7]

Such banks are also resisting appeals to modify the terms of mortgages in trouble, citing "the sanctity of contracts" where their interests are concerned.[8] Reductions in monthly payments are being made, but the notion of

---

cases involved in abusive lending practices was called a "go easy" approach, circumventing banker accountability. Paul Krugman, "Letting Banks Walk," *New York Times*, 18 July 2011, p. A17. In early 2013, a more scathing exposé of the banks' continuing lack of transparency and obscure reporting, with a focus on Wells Fargo, suggested remedies. Frank Portnoy and Jesse Eisinger, "What's Inside America's Banks?" *Atlantic*, January/February 2013, pp. 60-71. In October 2013, the Justice Department reached a possible $13 billion settlement with JP Morgan Chase over mismanagement involved in the 2008 mortgage crisis and afterward. But both the operations of huge banks, such as Jamie Dimon's, and their supposed regulators have not yet been sufficiently checked, much less restrained. Gretchen Morgenson, "A $13 Billion Reminder of What's Wrong," *New York Times*, 27 October 2013, http://www.nytimes.com/2013/10/27/business/a-13-billion-reminder-of-whats-wrong.html. This extraordinary deal between the government and a private financial institution is another example of the country's two sets of rules: "one for the rich and another for the rest of us," said Gretchen Morgenson of the *New York Times*. Further, JP Morgan's shareholders will pay this fine, not the bank or its officials. The bank, in fact, may write off the settlement as a tax liability. Gretchen Morgenson, Interview, "Moyers and Company," PBS, 26 October 2013. JP Morgan faces more federal charges about favoritism to advance their interests in a "Sons and Daughters" hiring scheme that came to light in China. Now the inquiry is extending into similar policies that they may have pursued in South Korea, Singapore, and India. Jessica Silver-Greenberg and Ben Protess, "US Inquiry Broadens into JP Morgan's Asia Hiring," *New York Times*, 1 November 2013, http://dealbook.nytimes.com/2013/11/01u-s-inquiry-broadens-into-banks-asia-hiring/. However, on 4 November 2013, Steven A. Cohen's hedge fund firm pled guilty to all five counts of insider trading violations and agreed to pay a record $1.2 billion penalty. Billionaire Cohen, who owns 100% of the company, is personally liable. "No institution should rest easy in the belief that it is too big to jail," said Preet Bharara, United States attorney in Manhattan, who led the case against Cohen. Ben Protess and Peter Lattman, "After a Decade, SAC Capital Blinks," *New York Times*, 4 November 2013, http://dealbook.nytimes.com/2013/11/04/after-a-decade-sac-capital-blinks/?_r=0. — *Ed.*

7. Pradnya Joshi, "We Knew They Got Raises: But This?" *New York Times*, 3 July 2011, p. BU1. High compensation for executives whose firms were bailed out by the government in 2009 continues in 2013. Annie Lowrie, "Pay Still High at Bailed-Out Companies, Report Says," *New York Times*, 28 January 2013, http://www.nytimes.com/2013/01/29/business/generous-executive-pay-at-bailed-out-companies-treasury-watchdog-says.html. — *Ed.*

8. In July 2010, President Obama signed the Wall Street Reform and Consumer Protection Act — the Dodd-Frank Act — declaring it to be the most sweeping financial regulatory reform of the century. Designed to restrict banks in lending practices, make such activity more trans-

downward revision of principal amounts to correspond to lowered home values is being stubbornly resisted by bank lobbyists and in Congress. A provision to this effect was left out of the bill signed by President Obama on June 4, 2009. Political lobbyists are opposing every proposed or enacted regulation of financial institutions and markets.[9] Though some see "recovery," the gap

---

parent, and protect consumers through the creation of the Consumer Financial Protection Bureau (CFPB), the implementation of this complex law has been slow and challenged by the mortgage banking industry since its inception. In 2011, these measures remained precarious. Two dozen bills brought before Congress sought to dismantle the act. Edward Wyatt, "Dodd-Frank Under Fire a Year Later," *New York Times*, 19 July 2011, p. B1. Interestingly, the derivatives industry supports the recognition of its business model by the regulations in Dodd-Frank. Ben Protess, "Unlike Banks, This Wall St. Group Embraces Dodd Frank," 21 August 2011, www .nytimes.com/dealbook. In July 2011, President Obama named Richard Cordray, former attorney general of Ohio, to be the CFPB's first director over its originator, Elizabeth Warren, who was assessed to be too controversial to win Senate approval. "Bureau Consumer Reform," *New York Times*, Times Topics, 18 July 2011. On its first anniversary, 21 July 2012, the CFPB advanced on requiring clearer mortgage contracts and improving operations in mortgage and payday loan companies as well as the student loan market. Jessica Silver-Greenberg, "Consumer Bureau Proposes New Mortgage Disclosure Rules," *New York Times*, Legal/Regulatory, 9 July 2012. The CFPB's first enforcement action in the financial industry came against Capital One, a leading national bank. It had to pay $150 million to more than 2 million clients for selling credit card products that were unwanted, unusable, or not requested. In June Hawaii's attorney general sued Bank of America, JP Morgan Chase, and HSBC for also offering such products. Ben Protess and Jessica Silver-Greenberg, "In Its First Action, Consumer Bureau Takes Aim at Capital One," *New York Times*, Legal/Regulatory, 18 July 2012. In October 2013, the House targeted Dodd-Frank with two bills that would remove an array of derivatives trading from new regulation. Despite help from Citigroup lobbyists in writing one of the bills, and sure defeat — like others — in the Senate and White House, both bills had wide bipartisan support. But the anticipated reward for these votes was huge: "hundreds of thousands of dollars in campaign contributions." Eric Lipton and Ben Protess, "House, Set to Vote on 2 Bills Is Seen as an Ally of Wall St.," *New York Times*, 30 October 2013, http://dealbook.nytimes.com/2013/10/28/ house-set-to-vote-on-2-bills-is-seen-as-an-ally-of-wall-st/. — *Ed.*

9. On the first anniversary of the Dodd-Frank Act, Phil Angelides, former chair of the Financial Crisis Inquiry Commission, observed that massive lobbying against regulatory reform in Washington had served to "eviscerate" many of the provisions designed to restrain Wall Street lending practices. Angelides concluded that bankers enjoy the status quo "while working families are struggling to survive." "On the Anniversary of Dodd-Frank: Wall Street Fights Back and American Families Fight to Survive," *Huffington Post*, 21 July 2011, http://www .huffingtonpost.com/phil-angelides/dodd-frank-anniversary. In the wake of the Fed's stimulus measure of purchasing bonds backed by mortgages to reduce rates, banks are resisting by keeping them higher. Peter Eavis, "An Enigma in the Mortgage Market That Elevates Rates," *New York Times*, DealBook, 18 September 2012. In addition, longstanding financial abuses have been exposed, revealing new levels of institutional hubris and inadequate oversight, e.g., the fraudulent London Inter-Bank Offered Rate (LIBOR). Peter Eavis and Nathaniel Popper,

between rich and poor continues to widen. Simultaneously, unemployment grows, as do foreclosures, further spending reductions in education and public services, and increasing misery and violence in working families. Even if markets rebound, here is a set of formulae for increasing social destitution among the already poor, and even for many of the not-so-poor.

One is reminded of the Parable of the Unjust (or "Merciless") Servant in Matthew 18:23-35. A tenant farmer's enormous debts (resulting, it seems, from the impact on him of first-century exploitative lending practices) have been forgiven. The forgiven one then refuses forgiveness to a fellow debtor for a much smaller sum. His fellows denounce this merciless one to the authorities. He is led before the king, and for his unforgiving response to being forgiven, is sold into slavery with his wife and children.

Could there be some echo of this story in the situation of today's big banks, "bailed out" (i.e., forgiven) with huge sums of public money to relieve them of debts they cannot pay, who then turn around and refuse relief to small mortgage borrowers who are now "under water," faced with foreclosure because of layoffs, uninsured medical expenses, and the like. Granted the much greater complexity and nuance of the modern situation, is not some form of popular denunciation, followed by retribution, still the just reaction?[10]

"Libor Scandal Shows Many Flaws in Rate-Setting," *New York Times*, DealBook, 19 July 2012; see also Joe Nocera, "Financial Scandal Scorecard," *New York Times*, DealBook, 21 July 2012, p. A19. James Surowiecki calls the guesswork and manipulation of the LIBOR index outright lies. Besides reforms, he recommends sending guilty bankers to jail and changing regulators' "gentlemen's club ethos" to become more active in preventing fraud. "Bankers Gone Wild," *The New Yorker*, 30 July 2012, p. 25. Major plans to regulate LIBOR are underway by the British government. Mark Scott, "British Regulators Plan Changes to Libor Oversight," *New York Times*, DealBook, 10 August 2012. But Floyd Norris argues that LIBOR cannot be fixed. "The Myth of Fixing the Libor," http://www.nytimes.com/2012/09/28/business/the-myth-of-fixing-the -libor-high-low-finance.html?emc=eta1&_r=0. — *Ed.*

10. See note 5 for the start and continuing process of such reaction. Also, by January 2013, the Consumer Financial Protection Bureau's new, more stringent rules about loans are designed to further protect consumers and encourage banks to make loans. Edward Wyatt, "U.S. Consumer Watchdog to Issue Mortgage Rules," http://www.nytimes.com/2013/01/10/business/ consumers-win-some-mortgage-safety-in-new-rules.html?_r=0; interview of CFPB's Richard Cordray, *The News Hour*, PBS, 10 January 2013. But major problems remain. Not only are banks' reports suspect because opaque and unreadable (see Portnoy and Eisinger article, note 6), but international banking procedures are relaxing key regulations. Simon Johnson, Professor of Entrepreneurship at the MIT Sloan School of Management, notes: "This week the Basel Committee on Banking Supervision, as it is known, let us down — once again. Faced with renewed pressure from the international banking lobby, these officials caved in, as they did so many times

From the beginning of the recession, Marta Pelaez, CEO of Family Violence Prevention Services in San Antonio, Texas,[11] has regularly been supervising a cascade of personal and family tragedies arising from reduced pay and unemployment: leaner meals, tighter budgets, loss of medical insurance (if any existed), and lost homes, all in a setting of increasing domestic violence. As Pelaez continues to witness, the husband dares not express his anger to employers at being laid off, so he beats up his wife and often his children. (Of course, women are being laid off too, which compounds the problem.) Draconian immigration enforcement in certain communities also gives men additional power over women. "You report me for having beaten you up and I'll get you deported and keep the (American-born) children here." More deterioration ensues, if fathers abandon their families or malnutrition and infection lead to serious illness.

Men require help, too. Before they physically do damage to their families, they need to be shown better choices. Those returning from Iraq or Afghanistan who cannot find employment have the additional handicap of speaking a language of combat better suited to the violence they have known than to the needs of their reunited families. And it's well known that family strife suffered by young children and teenagers is directly connected to their later dysfunction: dropping out of school and work, joining gangs, taking up drugs, and regularly engaging in violent behavior. These social maladies existed before this crisis. But now they are worse.

This situation is unlikely to get better soon. Unemployment and inner-city blight are likely to grow long after the banks and stock markets are doing better. Rightly outraged, the general public needs to be aware of what is happening nearby. People of faith should know the status of their own

---

in the period leading to the crisis of 2007-8. As a result, our financial system took a major step toward becoming more dangerous." Johnson writes that the euro zone in particular is trying to emerge from its present crisis by allowing banks to take higher risks with more debt and less equity. Johnson's solution: "The United States must go it alone. Basel agreements should be a floor on our bank regulation (including bank capital, leverage and liquidity), not a ceiling. If our tighter rules induce dangerous banking activities to leave the United States, that is fine. In fact, we should offer to help them pack." "Betrayed by Basel," *New York Times,* 10 January 2013, http://economix.blogs.nytimes.com/2013/01/10/betrayed-by-basel. But the U.S. was among the two dozen countries that agreed to this rollback of the so-called Basel III rules of 2010. The new assets on which increased liquidity will be based are the same as those the banks found difficult to value and trade in 2008. Anat Admati, professor of finance and economics at Stanford, calls this move a recipe for disaster. Editorial, "A Step Backward in Bank Regulations," http://www.nytimes.com/2013/01/10/opinion/a-step-backward-in-bank-regulations.html. — *Ed.*

11. Interview of Marta Pelaez, *Bill Moyers' Journal,* PBS, 20 March 2009.

members. Where they can, everyone should support agencies that confront such conditions, and with proper orientation and training, volunteer to help. But outrage and action need to go hand in hand with analysis by both professional and volunteer groups to study the root of these issues.

Such analysis must be of a "situation-sensitive" sort. We simultaneously see people's problems, hear their stories, and offer immediate help, while we also critique our larger financial structures: corporations, banks, and international organizations. To do so requires becoming liberated from the false assumption that workable economic systems can only be designed in one way. Then we are more likely to find categories that keep us at once in the double world of human misery and abstract critical thought. Such simultaneous situation-sensitive analysis is the goal of this book. And faithful people who have a common heritage in the Abrahamic tradition are particularly suited to take on this job.

Economics and Its Religious Critics

Someone has said that economics deals with matters too important to be left to economists. Even if many have so far been insulated from this downturn's worst consequences, silence cannot remain the answer. Middle-class Christians and their Jewish and Islamic counterparts are naturally led to enter the debate about future developments for several good reasons. First, we are deeply implicated in what has occurred. For generations, our religious bodies have been dependent on the generous gifts of people who, if they do not themselves own stocks and bonds, either already do, or soon will, benefit from pension funds deeply invested in the world's financial markets. In addition, the global missions of our faiths heavily depend on an established pattern of money donated and invested for that purpose. In brief, we are simultaneously players and beneficiaries of an economic system that has suffered debilitating losses, seemingly through a variety of irresponsible, unjust, or illegal decisions.

But second, as we've seen, these losses more severely impact the structurally disadvantaged. Christians and others have a track record of making this moral responsibility our prior concern. For half a century now, the World Council of Churches has embraced "a preferential option for the poor." More recently, documents such as the *Accra Confession* of 2004, a statement issued by an international council of the World Alliance of Reformed Churches, have prioritized support for the oppressed and impoverished.[12] So we have a well-established duty in helping these voices speak in the world's centers of power. These institutions are a vital conduit allowing the poor to directly announce their needs there. In this process, our own reasons for such action are useful to recall and renew.

Scriptural Warrants

Today the Bible is primarily seen less as speaking of unworldly spiritual truths and more as recording the ways that the faithful wrestled with the ethics of concrete economic problems. Reading the Torah, New Testament, and the Qur'an for guidance on these matters, we need to remember that though we wish to honor the meanings such texts may have had to their original authors or readers, not only is this information impossible to recover for sure, but our present situation also shapes our understandings. Throughout this book, I follow a version of Paul Ricoeur's insight that texts inevitably pass through many interpretive contexts, the more so if they are strongly allegorical or metaphorical.[13]

With this important proviso, the economic crisis allows us to see striking parallels between the Leviticus 25 Jubilee tradition and present attempts to find positive consequences that could come from the downturn. Ancient Israelites of great practical insight were responsible for beginning the Jubilee tradition, which involved the remission of debts and the liberation of slaves. They saw that unacceptable debt could pile up generation after generation, especially among the poor. When homes and fields were lost, former owners would become tenant farmers. Exactions from their new masters and onerous taxes continued to exploit them, so that again falling into debt, they would finish as slaves along with their spouses and children. The eighth-century BCE Hebrew prophets (Amos, Hosea, First Isaiah, Micah) often talk precisely about such injustices against the poor.[14] Meanwhile, landlords and financiers grew increasingly powerful, joining former small farms together into vast real-estate holdings.

Since these holdings continued into Jesus' time, he echoed these Jubilee

12. *The Accra Confession: Covenanting for Justice in the Economy of the Earth* (Geneva: World Alliance of Reformed Churches, 2004), p. 4.

13. Lewis S. Mudge, ed., Introduction, *Essays on Biblical Interpretation,* by Paul Ricoeur (Philadelphia: Fortress Press, 1980), pp. 4ff.

14. *Holy Bible, New Revised Standard Version* (Oxford: Oxford University Press, 1989). All subsequent quotations from the Bible are from this source.

expectations in identifying his own mission with that of Isaiah, implying that he had the same mandate: ". . . to let the oppressed go free, to proclaim the year of the Lord's favor" (Luke 4:18-19). Again, in announcing the Beatitudes, he says, "Blessed are the meek, for they will inherit the earth" (Matt. 5:5), and in the Lord's Prayer: "And forgive us our debts, as we also have forgiven our debtors" (Matt. 6:12). Matthew's chapter 25 tells of Jesus on the Mount of Olives speaking to his disciples in parables. In the last one, he distinguishes the "goats" from the "sheep," those who have served the hungry, thirsty, homeless, unclothed, sick, and imprisoned, and thereby have also served him. Jesus so fully identifies with the poor as his family that he himself is present *in* them and in their condition: "Truly I tell you, just as you did it to one of the least of these who are members of my family, you did it to me" (Matt. 25:40).[15]

A Protestant Reformed Legacy

Reading the Bible in such ways has helped Reformed Christians to rediscover that ethical struggles with economic questions have long been in their genes. The sixteenth-century origins of the Reformed tradition coincided historically with a major start in the development of entrepreneurial consciousness in Europe. Controversy now simmers over the nature of that exact relationship.[16] But Max Weber's celebrated thesis, as elaborated by

15. [In 2012, an arm of the Occupy Wall Street group, Strike Debt, gained the support of religious groups for their Rolling Jubilee program. This program terminates defaulted loans by buying them up for pennies on the dollar. Hugely successful, to date about $10 million in debt was slated to be abolished. Nathan Schneider, "How Occupy Wall Street Got Religion," *Nation of Change*, 21 December 2012, p. 2, http://www.nationofchange.org/how-occupy-wall-street-got-religion-1356104826. See more about the Occupy Movement, Ch. 2, n. 107. — Ed.]

16. Testing the Weber-Tawney hypothesis, social philosopher Michael Walzer studied hundreds of sixteenth- and seventeenth-century English Puritan sermons in search of explicit connections between Calvinist faith and capitalist presuppositions and practices. He found very few such links. Walzer concluded that socioeconomic factors such as migration from the countryside to the cities, rather than theological arguments, taught Puritans the need for certain economic survival virtues. Furthermore, comparable "capitalist" virtues have been found in many non-Reformed and non-Christian people such as Korean, Chinese, and other Asian merchants both in their home situations and migrating to North America. But, then, does the success of Presbyterianism among Koreans in both Korea and North America stem in part from some sort of mutual reinforcement between Calvinist preaching, Confucian

R. H. Tawney, still stands: that Christians in the Calvinist tradition tended to be anxious about whether they had personally been predestined to salvation in heaven, since in this life they could not know. For them, worldly success was at least a clue of God's favor. Naturally, then, they would strive for material rewards to increase their reassurance. Besides, salient character traits abetted this need: assiduous bookkeeping, honesty, and reliability. John Calvin, the controversial sixteenth-century French reformer-pastor who helped make Geneva, Switzerland, a center of Reformed church and government, became a towering establishment figure. Today's irresponsible mismanagement of wealth by the West's great financial institutions would have appalled him, and its disastrous effect on millions would have appalled him all the more. Calvin observed, "Many so enslave all their senses to delights that the mind lies overwhelmed. Many are so delighted with marble, gold, and pictures that they become marble, they turn, as it were, into metals. . . ."[17]

An important part of the connections between economics and theology may be told in terms of consistent, yet ever-adapting Reformed attitudes toward money lending, or "usury." Much that has gone wrong in both national and global economies has had to do with lending and borrowing in varieties of complex ways, from payroll loans and mortgage lending, to individuals, to massive transactions involving corporations and governments. Biblical warnings (Exod. 22:25; Lev. 25:35-36; Deut. 23:10-20; Luke 6:35) focus on lending practices that take advantage of others' financial distress, and especially on the evils of exploiting the poor.

Calvin, writing in the *Institutes of the Christian Religion* (first published 1536) and elsewhere, continues the prohibition of charging interest to the needy. But he also acknowledges that commercial, as opposed to personal, loans can mean gains for both lender and borrower.[18] Borrowing money to

---

values, and existing economic opportunities? *The Revolution of the Saints* (Cambridge, MA: Harvard University Press, 1982).

17. *Institutes of the Christian Religion*, 3.10.3, ed. John T. McNeill, trans. Ford L. Battles (Philadelphia: Westminster, 1960), p. 722.

18. Calvin wrote in his Biblical Commentaries, Exodus 22:25: ". . . Usury is not now unlawful, except insofar as it contravenes equity and brotherly union." Tolerating usury, Calvin nevertheless observed: "It is scarcely possible to find in the world a usurer who is not at the same time an extortioner and addicted to unlawful and dishonorable gain. Accordingly, Cato of old justly placed the practice of usury and the killing of men in the same rank of criminality, for the object of this class of people is to suck the blood of other men." Comm. Psalm 15:5. William J. Bouwsma, *John Calvin: A Sixteenth-Century Portrait* (New York: Oxford University Press, 1988), pp. 198, 285 n. 85.

make money thus began to become commonplace. The question then became, what constitutes *excessive* interest? In *The Book of Confessions* of the Presbyterian Church (USA), the topics of borrowing and lending are treated largely in commentaries on the Eighth Commandment, "Thou shalt not steal." See, for example, the *Heidelberg Catechism* (1562) on "exorbitant interest" under "pretext of right," and the *Westminster Larger Catechism* (1547) on "fraudulent dealing" and "injustice and unfaithfulness in contracts." In this last, the duties required by the admonition not to steal include, in addition to the above:

> . . . giving and lending freely according to our abilities and the necessity of others; moderation in our judgments, wills and affections regarding worldly goods; . . . frugality; and an endeavor by all just and lawful means to procure, preserve and further the wealth and outward estate of others, as well as our own.[19]

Seventeenth-century civil law, enacted under strong Reformed influence, particularly in Britain and the Netherlands, generally permitted charging interest in business transactions, but maintained, with Calvin, that charging interest to the economically distressed was an immoral act, because it adds to rather than relieves that distress.[20]

Much has changed, of course, in five hundred years. Industrialization, the rise of the modern corporation, and the emergence of giant banking

---

19. *The Constitution of the Presbyterian Church (USA), Part I: Book of Confessions* (New York and Atlanta: Office of the General Assembly, 1983); see 4.110, 7.251, and 7.252.

20. See the lucid summary on these subjects, with historical quotations, in *A Reformed Understanding of Usury for the Twenty-first Century*, Report of the Advisory Committee for Social Witness Policy, 217th General Assembly (Louisville: Office of the General Assembly, 2006). [The author's friend Don Shriver, former president of Union Theological Seminary, and his wife recommend exploring this ACSWP draft report further, and ask, "Why is 5% interest legitimate and 30% not? Here, the old idea of 'just price' [is relevant to] your discussion of the difference between making money from money ad infinitum and making things for human need. Official capitalism abandoned just price centuries ago — e.g., the cost of production does not determine price. Only the market determines price, with no limit on profit. The same issue abounds in questions of compensation: you buy wage workers at the lowest possible price, then you sell their products at the highest possible price for the largest possible return to investors — and top executives. One has to confront this 'ethic' head-on with another ethic. One does not have to be a Marxist to do so! It would be worth studying the perplexities and cautions of two parables, Matthew 20 and 25. In the one, all workers get equal wages. In the other, all investors get returns according to their wise or no-use of capital." Donald and Peggy Shriver, email attachment to author, 8 August 2009. — *Ed.*]

and brokerage institutions doing nationwide and international business have called for the availability of enormous quantities of capital. In the light of their development, seventeenth-century financial admonitions seem simplistic and almost naïve. Clearly, Presbyterians and other Christians in today's business community have largely forgotten these confessionally enjoined economic principles, as shown by skyrocketing levels of credit card interest, and biblical prohibitions of lending practices that exploit the poor, as in banks' widespread resistance to modifying the terms of mortgages for clients who are "under water" with homes worth less than their mortgage value.[21]

The lending and borrowing practices from Jesus to Calvin to today's financial complexities may seem far apart. But the principles of lending and borrowing, borrowing and lending, *still* stand as essential actions in contemporary economics in both mortgage markets and the most intricate Wall Street transactions. Lending and borrowing are at the heart of leveraging in which financial assets are bought with borrowed money in hopes that their value will rise, making it possible to pay off the original loans and still make

21. The government's Home Affordable Modification Program (HAMP), designed as an incentive payment plan for mortgage banks to assist "distressed homeowners," has been undersubscribed in spite of the $50 billion committed as part of the bank bailout program. The three big mortgage banks (Wells Fargo, JP Morgan Chase, and Bank of America) have been encouraged by the Treasury Department to improve their respective lending practices. Andrew Martin, "Banks Penalized for Performance in Mortgage Modification Program," *New York Times*, 10 June 2011, p. B4. In early February 2012, a federal and state effort made a $26 billion settlement with five of the largest home lenders, the above-mentioned three plus Citigroup and Ally Financial. Obama announced that this would be a start in helping the collapsed housing market, especially for "underwater" properties (owing more than their worth). Negotiations are underway to increase this settlement to $30 billion by including nine more other major servers. Chris Isidore and Jennifer Liberto, "Mortgage Deal Could Bring Billions in Relief," CNNMoney, 15 February 2012. However, this deal was seen at the time as too lenient for the banks. Editorial, "Too Many Unanswered Questions, and Too Little Relief," CNNMoney, 11 February 2012. By May, most of this money was not reaching its intended parties. Twenty-seven states had already diverted the funds to cover other priorities. Those most affected were minorities, especially African Americans, who in some cities were the principal victims of the housing crisis. Shaila Dewan, "Needy States Use Housing Aid Cash to Plug Budgets," *New York Times*, 16 May 2012, p. A1. As of mid-July 2012, more than 11 million U.S. homeowners were underwater five years after house prices began their plunge. Dean Baker, Center for Economic Policy and Research, "California Gold Rush? Righting Underwater Mortgages," www.nationofchange.org, 17 July 2012. By the end of the first quarter of 2013, despite the rise in housing prices, 25.4 percent of homes, affecting 13 million homeowners, were underwater. Zillow Report, "The U.S. Housing Crisis: Where Are Home Loans Underwater?" http://www.zillow.com/visuals/negative-equity/#4/39.98/ -107.01. — Ed.

a profit. But when leveraging produces gigantic pyramids of promissory notes that come due when the underlying assets have lost their market value, a collapse of the sort that is now globally felt ensues. And such financial disaster hurts the poor most of all.

Lessons from the Global South

A few decades ago, contemporary Christians in the South, determined to put an end to American and European imperialism and to secure justice for the poor, reminded the paper titans among today's Christians of their biblically and confessionally mandated economic duties. Liberation thinkers showed us how resistance to these duties has sunk into the assumptions of Western economic life for several centuries. Today, Christian ethicists are in the forefront of those pointing out how the market has become so taken-for-granted and determining in our economic thinking that we deceive ourselves into believing our behavior is moral, when it is not.[22]

Can "liberation economics," North and South, now be considered validly grounded in sixteenth- and seventeenth-century Reformed standards for conduct in business? Yes and no. Concern for the impact on others of what we do is still basic. But categories of thought and a new totally global scale of economic life in this century have emerged. Christian ecumenists, many of them Reformed, have recently produced numerous thoughtful statements bearing on global economic justice. The Kairos Document, the Belhar Confession of South Africa, and the World Council of Churches (WCC) Agape process, to name leading examples among many, have been a series

---

22. See Rowan Williams, "Theology and Economics: Two Different Worlds," speech given at 40th National Conference, Trinity Institute, New York, 27 January 2010, http://www.trinity wallstreet.org; Gary Dorrien, "Economic Crisis, Economic Democracy, Religious Awakening," www.tikkun.org/article.php?stor=sept2010dorrien; Jim Wallis, *Rediscovering Values: On Wall Street, Main Street and Your Street* (New York: Howard Books, 2010). Cherie Blair and Desmond Tutu, "Ubuntu Declaration for a Just and Sustainable World Economy," Emergency Congress, London, 23-25 February 2009. This congress, jointly organized by the South African Human Rights Commission and Tomorrow's Company, was endorsed by former UK Prime Minister Gordon Brown. It brought together a unique gathering of two hundred leaders from the UK and other governments, UN agencies, the World Bank, the corporate sector, trade unions, civil society, academia, faith communities, and the media. See also Jonathan Sacks, *The Dignity of Difference* (New York: Continuum, 2002), where Sacks, chief rabbi of the United Hebrew Congregations of the British Commonwealth, focuses on the role of religion and morality in a global market economy, well before this current crisis. — *Ed.*

of efforts to see global household management, or *oikonomia,* through the lenses of the gospel.[23]

In particular, over recent decades, the World Alliance of Reformed Churches (WARC)[24] has sought its members' support for a liberationist perspective. The effort began in Ottawa in 1982 with WARC's declaration that the theological defense and ecclesiastical practice of *apartheid* by white Dutch Reformed churches in South Africa constituted a *status confessionis,* a situation in which integrity in the faith was at stake. At Debrecen, Hungary, in 1997, the Council adopted a strong statement on injustice in the global economic order.

How is this recent activity linked to historic Reformed conceptions of middle-class worldly responsibility? While few, if any, explicit connections are claimed in the Debrecen and Accra declarations, there can be no doubt that the tradition engenders a sense of freedom to "let new truth spring forth" from God's word. Debrecen and Accra exercised their responsibilities to God's promises in a new global situation, just as Reformed forebears exercised their responsibilities in previous situations. How so?

Debrecen, in addition to its acute economic analysis,[25] made one attempt to graft new meanings into an old text. In Book III, chapter 7, section 1 of the *Institutes,* Calvin repeats over and over the words "we are not our own," adding codas each time that express social and other concerns in the language of his day. Debrecen rewrote Calvin's words, inserting both traditional and liberation themes after each repetition within Calvin's litany. The resulting "Declaration of Debrecen" was signed by most of the participants and spoken in unison at the closing event of the Council. Two of its clauses give the flavor:

> *WE ARE NOT OUR OWN:* We know that in Jesus Christ we were bought with a price. We will not patronize, exclude or ignore the gifts of any person, male or female, young or old. We declare our solidarity with the poor, and with all who are suffering, oppressed or excluded.

23. The Kairos Document (2007) focused on conflict resolution between Israel and Palestine. The Belhar Confession, originally adopted in South Africa (1986), addressed racism. Initiated in 1998 in Harare, the AGAPE process (2005) involves several projects concerned with economic globalization and its implications for people and the earth (Geneva: World Council of Churches, 1986, 2005, and 2007).

24. As of 2010, WARC was renamed the World Communion of Reformed Churches (WCRC). — *Ed.*

25. Debrecen's economic analysis was the work, among others, of Kim Young Bok of South Korea and Bob Goudzwaard, now professor emeritus of economics at the Free University, Amsterdam, and former member of the Dutch Parliament.

WE ARE NOT OUR OWN: We believe in the Holy Spirit who will guide us into all truth. We refuse the false assumption that everything, including human beings and their labor, is a commodity and has a price.

The Accra Declaration of 2004, based upon a theology of empire, reflects a desire to denationalize such empire in global trade and finance. But it could also be specifically understood as an exercise of the responsibility to resist unjust rulers as taught by Calvin in the *Institutes*. Although Calvin was inclined to find social good in the support of established orders, he also spoke of the need to oppose injustice by organized political means. WARC has tried to embody this opposition for our times, condemning the manner in which our current established orders have organized the economic world. Perhaps doing so has opened a new chapter in the long argument about what it means to be Reformed Christians. Accra announced:

> As we look at the consequences of globalization for the most vulnerable and for the earth community as a whole, we have begun to rediscover the evangelical significance of the biblical teaching of empire.
>
> We recognize the enormity and complexity of the situation.[26] We do not seek simple answers. As seekers of truth and justice and looking through the eyes of powerless and suffering people, we see that the current world (dis)order is rooted in an extremely complex and immoral economic system defended by empire. In using the term "empire," we mean the coming together of economic, cultural, political and military power that constitutes a system of domination led by powerful nations to protect and defend their own interests.
>
> We see the dramatic convergence of the economic crisis with the integration of economic globalization and geopolitics backed by neoliberal ideology.[27] This is a global system that defends and protects the interests of the powerful. It affects and captivates us all. Further, in biblical terms, such a system of wealth accumulation at the expense of the poor is seen as unfaithful to God and responsible for preventable human suffering and

26. The "situation" referred to here is that of 2004, not that of the 2008-9 meltdown, and yet Accra anticipated many of the latter's causes and characteristics.

27. The word "neoliberal," even now not well-known in North America, is explained by the Accra drafters as "a political-economic philosophy that de-emphasizes or rejects government or other intervention in the economy; it would allow the market to operate without restraints or protections. Neoliberal economics focuses on property rights rather than human rights. It promotes the market as the primary engine of human economic activity, emphasizing competition and growth, and upholding individual self-interest over the common good."

39

is called Mammon. Jesus has told us that we cannot serve both God and Mammon (Luke 16:1-3).[28]

Here is an implicit move from the classical Reformed dependence on Romans 13 for teaching about obedience to authority to the condemnation of world empires. Luke 16:1-3 is a favorite passage of the three "historic peace churches" — the Mennonites (including the Amish), the Church of the Brethren, and the Religious Society of Friends, or the "left wing of the Reformation." So we learn from experience, and from the experience of others. The Reformed tradition is today less an "establishment" tradition than it was in Calvin's time and through much of its history. It has moved from a social location at the center to the margins of power. Doing so, it is now in a better position to grasp the meaning of solidarity with those whose lives have been cursed rather than blessed by market ambitions.

Responses in Europe and North America

European and North American theologians and ethicists were deeply involved in drafting the Accra Confession and in other moves and statements made by WARC and the WCC. Many of them have done their work alongside and in solidarity with thinkers whose contexts have been largely marginal to contemporary "turbo-capitalism." North Americans have gained indispensable insights from these connections. In particular, feminists have contributed much to the discussion of the marginalization and oppression of women worldwide, a parallel to that same exclusion of both sisters and brothers in the South.[29] In particular, the Presbyterian Church (USA) through its Advisory Committee on Social Witness Policy (ACSWP) has produced a series of more detailed studies directly or indirectly bearing on these questions, before and after Accra. They also reflect the denomination's less-dominant social location. Among these are *Hope for a Global Future*

---

28. *The Accra Confession*, pp. 3-4.

29. Rosemary Radford Ruether's writings on globalization and liberation theology are exemplary testimony to the marginal status of women. See her *Integrating Ecofeminism, Globalization, and World Religions* (Lanham, MD: Rowman & Littlefield, 2005). [At the 2013 World Economic Forum in Davos, only 17 percent of the global business and political leaders were female. Nicholas D. Kristof, "She's (Rarely) the Boss," Op-Ed, *New York Times*, 26 January 2013, http://www.nytimes.com/2013/01/27/opinion/sunday/kristof-shes-rarely-the-boss.html ?_r=0. — *Ed.*]

(1996), *The Globalization of Economic Life: Challenge to the Church* (2001), *Just Globalization: Justice, Ownership and Accountability* (2006), and *The Responsibilities of Global Citizenship: A Study Guide* (Draft, 2008). With such documents as guides, now is the time to grasp the opportunities that go with our anxieties. Now is the time to begin to envision for a post-crisis world the sorts of just economic policies that Christian and other thinkers have been urging for many years.

In short, people of faith in North America and Europe are now in a strategic position to become liberationists themselves. They are ready to truly hear what prophets in the global South have long been saying: "We appreciate your solidarity with *our* struggles, but wish that you would also begin to fight your *own* battles, for these are ours as well." American religious bodies now begin to realize that they are living at the epicenter of the global financial irresponsibility that threatens the well-being of the entire planet. It is *our* institutions that need radical reform. The big banks, guilty of irresponsible lending and wildly undercapitalized leveraging of derivatives to produce financial obligations alienated from the real economy of goods and services, are the same institutions that have branch offices on main streets all across the land. We see what our own greed and consumerism, in combination with theirs, have done in leading to the foreclosure signs dotting our residential streets. We must learn from the global South, but we must also think biblically *for ourselves* in solidarity with them, deriving our *own* strategies for revision of our attitude and reform of our economic institutions.

Spurred by this message from the South, enforced by our own tradition, it is most appropriate for the Abrahamic faiths to respond to the effects of this global meltdown. Our scriptural and theological resources are at hand. With a renewed sense of responsibility we may use these resources constructively and justly.

Historical Analogies in the Search for Justice

Similar troubled times in the past are instructive. The period just before and during World War II was an economic and spiritual moment both like and unlike our own crisis. With the Great Depression still a grim reality and armed conflict already on the horizon, religious thinkers were both struggling with economic realities and creatively imagining what a post-crisis world might be like. These glimmerings within a crisis of a post-crisis world emerged as early as the World Conference on Church and Society in

Oxford in the summer of 1937, followed by a smaller meeting for ecumenical planning in Utrecht in 1938. When war broke out, these efforts had laid the groundwork for continuing communication between Christians despite living on both sides of the belligerent nations. They also led to the postwar formation of the World Council of Churches in 1948 with its theme of "responsible society."

At roughly the same time, politicians and economists were beginning talks that eventually led to the Bretton Woods Monetary and Financial Conference of 1944. It formulated the notions of a World Bank, an International Monetary Fund (IMF), and a General Agreement on Tariffs and Trade (GATT), all subsequently actualized by international treaties and put into operation in 1959. The GATT later became the World Trade Organization (WTO). The same kind of process, begun during the war, led to the United Nations and subsequently its many agencies, as well as to the Universal Declaration of Human Rights of 1948.

Unlike the ecumenical moves and meetings cited, the original wartime Bretton Woods Conference and the institutions it spawned touched very lightly, if at all, on principles of comprehensive economic justice. Rather, the Bretton Woods preoccupation might have been called, after Adam Smith, "the wealth of nations," especially the victor nations in World War II. The war had at last put an end to the Great Depression, and the idea was to create institutions for a new global financial system, making the world safe for corporate and national entrepreneurship. The principal players in this effort were the U.S. and Britain, whose representatives (most notably Britain's John Maynard Keynes) seem to have dominated the discussion.[30]

Little, if any, interaction apparently took place between the fledgling Christian ecumenical organizations and the emerging Bretton Woods in-

---

30. The revolutionary, controversial Keynes (1883-1946) is acknowledged to have been the major architect of these meetings. However, his hopes for the location of the IMF and an international currency did not materialize in his favor. Scott Neuman, "Is the World Ready for a New Bretton Woods?" National Public Radio, 29 October 2008, www.npr.org. [Keynes, one of the most lastingly influential macroeconomists of the twentieth century, introduced the concept of aggregate demand at the base of all economic activity. He also attempted to show that full employment is dependent upon government spending. "John Maynard Keynes (1883-1946)," The Concise Encyclopedia of Economics, http://www.econlib.org/library/Enc/bios/Keynes.html. The chief UK representative at Bretton Woods, Keynes urged the adoption of an International Clearing Union (ICU), a bank with its own currency, in regulating the balance of trade, hoping to help countries unable to rid themselves of trade deficits. The U.S. and others, firmly opposed, carried the day. www.wikipedia.org/wiki/United_Nations_Monetary _and_Financial_Conference. — Ed.]

stitutions. Justice discussions among the ecumenical conferees did not sufficiently go into international economic issues to justify contact or co-operation. "Responsible society" thinking, for all its value, quickly became associated in many minds with Western imperial aspirations, as reflected in Kipling's phrase "the white man's burden." Early postwar ecumenical thinking of this nature found itself progressively eclipsed over subsequent decades by the rise of "liberation theology." This was so especially after the 1966 Geneva Conference on Church and Society at which Richard Shaull, then a professor of ethics at Union Theological Seminary, made his famous attack on "responsibility" discourse as oblivious to growing revolutionary ferment among the "third world" poor.[31] There followed at least two ecumenical generations of primary (and very necessary) emphasis on economics "from the underside" and the emergence of the "preferential option for the poor" as perhaps its most memorable expression.

We now need to bring the knowledge, experience, and above all conviction that have been expressed in liberation themes as well as earlier perspectives to bear on our present opportunity to reshape the character of global economic institutions. The task will not be easy. We will not all see these institutions as worth revising. Some will judge the crisis as an opportunity, not for revision, but for sweeping the present economic order away entirely. Such a strategy, if history is any guide, would pile anarchy upon meltdown, followed by some form of tyranny. Perhaps *some* radical deconstruction might prove to be necessary to secure economic justice, but justice could not be guaranteed to be the result. The present proposal is more moderate. It looks toward a phase beyond both "responsible society" and "liberation theology" that learns deeply from both but tries to seize the moment to do something new.

Already a host of proposals for reconstructing the global financial system is coming out of the present financial meltdown. In November 2008, the Bush Administration called a "Bretton Woods II" meeting that seems to have produced very little, but at least it made public the idea. Post-collapse economic reconstruction strategies continue in Washington. All this suggests

31. See Paul Abrecht, "The Development of Ecumenical Social Thought and Action," in *History of the Ecumenical Movement: The Ecumenical Advance, 1948-1968,* ed. Ruth Rouse, Stephen C. Neill, and Harold E. Fey, vols. 1 and 2 (Geneva: World Council of Churches, 1993), pp. 235-59; and Lewis S. Mudge, "Ecumenical Social Thought," in *History of the Ecumenical Movement, 1968-2000,* vol. 3, ed. John Briggs, Mercy A. Oduyoye, and George Tsetsis (Geneva: World Council of Churches, 2004), 279-321. See also Michael Kinnamon and Brian Cope, eds., *The Ecumenical Movement: An Anthology of Key Texts and Voices* (Grand Rapids: Eerdmans, 1997).

another attempt by the U.S. to dominate the reconstructive process with a focus on the "Group of Seven" (G-7, sometimes G-8), or "Group of Twenty" (G-20) powers, and perhaps continued avoidance of comprehensive justice issues in the process. America must fully take into account the rise of Brazil, Russia, India, and China (the BRIC countries) and perhaps others (such as Argentina and a pan-Arab entry). Certainly, these nations represent very diverse economic assumptions and cultures that arise from a variety of religious roots shaping their respective value systems. Whatever these systems, the poor are largely left out.

The Challenge to an Involved and Divided Religious World

As we've seen, religious bodies are fully implicated in the economic system as it stands. Recently, Philip Wickeri has trenchantly outlined Christians' deep ties to the present order in his article, "The Political Economy of Christian Mission."[32] But the path toward remedying this situation will spawn a spectrum of dissent, making any new move difficult. Some years ago, Heidi Hadsell pointed out a postmodern multiplication of ethical perspectives.[33]

Whether Christian, Jew, Muslim, or secular, we all now live in a moral world of many voices, each having every right to be heard, and raising the question of confidence in moral generalizations of any sort. Certainly, efforts from the West alone to put *this* economic world back together risk accusations of racism, neocolonialism, or male chauvinism. Suspicion about any programs to surmount our present difficulties is thoroughly justified. Yet even if social ethics from a religious perspective start by being compromised and continue in disagreement about solutions, the effort to construct new global economic institutions is a covenantal human duty, especially for those in the Abrahamic tradition. We are bound to seek the well-being of all the earth's families (Gen. 12:3).[34]

32. Philip L. Wickeri, unpublished essay given as a lecture in Lew Mudge's class on "Globalization, Ecumenism and Ethics," the Graduate Theological Union, Berkeley, California, October 2008.

33. "Ecumenical Social Ethics Now," in *Beyond Idealism: A Way Forward in Ecumenical Social Ethics*, ed. Robin Gurney, Heidi Hadsell, and Lewis Mudge (Grand Rapids: Eerdmans, 2006), pp. 17-29.

34. The Hebrew term in Genesis 12:3 literally means "tribes," hence the Septuagint translation *phulai*. The Bible's King James and New Revised Standard Versions translate the word as "families." I use the even more neutral term "households" to emphasize that we are dealing

Of course, when we ask "Can any good come out of it?" the real question is "good for whom?" It seems unlikely that we will go back entirely to the *status quo ante*. We are undergoing a very substantial "reset" of our assumptions and structures, which makes the role of the Abrahamic faiths potentially even more important. Not only do their traditions have wisdom to offer, but being a worldwide presence, they have a crucial part to play in the foreign policy challenges that are simultaneous with this economic recovery.

Obviously, the human consequences of the downturn take priority. And solidarity with its most powerless victims is not only a pastoral duty for believers; it's also an indispensable angle for fully understanding the world's misery. Adopting the eyes of the world's poor moves us beyond previous arguments for the system's repair to visions for its transformation. This view from the "underside" could also help detach "the rich, the well-born, and the able" from their prejudice for unbound individual autonomy and the pursuit of personal and corporate wealth as first goals. Standing with the poor, we have to insist on justice as playing a central role. Our position, privileged but marginal and one with the impoverished, would help us influence decisions in their favor in any new "Bretton Woods" conversation. In short, this downturn gives interfaith bodies a great opportunity to probe and change centuries-old ideas about the way the world works and must work.

No doubt it's unrealistic to demand "a seat at the table," although existing ties to the UN and its agencies, through accredited nongovernmental organizations (NGOs), offer more opportunities than many imagine. Besides, getting too close to power puts one in danger of being co-opted by that power. A better way would be to set up a kind of parallel or shadow dialogue that would closely follow and critique the secular economic arguments now beginning to appear. Such a shadow dialogue would effectively include impoverished voices — both those who pre-date the crisis and those who have become its victims.

Some, of course, will dismiss such spiritual imaginings as a flight from present burdens toward a more happily foreseen world. Utopian philosophizing can be comforting. But any worthwhile imagining needs to be solidly grounded in confronting present conditions. In them lie the devil's details.

---

with all kinds of intimate economic units held together by preferred human ties, whether biological or simply associational. The word "families" may convey notions of the "traditional family," which is certainly included. But there are many other kinds of households that likewise function as morally nurturing primary communities, which is basic to my argument.

Our present focus will lack perspective if it does not represent a hopeful *realism* in touch with these details. Guided by ideals of justice, we need to grasp what the economists and politicians on the ground are dealing with.

Key Historic Economic Ideas

A brief look at Western economic history is necessary to fully understand our present plight. Economic life, as we know it today, is a partially corrupted product of a relatively long-term and highly complex process. The axis of cultural, scientific, and economic concern gradually shifted from what had been laid down in the past by authority and tradition to what human beings could achieve on their own. It fell to eighteenth-century Enlightenment philosophers to relieve established institutions of their responsibility for human well-being and to assume it for themselves. Thinkers such as Adam Smith pressed further, arguing for the autonomy of economic institutions and economic reasoning. In time, that view led to the idea of economics as a self-regulating field based on the informed pursuit of self-interest and illuminated by "rational choice theory."

This view continues to be taught in business schools with elaborate formulas and graphs, insulating economics from non-quantifiable value considerations. It insists that to function and produce annual growth, bankers and corporate leaders must be left alone, even if doing so leads to periodic recessions — like forest fires clearing underbrush — in which weak actors are weeded out. Indifference to the resulting effects on human life is justified by the principle of independence for economic reasoning wherever it leads. This sort of thinking has now led to disastrous consequences. People's homes, not just patches of underbrush, are consumed. Diagnosing today's downturn thus calls for attention to a history of ideas that help explain how we got to where we are.

Enlightenment Economic Philosophies

Our Enlightenment forebears anticipated little of what has now happened to us. In fact, many of them were simply fascinated with understanding the way things worked, especially in ethics, economics, and society. They were fond of the notion of *Homo faber*, "man" (sic) the maker or manufacturer, including in this case the maker of his/her own nature. Yet the story of these years may justly be called the story of a revolutionary kind of individual responsibility-taking for what humanity would do and therefore *be,* after centuries of generally accepting answers to these questions from established religious and political authorities.

Probably the most crucial idea behind such projects was that of personal *autonomy,* or finding one's authority in oneself or in the rules of what one does, as opposed to finding it in external or traditional sources. Human self-directedness implies responsibility; whatever we do is acknowledged to be morally *imputable* to us, making us subject to blame or to praise, to reward or punishment. The act is *my* act. I am the author of it. I am identified with it.[35]

Yet easily forgotten is the fact that this whole Enlightenment process of societal self-authorization began and continued for some time within a world of orthodox religious presuppositions. Carl Becker, in *The Heavenly City of the Eighteenth-Century Philosophers,*[36] argues persuasively that the *philosophes* still lived in a medieval world of established moral assumptions that they then sought to reproduce in naturalistic terms. As someone has said, they "demolished the Heavenly City of St. Augustine only to rebuild it with more up-to-date materials." For Becker, both Christians and Enlightenment revisionists "held fast to a revealed body of knowledge which provided for Christians salvation in the world to come and for the philosophers salvation in the world here and now."[37] Rejecting the Christian paradise, eighteenth-century philosophers constructed their own heavenly city. "For the love of God, they substituted love of humanity, for the vicarious atonement, the perfectibility of man through his own efforts; and for the hope of immortality in another world, the hope of living in the memory of future generations."[38]

John Locke, the seventeenth-century English philosopher-physician, is a perfect predecessor to Becker's *philosophes* of a century later. Now known as the "father of liberation," Locke's social philosophy reflects the influence of Calvinism in constructing a rational understanding of civil government. As a thinker in the social contract tradition, he saw community created not by revelation or custom but by the decisions of individual human beings

35. See Alan R. Mittleman, "The Modern Jewish Condition," *First Things* (October 1994), pp. 30-34.

36. Carl L. Becker, *The Heavenly City of the Eighteenth-Century Philosophers* (New Haven: Yale University Press, 1932).

37. Words of Donald K. Pickens, H-Net Review, June 2000, dpickens@unt.edu.

38. Trevor Colbourn, ed., *Fame and the Founding Fathers: Essays by Douglass Adair* (New York: Norton, 1974), cf. Becker, *Heavenly City,* p. 3.

in a "state of nature."[39] People are at the starting point of their forms of life-together, banding together to secure shared advantages not otherwise available. Preexisting communities are no longer *a priori* conditions of our humanness. Community is constructed, not piously received. Communal norms bind us only to the extent that we consent to them.

Locke's text was a self-aware attempt to give contractual shape to certain Calvinist presuppositions. Humanity's rights and privileges in the natural state derive from the medieval tradition of natural law, but even more, a set of recognizable theological assumptions. Persons in the "state of nature," an idealized (but not primordial) community of individuals, exist under, and in virtue of, God's dominion. These persons engage one another to make and maintain contracts in their shared status as creatures of God. Their status as moral actors rests on their responsibility as individuals before God. Contracted structures of authority are therefore also expressions of God's will.

Yet from Locke's time onward the religious context and sometimes unspoken religious presuppositions of social contract reasoning steadily weaken, while assertions of unlimited human autonomy grow stronger. By the eighteenth century, Locke's image of persons constituted not only by their relations as individuals to God, but also by their participation in a divinely validated network of social relations, begins to be challenged by a sense of the autonomous social actor pursuing his or her (mostly his) individual interests in the public realm. Locke's concept of society is superseded by one in which an ensemble of many individuals join together as citizens in rational pursuit of their various forms of self-interest.

But the result fails to ensure social cohesion. No framework of laws and values designed to trump individual acts of will emerges until thinkers of the Scottish Enlightenment begin to speak of "moral sentiments and natural affections." This is certainly not an explicitly religious, let alone a Calvinist, way of speaking. It is a general description of virtues liable to be found in any stable Protestant Christian culture, but certainly in principle replicable in other cultures, religious or otherwise. This description of the basis of social coherence appears in what is for some an unexpected place: the work of Adam Smith.

Smith's *Theory of Moral Sentiments* seeks to identify the kind of social

39. John Locke, "An Essay Concerning the True Original, Extent and End of Civil Government" (1690), in *Social Contract: Essays by Locke, Hume and Rousseau*, ed. Ernst Barker (New York: Oxford University Press, 1960).

bond still existing among newly emerging individual, self-interested social actors. He finds it in the universal human need for recognition and consideration by others. Every human being, for Smith, is interested in being the object of attention and approbation. This desire generates the primary sphere of human interaction within which there arise the different forms of economic life. Economic activity itself is thus rooted in noneconomic but certainly reasonable considerations, the need for appreciation and sympathy. The idea of a *moral* world within which economic activity is one expression among others underlies the later development of the notion of "civil society."

Smith, of course, is far better known for his book *The Wealth of Nations* and for his alchemy of the Invisible Hand, "turning the dross of rational self-interest into the gold of the public good."[40] This is, of course, the idea that the interaction of the rational self-interests of many different economic actors will lead to economic justice, for example, providing for the equitable distribution of grain. As stated by Smith, market forces and relationships alone drive his theory. It does not need moral sentiments or even recognition from others in order to work. In his effort to show how a just economy can be based on a confluence of individual economic choices, Smith seems to have forgotten his earlier book. One may even wonder whether the Invisible Hand, in which metaphor the logic shaping these economic choices is given a quasi-personal quality, may not actually function just because of the moral sentiments described in Smith's earlier work. Economics, in short, needs to be surrounded and undergirded by human meanings if it is to work in the real world as Smith's theory says it should.[41]

How do people decide whether or not to consent to the social contract with which they are confronted? In contract theory, the *polis* is constantly re-created by our consent to it. So society is a result of the concurrence of many rational acts of will. How otherwise do we get from individual autonomy to sociality or solidarity? From whence comes the political obligation to do any such thing at all? Does a sense of duty generate the obligation to consent to a *polis,* or may it just as well produce myriad individual ideas of what duty requires? One suspects that consent to any social arrangement issues from some sort of covert calculation of gains and losses, duty meaning pursuit of my own personal interpretation of obligation or responsibility, just as others

---

40. Adam B. Seligman, *The Idea of Civil Society* (New York: Free Press, 1992), p. 32.

41. See Gordon Brown, *Beyond the Crash, Overcoming the First Crisis of Globalization* (New York: Free Press, 2010), pp. 239-42. Recent biographies of Smith include: Nicholas Phillipson, *Adam Smith: An Enlightened Life* (New Haven: Yale University Press, 2010), and Ian Simpson, *The Life of Adam Smith* (New York: Oxford University Press, 2010). — *Ed.*

may freely pursue their own purposes. On such grounds, we come to live in a society in which pursuing such personal logic is taken as the universal law. Consent comes closer and closer to being calculation of what is best for *me*. I determine that *this* is a society in which I can pursue my personal aims while others do the same.[42] If I recoil at this utterly individualistic view of freedom, modernity offers the absolute control of the totalitarian state as an alternative.

"Rational Choice Theory"

Events and developments of many kinds separate us from the age of the *philosophes*, their predecessors and successors. But the character of modernity still owes much to them and the Western civilization they helped to bring into being. A globalizing version of autonomous aggrandizing behavior as normative human behavior rose concurrently with eighteenth-century colonialism. It continues today as an economic version of the principles of autonomy and globalization, precisely the scheme behind capitalism's universal projection of its values. Such a moral position threatens to unite humankind around purely acquisitive goals, leaving out all those incapable of playing such a game, or poorly positioned to do so. The right of the autonomous rule-giver, of the one who takes responsibility for making human life what it will be, is extended into the autonomy of economic conduct in the market. In this perspective, "human rights" are often interpreted as the "right to be left alone" to pursue whatever economic schemes one wants, ignoring any impact on others.

Today, we have moved from the mere fascination with devising how to be efficient to a crass aggrandizing of economic purposes that appears to sweep all human values before it. This is modernity expanded into globalization, and it needs to be saved from itself. Or more precisely, it needs to be saved from what it has made of the "common morality" that philosophers and theologians from time immemorial have sought. While these wise ones bent over their manuscripts, nations seeking wealth and power, in cooperation with private economic enterprises after the same goals, created a global

---

42. Such extreme self-interest was apparent in the Republican charge that President Obama's call for the wealthy to pay higher taxes amounted to "class warfare" at the same time that the Republicans called the country's deficit an "existential threat." Paul Krugman observed, "That amounts to a demand that a small number of very lucky people be exempted from the social contract that applies to everyone else. And that . . . is real class warfare." Krugman, "The Social Contract," Op-Ed, *New York Times,* 23 September 2011, p. A27. — *Ed.*

passion more powerful than any philosophically grounded universalism. The Enlightenment notion that human beings take autonomous responsibility for determining what society is to be has now produced a worldwide project of egregious irresponsibility toward the gifts that characterize us as human beings. We need now to be saved from a way of thinking that disastrously distorts the benefits that economic globalization might potentially confer.

The French scholar Pierre Bourdieu[43] stresses that we are dealing not merely with an economic agenda but with a "totalizing" ideological position. He has defined this perspective: "neoliberalism," a coinage still little known in the U.S. but now widely used elsewhere.[44]

Bourdieu uses the words "ideological" and "ideology" to mean ideas, including many with deeply historical, spiritual, or motivational contexts, that have at a certain time or place been "bent out of shape" to serve certain political or economic interests. Ideas such as "self-reliance," "property rights," "shareholder value," or "keeping the American (or British, or French, or Iraqi) people safe" have been attached to particular partisan ends, either by the social classes whose ends they are or by politicians trying to appeal to such voters. Concepts so bent are used to justify unjust policies, indeed to mislead people and their leaders about the true meanings and consequences of their actions. People can be led by ideologies to forfeit their own critical capacities for seeing "what is really going on."

With many others, Bourdieu sees "the market" as having become so dominant an ideological model in this sense as to be largely beyond question for a huge majority of today's movers and shakers. This is the case not only for the power elites that prosper under its assumptions but for many injured by those assumptions as well. Here is the "truth" that Western elites seemingly now hold "to be self-evident," as if it were pure rationality in practice. So pervasive has this logic become in our time that criticism of it begins to be considered irrational, as lying outside the boundaries of plausible discourse.

This logic consists mainly of cost-benefit analyses that sometimes make use of "rational choice theory." In this theory, self-interest and profit maxi-

43. Pierre Bourdieu (1930-2002) was a professor at the Collège de France and the author of books such as *The Field of Cultural Production* (1994), *Homo Academicus* (1988), *Invitation to Reflexive Sociology* (1992), *Language and Symbolic Power* (1993), and *The Logic of Practice* (1992).

44. The term "neoliberalism" in this sense is negligibly heard in North America and, if uttered here, is likely to be misunderstood as some sort of new Rawlsianism. The minute one travels to Western Europe or to Latin America, however, one hears the term being used, as Bourdieu does, to mean the dominance of the "market" model for all human interaction.

mization are assumed to be the only really rational (as opposed to unrealistically idealistic) human motivations. In effect, we have a new and greatly narrowed kind of social contract. By applying complex mathematical formulas, it is believed to be able to predict human actions and reactions. The Chicago economist Gary Becker even won the Nobel Prize in Economics for a book extending such calculations to the understanding of all human behavior.[45]

Such reasoning "colonizes" our life-world in ways that are often systematically and cleverly hidden.[46] This ideology has the means, largely through capture of the media, of making itself seem quite simply true, thereby forcing the progressive disappearance of "autonomous universes of cultural production." Independent publishers and filmmakers, independent media outlets, and other cultural institutions are forced to make their way with ever-diminishing public support. The neoliberal ideology, as Bourdieu sees it, eventually takes over all that lies in its way, but does so in an imperceptible manner, "like continental drift." Paul Treanor, a Bourdieu interpreter, has described the process in this directive:

Act in conformity with market forces.
Within this limit, act also to maximize the opportunity for others to
    conform to the market forces generated by your action.
Hold no other goals.[47]

In short, one is to keep to the spheres and objectives where rational choice, mathematical models, and the search for strategic advantage prevail.

45. See Gary Becker, *The Economic Approach to Human Behavior* (Chicago: University of Chicago Press, 1976). A useful brief discussion of Becker is in Larry Rasmussen, *Moral Fragments and Moral Community* (Minneapolis: Fortress Press, 1993), p. 49. As Rasmussen says, Becker is "arguing against Adam Smith's refusal to extend the logic of self-interest into non-economic territory, together with Smith's corollary conviction that different spheres require different moralities. In this scheme individuals are all 'utility maximizers' who operate from a relatively stable set of personal preferences. Quite apart from markets, then, there is a mental process of market behavior and logic that supplies all the guidance needed for moral and other considerations necessary to the thousands of decisions we make." One may add, however, that some forms of rational choice theory, particularly in the work of John Nash, stress the advantage-maximizing properties of market cooperation. But this hardly reduces the primacy of self-interest in the equation. Cooperation here is not altruism. It is a strategy of self-interest in itself.

46. Jürgen Habermas, *Theory of Communicative Action,* vol. 2 (Boston: Beacon Press, 1987), pp. 338-42.

47. This trenchant summary is found in "Neoliberalism: Origins, Theory, Definition," www.paultreanor/neoliberalism.html.

Doing so will make one powerful, wealthy, and, by definition, irresponsible to the people around one, their aspirations, their lives. This seems a terrible diminishment of the possibilities of the human spirit. Hold no other goals? The commercialization of all values? No wonder such a "totalizing"[48] mentality is blind to the consequences such attitudes have for most of the world's poor. No wonder they feel sidelined, diminished, and are justly resentful.

The predominance of "rational choice theory" in economic reasoning has more recently led to the "efficient market hypothesis," a theory that proclaims the stock market, in particular, to possess a form of rationality in itself. Economics, as taught in leading business schools since the 1970s, has become a matter of formulas and graphs claiming to describe, and often to predict, how economies based on competitive, rationally reasoned pursuit of interests and maximization of profits must necessarily work. If one wants growth and prosperity, then one must give the logic of the market free rein. Regulation is considered as interference with market logic. The money machine must be left alone to do its work. Such reasoning, practiced by commercial and investment banks as well as hedge funds and other financial institutions, underlies the processes that have led to the meltdown. To generate wealth, one must follow this reasoning above all other values. One must "hold no other goals."

Clearly, from Bourdieu's perspective, this economic ideology has taken on global political as well as economic dimensions. Critics see this globalization of capitalist production and exchange as fueled by American and Western European ambitions for world domination. The global South decries this pursuit of economic neoliberalism as the advance of "empire," to be resisted by every means possible. Such a view is everywhere, as mentioned above, in such documents as WARC's *Accra Confession* of 2004, and other publications.

Globalization based on a neoliberal ideology becomes Empire. In their book of that title, Michael Hardt and Antonio Negri state this thesis, "Empire is materializing before our very eyes. Over the past several decades . . . we have witnessed an irresistible and irreversible globalization of economic and cultural exchanges. Along with the global market and global circuits of

---

48. The terms "totalizing" and "totalization" have been used, particularly by such philosophers as Paul Ricoeur and Emmanuel Levinas, to refer to conditions under which some single vision of life is given politically dominant or even metaphysical status. In *Totality and Infinity*, Levinas refers to the moral struggle against metaphysical totalizations of ideology maintained in force by constellations of economic, political, or military power. *Totality and Infinity* (Pittsburgh: Duquesne University Press, 1962), p. 55.

production has emerged a global order, a new logic, and structure of rule — in short a new form of sovereignty."[49]

Among many consequences drawn by these authors is one already stated here in different terms. Economic reasoning going on in corridors of power has come to be thought autonomous and inevitable. It has been pried loose from political or cultural control, and thus from all social considerations other than the maximization of profit. "Our basic hypothesis," write Hardt and Negri, "is that sovereignty has taken a new form composed of a series of national and supranational organisms united under a single logic of rule."[50]

Naomi Klein's controversial book, *The Shock Doctrine: The Rise of Disaster Capitalism,* builds on this thesis by emphasizing the international corporate exploitation of human tragedies and disasters.[51] Klein attacks neoliberal economics and market fundamentalism. Her aim is to show how economic opportunists promote and profit from misery and disaster worldwide. One of her examples is the collapse of the Soviet Union leading to virtually unregulated "turbo-capitalism" that has brought misery to many and huge profits to the few. Another is the exploitation of circumstances following Hurricane Katrina in ways that have little aided the people most in need. Klein seeks to show how the U.S. military and intelligence services have consciously sought to aid global corporate interests bent on such opportunistic policies.

From books like these, it follows that today's global markets cannot be the servants of social welfare goals. Rather, their activity has gone on without heed to social consequences for good or ill, leading to much of the financial woe the world has experienced over the past years. As economic reasoning stood apart from all other considerations, playing by its own autonomous rules, it gave birth to a general assumption pervading society that things *have to be this way* in order to foster the continuous growth that makes for prosperity. As Margaret Thatcher famously said, "There is no alternative."[52]

We reject this sort of globalization and its imperial spread. But we differ from others who seem to find no benefit at all in an interlinked world economy. If the distribution of economic gains were regulated to be fair by a host of international bodies, the capacity to exercise human rights,

49. *Empire* (Cambridge, MA: Harvard University Press, 2000), p. xi.

50. *Empire,* p. xii.

51. (New York: Picador, 2007).

52. This iconic phrase, commonly known as "TINA," represents Thatcher's ideological perspective. Its substance embraces neoliberalism, free market capitalism, and maintenance of the status quo. See George Black, "The TINA Syndrome: Is There Life After Thatcher?" *Nation,* 8 May 2009, p. 46.

including the rights of women, would be greatly enhanced. National economic capacities for most if not all countries and the development of their citizens' personal capabilities would increase.[53] Personal growth and genuine self-determination beyond traditional limited expectations would also be advanced. Around the globe, people would become current with news and opinion, have a chance to express their views, and build networks of opinion-exchange across the Internet. Such possibilities would be an obvious educational boon to democracy. Which makes the unjust distribution of such assets the more reprehensible.

Studies of globalization leave us with an overwhelming and ironic question: Does the economic system that could generate such beneficial possibilities also need, for its competitive success, to be pursued with a single-mindedness that devalues, if it does not eclipse, all other ends for human life?

Neoliberal Market Rationality and the Present Downturn

The consequences of neoliberalism in action appear everywhere in accounts of today's ongoing global financial crisis. Bourdieu, Hardt, Negri, Klein, and others could almost say, "We told you so." Yet none of these writers actually predicts the sort of unraveling we have experienced. More important, this crisis may not mark the end of neoliberal economics. "Business as usual," only briefly interrupted, could return with vigor, leaving behind increased levels of misery for its prey. In any case, the numerous real-time analyses of the 2007-9 downturn have made little reference to the neoliberal ideology of empire. An explicit connection still needs to be made.

The connection may lie in the realm of the "structural."[54] Even in good times, the overlapping power structures of both neoliberalism and domestic American financial institutions exploit the poor. Our major banks and corporations do business both at home and abroad following a single seamless financial logic that puts profit first. That logic is then justified with arguments that ostensibly are purely economic but that contain ideological elements.

---

53. I allude to the "capabilities" approach of economist Amartya Sen. [See note 56. — *Ed.*]

54. A recent study of long-term racism and economic discrimination in the city of Detroit, now disclosed and exacerbated by the meltdown, turns on such structural analysis rather than on liberal, ameliorative moves that fail to grasp what is really going on. Gloria Albrecht, "Detroit: Still the 'Other' America," *Journal of the Society of Christian Ethics* 29, no. 1 (Spring/Summer 2009): 3ff.

For big business, with its own prosperity as a first priority, this is the way things have to be.[55]

Many who make these arguments fail to see that they are ideologically spouting self-deluding justification for the maintenance of power and privilege. These mandarins are unable or unwilling truly to see what is happening to either the domestic or global poor. Part of the self-delusion takes the form of covert racism that takes for granted that nonwhites cannot handle their financial affairs without supervision (read subprime mortgages, and ruinous lending rates for credit cards and payroll loans). That supervision may be designed to exploit them.

Most analyses of our downturn seem largely innocent of the fact that economic downturns are exacerbated because they disclose preexisting exploitative conditions in the economy, both global and domestic. Little of this appears in the otherwise useful observations coming from leading economists and observers such as Paul Krugman, Amartya Sen, George Soros, Joseph Stiglitz, Simon Johnson, Thomas Friedman, and many others. Our analysis does not offer any adequate critical account of these opinions. Rather, it sketches a storyline that generally reflects these economists' views without accounting for diverging interpretations of details.[56]

Reasons for the Crash: The Consensus Story

The heart of the mainstream narrative seems to be that our downturn is most of all the result of paper-thin, highly leveraged financial structures built to

---

55. See Gretchen Morgenson and Joshua Rosner, *Reckless Engagement: How Outsized Ambition, Greed and Corruption Led to Economic Armageddon* (New York: New York Times Books/Henry Holt, 2011). — *Ed.*

56. In 2008, I noted economist Amartya Sen's persuasive idea of using human capabilities — what a people are able to be and do — as an alternative measure to a quantitative assessment of a country's wealth, or Gross Domestic Product (GDP). Classical philosopher Martha Nussbaum, once academically linked with Sen, builds on this capability theory, listing distinctive human capabilities that justice demands we should respect and enhance — from life itself, to thought and imagination, to opportunities for play. Among other matters, Nussbaum's work has been criticized for being too individualistic and not contributing to "social capital." In addition, one capability that she does not mention is the virtue that Hannah Arendt felt is the most important to society's optimum functioning: the capability of receiving, making, and keeping promises. This capability is the gift of responsibility. Derived from Abraham's covenant narratives, it leads to society's blessings. This sort of motivation is needed for any capability to become more than simply personally satisfying. See my *Gift of Responsibility,* pp. 291-93.

maximize the wealth of financial elites, or oligarchies. Before 1985, their operations constituted no more than 16 percent of domestic corporate profits. In this century's first decade, they have grown to constitute 41 percent of those earnings, effectively taking over many of the functions of government. Simon Johnson of the Sloan School of Management at MIT largely blames this financial oligarchy for our global economic crisis.[57] Following Johnson's lead, we seek to show that the economic excesses of members of this oligarchy have closely adhered to the distinctive rationality of the economic realm, i.e., profit-maximizing by way of "rational choice theory," or "efficient market hypothesis," as described above. An alleged independence of economic reasoning from all other influences, moral or otherwise, led these oligarchs to make complex moves to isolate their operations from criticism. This hiding of the real facts involved enormous self-delusion and, objectively speaking, amounts in many ways to fraud.

As is well known, the meltdown in America began with the "subprime mortgage" crisis, and quickly involved the whole economic system. Ironically, mortgages were purposely contracted to entail borrowers with debt they could not afford in the name of "the American dream." In fact, in the business, these subprime mortgage loans were blatantly termed "liars' loans." Dishonesty began by banks pushing "subprime" loans on first-time, unsuspecting borrowers. These short-term, adjustable loans with interest rates lower than longer loans nevertheless had elevated contract costs for the greater risk. These adjustable rates would be reset, and a new contract with fees signed every few years. Clients might initially lie about their assets to meet the down payment, but often banks only required a minimal or even zero amount and without documented collateral. In a rising housing market, the bank presumably couldn't lose. If defaults led to foreclosure, the bank would profit by owning an appreciated property.

Then more often than not, the bank would "bundle" many loans, selling them as securities to faraway financial institutions. Afterward followed a process of securing AAA ratings for the "securitized" loans. (The rating agencies knew better; they were in on the character of these deals.) Finally, the insurance giant, AIG, among other similar institutions, insured these transactions against default, or credit default swaps. It was highly lucrative to do so, and the risk of having to make good on defaults all at once was thought to be remote.

---

57. Simon Johnson, "The Quiet Coup: How Bankers Seized America," *The Atlantic,* May 2009, www.theatlantic.com/magazine/archive/2009/05/the-quiet-coup/7364.

When housing values plunged, the premise for profits in the system collapsed. Banks could not resell properties in default for expected returns. The big government-supported mortgage firms Fannie Mae and Freddie Mac became insolvent. Other large private financial institutions and hedge funds had borrowed to further invest so that actual stakes in transactions might be a small percentage of their on-paper amounts, i.e., leveraging. They, too, were near fatal distress as awareness of the thinness of underlying values spread throughout Wall Street. Many supposed assets became "toxic," meaning that no one could determine their worth; thus they became nearly valueless. Virtually all lending activity ceased, and with that the engines of entrepreneurship, if not silenced, were greatly subdued.

In the emergency, the Treasury Department intervened and allowed Lehman Brothers to fail (as an object lesson to other firms?) while pumping taxpayer money into a variety of other financial institutions such as AIG and then into corporations such as General Motors and Chrysler. Stock prices kept dropping. Large and small banks could not make good on their obligations, since so many fell due at once. Suddenly the whole financial system teetered for lack of public confidence. The discovery that much of the taxpayer bailout money to AIG passed through to institutions such as Goldman Sachs where the then Treasury Secretary Henry Paulson had been CEO further diminished confidence, as did the revelation that Wall Street firms were paying huge bonuses — as if nothing had happened — to the very executives responsible for disastrous failures in judgment.[58]

The sort of thinking that allowed this system to implode was a result of the neoliberal ideology outlined above. The paper pyramids built by financial oligarchies on Wall Street reflected a view of economic rationality

---

58. Legal cases designed to erode financial regulatory reform have begun to enlarge and strengthen the work of lobbyists. A ruling by a federal appeals court limiting a provision in the Dodd-Frank Act for more open access by stockholders to nominate corporate directors will have the effect of inviting many more suits against the government's regulatory efforts. Ben Protess, "Court Ruling Offers Path to Challenge Dodd-Frank," *New York Times*, DealBook, 18 August 2011, p. 3. "Now [2012], Wall Street pay packages routinely include deferred cash payments and restricted stock awards that can be redeemed only after multi-year waiting periods." And companies rely on outside consultants to set these packages. Kevin Roose, "The Invisible Hand Behind Bonuses on Wall Street," *New York Times*, 16 January 2012, p. B1. Still, *Equilar* reports, despite "a scant 2 percent" increase over 2010, among the one hundred top-paid CEOs, the "median chief executive in this group took home $14.4 million — compared with the average annual American salary of $45,230." Natasha Singer, "In Executive Pay, a Rich Game of Thrones: C.E.O. Pay Gains May Have Slowed, But the Numbers Are Still Numbing," *New York Times*, 7 April 2012, p. BU1. For more on CEO compensation, see this chapter, note 100. — *Ed.*

as a realm unto itself with its own rules. The drive for profits, the search for every possible means to maximize gain, was justifiable motivation. In the process, it was quite alright if some at the top became very rich. Only with this sort of material incentive would others support the game, like hapless casino players hoping to be among the few who won immense payoffs. The lure of gain for its own sake was even the moral rationale for these players. If wealth were to be generated for the nation's purposes, the argument ran, greed needed to stimulate everyone. Otherwise, there would be no funding for pension funds, religious groups, universities, and social safety nets. For *this* reason "greed is good." So still runs the argument.[59]

A friend has pointed out that certain banks that refused to participate in the subprime mortgage market — even global ones such as ABN AMRO — did not succeed in that risky market and were bought out. That led to thousands losing their jobs in banking and related industries, such as accounting, law, and technology. In short, banks with moral scruples and their business associates were as much victims of the greed factor among their cohorts as were direct borrowers. This circumstance gives even more reason to reform the system and to call upon people of faith, already within the banking and financial worlds, to help bring that about.[60]

Economic Behavior, an Expression of the Human Condition

Something more than pure economic rationality has been going on here, namely, human perversity. Bob Goudzwaard, economist and former member of the Dutch Parliament, besides commenting theologically on the market's worship of mammon has described our recent economic behavior in the light of Goethe's *Faust*, as follows:

> Goethe, a one-time finance minister of the German state of Weimar, describes Faust as a magician who at the price of his soul contracts with Mephistopheles, the devil, who can fulfill all of Faust's earthly wishes. Instead

59. William Saint, formerly of the World Bank and a committee member of ACSWP, wrote Mudge, "To my mind, greed has now become much more blatant in society. It is no longer enough to play by rules that give you an unfair advantage; now it is necessary to denigrate and eliminate anyone who challenges you." William Saint, email to author, 15 August 2009. Steve Lohr, "First Make Money. Also, Do Good," *New York Times*, 14 August 2011, p. BU3. Lohr asserts that shared value is "an elaboration of corporate self-interest — greed." — *Ed.*

60. John R. Buchanan, email to author, 10 September 2009.

of the unsuccessful alchemy of gold, the successful alchemy of printed money (pyramids of promissory paper) promises to realize Faust's vision of infinite economic and technological progress. This arrangement produces a continuous growth in wealth without any corresponding increase in human labor. The economy gains the transcendental character that humanity formerly sought in religion. This, of course, is possible only if finance takes the lead over the real economy. Money can be produced more quickly and easily than goods that must be laboriously obtained. The real economy now seems to dance to the enchanting flute tones of a new piper who has no horizon other than that of a lust for infinite acquisition.[61]

Just so. Today's wizards of finance have built a paper economy, composed of leveraged and releveraged financial instruments, on top of the real economy, goods and services. They have worshiped these imaginary assets as if they were gods. But now the paper gods have toppled from their pedestals. Wall Street's high priests, who had induced ordinary people to worship at the same shrines, made them devotees inside the inner sanctum of the great god "wealth." Then this worship of values consisting only of paper promises to pay was unmasked as false, as fraudulent, as empty.

This self-serving focus on the necessary motive of greed for generating wealth has consistently blinded financiers to the fraudulent character of their enterprises and their social fallout. For them, it is a matter of rational choice. "Business is business is business," a law unto itself because of its very nature, and not to be criticized because it is not theological ethics. "A thing is what it is, and not some other thing," as Bishop Joseph Butler said in the eighteenth century. With such a belief, one puts "extraneous" or "external" moral considerations well second to economic life. Self-criticism is deflected

---

61. Goudzwaard with Julio de Santa Ana, "The Modern Roots of Economic Globalization," in Santa Ana et al., *Beyond Idealism: A Way Forward for Ecumenical Social Ethics* (Grand Rapids: Eerdmans, 2006), pp. 109-10. Goudzwaard is drawing on the work of Hans Christoph Binswanger, *Money and Magic: A Critique of the Modern Economy in the Light of Goethe's Faust* (Chicago: University of Chicago Press, 1994). [A case in point is the New Year's Eve fiscal cliff deal of 2012. Amgen, the world's largest biotechnology firm, received a half-billion-dollar loophole: a second two-year relief from Medicare cost controls for kidney dialysis drugs, which included their product, Sensipar. Senate Republicans who have benefited from Amgen's largesse, Mitch McConnell, Max Baucus, and Orrin G. Hatch, are leaders of the Finance Committee, which holds great sway on Medicare policy payments. Eric Lipton and Ken Sack, "Fiscal Footnote: Big Senate Gift to Drug Maker," *New York Times*, 19 January 2013, http://www.nytimes.com/2013/01/20/us/medicare-pricing-delay-is-political-win-for-amgen-drug-maker.html?pagewanted=all. — *Ed.*]

by a self-deceiving good conscience, while fleecing the poor and wrecking the economy in the process.

Nobel prize–winning economist George Akerlof of the University of California has in effect undermined the notion of economics as a closed system unaffected by "externalities" in his book with Yale's Robert J. Shiller, *Animal Spirits: How Human Psychology Drives the Economy and Why It Matters for Global Capitalism.*[62] Psychology is not the only thing Akerlof and Shiller discuss. They take into account such "externalities" as theories of justice and action-shaping narratives. The title *Animal Spirits* (a term borrowed from John Maynard Keynes) suggests that the authors continue to think of such things as aspects of the lower, noneconomic self that unfortunately adulterate the purity of economic reasoning. But despite the predominantly psychological orientation of their work, these writers in effect display the ways in which economics belongs not only among the mathematical disciplines but also among the humanities. Theories of justice and action-shaping narratives are the stuff of history and phenomenology of cultures. Economic assumptions and systems are part of "the phenomenology of spirit" (Hegel) just as much as are works of art, literature, architecture, music, and the like.

In brief, economics is a human discipline whose alleged independent rationality is a self-interested illusion, driven by the passions. In truth, economic motivation is but a subcategory of all human motivation, defined as our "effort to exist and desire to be."[63] Here is Plato's *thumos,* or passion. Here is the "desire" that animates Hegel's dialectics of successive cultural syntheses. Here is Spinoza's *conatus,* or life-force. For the Germans, alongside *habsucht,* the desire to possess, stand *kraftsucht,* the will to power, and *ehrsucht,* the lust after honor or the good opinion of others. These philosophical references help show that financial greed is not exempt from moral critique because maximizing profit is necessary to make the economic engine go. Rather, greed in the marketplace is a destructive part of the common human condition, as much subject to philosophical or theological critique as any other form of human behavior.

In the West, that critique involves pointing to humanity's proneness to sell its soul to the devil, given sufficient temptation, with the justification that such acts bring general prosperity. It also reveals that such behavior

---

62. (Princeton: Princeton University Press, 2008).

63. This phrase comes from Jean Nabert and is quoted and explicated by Paul Ricoeur in *Freud and Philosophy: An Essay in Interpretation* (New Haven: Yale University Press, 1970), pp. 44-45, 528.

happens because, in our culture, it *can*. Goudzwaard's Faustian analysis of wealth-building out of paper pyramids is an opening of human consciousness to the analysis of self-deception. In theological terms, the different but converging work of Reinhold Niebuhr does the same.[64] Unlike Akerlof and Shiller's (as well as Keynes's) talk of "animal spirits," Niebuhr sees the driving force of greed as "pride," a disorder of the highest level of the self: a spiritual rather than an "animal" disorder, possible because human beings are self-transcending creatures. And this very capacity for self-transcendence makes people prone to overreach, leading to self-destructive acts and eventually to despair.

The Augustinian-Niebuhrian analysis of sin as pride *(superbia, hubris)*, when properly understood, is hard for any honest Western-educated person to escape. It is aimed particularly at the sort of self-deceiving idealism that takes pride in one's supposed purity of heart and good intentions. Some feminists assert that this definition of sin applies mainly to male but not female sinners. For such women, the primary sin is seen as failure to assert oneself, thus to submit to marginalization.[65]

But isn't the point in this economic crisis to go beyond gender and ask which women or men, and in what situations, are we talking about? No matter the sex, are not undue pride and undue self-abnegation often mixed? Isn't it excessive pride that keeps anyone from the rough-and-tumble and that may masquerade as self-abnegation? For many women and some men, too much stock in one's self-worth prevents taking on worldly matters considered beneath them. That then provides an inner excuse to hold back when others would get into the fray. For many men and some women, a kind of pride can make them insensitive to the need for others to care and step forward. Predictably, such pride arises no matter the place or gender.

History and current media constantly show us self-interest manifesting itself in many personal and cultural forms. Dishonesty apparently has had, and will have, more expressions across the globe than does honesty. Corruption continues to be rife everywhere, more blatant in some places, more refined in others, but always, at base, corruption. Power-seeking may characterize the publicly selfless, too. Excessive self-esteem and desire for recognition are present in many different voices, including multitudes of

---

64. See Reinhold Niebuhr, "Man as Sinner," particularly the section, "The Relation of Dishonesty to Pride," in *The Nature and Destiny of Man,* vol. 1 (London: Nisbet & Co., 1941), pp. 216-20.

65. See Mary Daly, *Gyn/Ecology: The Metaethics of Radical Feminism* (Boston: Beacon Press, 1990). — Ed.

social action groups, representing distinct ethnic and class identities. Many kinds of idealism may be self-deceiving because the pursuit of worthy ideals tends to block one's capacity for self-criticism. And all such actions operate regardless of geography or sex.

If economic rationality masks various forms of self-deception in both men and women, it can also, with appropriate regulation and structural changes within institutions, be made to serve higher human purposes. Touchstones lie in the Abrahamic tradition. The way to find such possibilities in our present global economic system is not to come up with an idealized alternative and expect its glad adoption. Instead, we need to explore locations in our various societies and cultures where realistic examples for overcoming self-justified greed may be appearing. This way is to draw a mental map of actual, rather than Niebuhr's "impossible," possibilities.

In a related matter — gender parity among resources for this study — two groups need to be separately identified: women ethicists and theologians who were invited to participate, and women economists reporting in the larger secular world. Of the first group, a handful of women were generally helpful but their own projects took priority, and they did not substantively respond. That fact may also reflect the wider world of economic news and literature where writers are predominantly white, male, and middle class, apart from seasoned reporter/authors such as the *New York Times'* Gretchen Morgenson and Sylvia Nasar.[66] This largely male group, despite being empathetic, well-informed, and even excellent writers, gives us a skewed sample of opinion. Does this fact impact the perspective and content of the literature and substance of this study? I think it does.

Women often see and respond to situations — particularly householding matters at home and on the job — in ways that men typically do not. And the recession may have made women even more perceptive; bearing the brunt of everyday poverty, they now feel it worse. The Grameen Bank has preferred to lend to women rather than to men in developing countries, because they are seen as more reliable entrepreneurs. In the developed West, certain women professionals in the U.S. spotted factors leading toward the economic crisis before men did, and were more vocal about what they saw. For their trouble, they were either not heeded or their ideas were dismissed. Brooksley Born, a Washington lawyer, became head of the Commodity Fu-

---

66. See note 55, referencing Morgenson's book, co-authored with Joshua Rosner. Nasar wrote the biography of game theorist John Nash, *A Beautiful Mind,* and more recently, *Grand Pursuit: The Story of Economic Genius* (New York: Simon & Schuster, 2011). — *Ed.*

tures Trading Commission in 1996, and shortly afterward warned Federal Reserve chairman Alan Greenspan that trading in the credit market was heading toward disaster. But he opposed any market regulation, and his absolutist views prevailed.[67] What Born foresaw has come to pass. Similarly in 2007, Meredith Whitney, at the time a young, relatively unknown Wall Street bank analyst, predicted "economic doom," based on her study of corporate reports, balance sheets, and other data that no one else pursued.[68] Again, Whitney's research represented extraordinary due diligence and suggests a professional stance that also protested largely male self-deception about the need to monitor the market, and thus fully oversee its stability. Women may be freer than men to face inconvenient financial truths. Is it also possible that women are not as ideologically encumbered by the dominant power structures, and are therefore more likely to see fraud and report it because they are not in an old boys' club?

Seemingly, women more readily "see through" the ideological justifications that blind men in power to the injustices that result from blinkered pursuit of their own economic interests. How far does such evidence hold up? As I have just argued above, women fully share men's potential for self-pride and corruption.[69] But their positive contributions in this crisis, previously ignored or slighted, deserve to be emphasized. How best to acknowledge and build on the encouraging data concerning women and the meltdown? This study partly reports such insights, which need to be extended.

I earlier referred to Marta Pelaez, of Family Violence Prevention Services in San Antonio, who reported on the particular hardships the crisis places on women. But I don't attempt an in-depth analysis of the recession's exposure of structural gender issues, involving minorities of all kinds. Even more revealing cases than Pelaez's should be included and their implications consistently elaborated. A number of publications, in print and via the Inter-

67. Rick Schmitt, "Prophet and Loss," *Stanford* (March/April 2009), pp. 40-47.

68. Jon Birger, "The Prophet of Dollars and Sense," *Brown Alumni Magazine* (May/June 2009), www.brownalumnimagazine.com/content/view/whitney2270/40.

69. In 2010, the press fully covered the arrests of Bernard "Bernie" Madoff's female bookkeeper and secretary for years of securities fraud and tax crimes in connection with his Ponzi scheme. Together, they were alleged to have pocketed over five million dollars. Three years before the crisis broke, in 2004, the insider trading case of Martha Stewart led to her serving a five-month prison sentence. Followers of Reinhold Niebuhr cannot be surprised. Jonathan Dienst, "FBI Arrests 2 Women in Connection with Madoff Case," 18 November 2010, http://www.nbcnewyork.com/news/local/Feds-Make-Another-Arrest-in-Madoff-Case-108923469 .html. "Martha Stewart Starts Prison Term," BBC News, 8 October 2004, http://news.bbc.co .uk/2/hi/americas/3726990.stm. — *Ed.*

net, are addressing these issues from a wide range of ideological positions. For example, the online independent news agency, *Scoop,* made public the International Trade Union Confederation's 2009 report on gender inequality and violence against Brazilian women under the headline, "To Change the World, We Need to Change the Lives of Women."[70]

Nicholas Kristof and Sheryl WuDunn, reporting on the education and empowerment of women in their book *Half the Sky,* affirm that the long history of women's subjugation in patriarchal societies must end. They argue that this liberation is the single key to human well-being across the globe. It can lift families and nations out of bigotry and poverty. Even more compelling is Kristof and WuDunn's argument that the more education and claim to power that women gain, the more they can provide an inside perspective on social and economic realities as they know them.[71] Such an alternative view calls into question long-entrenched, self-justifying assumptions protecting the privileged status quo. Are there similarities between the squandering financial activities of the Wall Street executive and certain elite wealthy men around the world who divert resources from education and broad social well-being? If women had been positioned so that they were listened to, perhaps they would have been able to forestall the present meltdown with its continuing miseries.

Meanwhile, women ethicists have long been important voices in Christian circles. Two have recently commented, not on the crisis itself, but on related aspects of it. Laura Stivers records her concern about homelessness and certain flaws in Christian thinking about the problem.[72] She critiques

70. International Trade Union Confederation. www.scoop.co.nz/stories/print.html?path =WO0903/800105.htm.

71. *Half the Sky: Turning Oppression into Opportunity for Women Worldwide* (New York: A. Knopf, 2009). [In 2012, women financial managers of hedge funds in the U.S. were found to deliver results several percentage points higher than men in parallel roles. The professional firm of Rothstein Kass, in its third-quarter 2012 report of sixty-seven hedge funds with women owners or managers, states: "Female financiers can have particular advantages over their male counterparts, including being more risk-averse and better able to avoid volatility...." Yet such women are still in a minority. William Alden, "Returns at Hedge Funds Run by Women Beat the Industry, Report Says," http://dealbook.nytimes.com/2013/01/10/ returns-at-hedge-funds-run-by-women-beat-the-industry-report-says/. — Ed.]

72. "Making a Home for All in God's Compassionate Community: A Feminist Liberation Assessment of Christian Responses to Homelessness and Housing," *Journal of the Society of Christian Ethics* 28, no. 2 (Fall/Winter 2008): 51-74. [Reviving the idea of a National Housing Trust Fund, created by Congress in 2008 but left behind in the recession, could provide a quantity of low-cost, mixed-income housing for the "nearly 3.3 million families with children

well-intentioned efforts to benefit the homeless, including the work of Gospel Rescue Missions, neighborhood soup kitchens, and Habitat for Humanity. Although not denying the contribution of such agencies, she argues for a deeper grasp of structural injustices that create conditions of poverty, and a firmer underpinning of such good works to the biblical sense of God's "compassionate community" to truly implement it. Although Stivers's article was published before the current subprime mortgage crisis became apparent, she exposes the hidden ideological biases of what our society has long seen as success and respectability. Her call for an ethic of "prophetic disruption" is challenging and, by implication, serves to question financial and government policies about foreclosure and their effect in this recession's new increase of homelessness.

Gloria Albrecht focuses on Detroit and its established social and economic conditions, a reminder that the downturn has a long history in inequitable practices.[73] She observes how "unshared social power" has contributed to Detroit's status as the poorest city in America. Her analysis of an "economic rationality" that both justifies and obscures unequal gender- and class-based power is critical and suggests the argument I make with respect to economic "rational choice theory" in these pages.

While analysis of the economic crisis is critical, the more important task is to fathom the ongoing social conditions and issues that the recession has so dramatically raised to attention that doubtless will continue when the downturn is declared "over." Whether the recession will turn out to have opened doors to social structural changes toward more just power-sharing remains to be seen.

Present and Future Scenarios

Any viable alternatives to the situation described will need to emerge in political as well as in economic circles. They will need to come from coalitions of interests located *somewhere*.

First, there are the efforts of largely Western governments, corporations,

---

living in 'worst case' situations — spending more than half their incomes on housing or living in hazardous buildings. . . ." Editorial, "Fight for the Housing Trust Fund, 12 January 2013, http://www.nytimes.com/2013/01/13/opinion/sunday/fight-for-the-housing-trust-fund.html ?_r=0. — Ed.]

73. "Detroit: Still the 'Other' America," *Journal of the Society of Christian Ethics* 29, no. 1 (Spring/Summer 2009): 3-24.

and financial institutions to reform themselves in the light of the meltdown. For convenience, this possible source of change may be called "Davos" after the Swiss resort where "the best and the brightest" of our economic establishments annually meet in a World Economic Forum (WEF). Secondly, there is the work of thousands of grassroots people's organizations and governments of the global South to envision replacements for today's dominant economic systems. Again, for convenience, this possible source may be called "Belem" after the Brazilian city where these interests meet biennially in the World Social Forum (WSF), and at varying locations throughout the world. And finally, after discussing the phenomenon of "tipping points" in such venues, the global economic (and military) strategizing of China will be discussed.

Evidence abounds that economists, politicians, and anti-Establishment activists are already combining reality-wrestling with their own projections. The watchword chosen for the January 2009 WEF in Davos was "shaping the post-crisis world." The simultaneous meeting in Belem of the WSF, originally conceived as a critical counterweight to Davos, proclaimed once more its perennial theme, "Another World Is Possible." In a November 2008 meeting in Washington, the "Group of Twenty" industrialized nations claimed in press releases to be a "Bretton Woods II" event, looking back for inspiration to the first summit of the world's economic leaders in 1944, as earlier discussed.

Davos: The World Economic Forum

Those government officials, bankers, and business people who gathered at Davos in 2009, dubbed by others "economic mandarins," were apparently unable to think beyond a scramble to find immediate solutions for their institutions and personal self-interests. The American delegation did not glitter. Many top decision-makers were not present. Beleaguered U.S. bankers for the most part also stayed away, or were not invited to begin with. Perhaps many who did come were motivated, to an extent even hidden from themselves, to keep their oligarchic, privileged worlds intact. Invited speakers Desmond Tutu and Jim Wallis did issue warnings of spiritual crises in the midst of economic chaos. These interventions were courteously, even gratefully, received. But they failed to lift most attendees out of thinly disguised panic about keeping control in a financial world whose levers of power could be slipping away from them.

An insipid closing communiqué seems to have left Davos founder Klaus Schwab so disappointed that he announced, perhaps prematurely, a follow-up effort that he characterized as a "global redesign initiative." "The key is global cooperation," Schwab said, "not only among governments but among all the stakeholders of our society." Further details were promised soon. One wondered whom he might mean by "all the stakeholders"? Could these be all the persons, or even all the life-forms, on our planet? One hopes to see this argument developed by Davos in the sequel.

High expectations at Davos were projected toward the Group of Twenty meeting scheduled for London on April 2, 2009. What degree of follow-through toward "shaping the post-crisis world" emerged from this meeting? Its evaluation depends on diverse expectations for it. The hopes of President Obama for a "global new deal" or even *The Economist*'s "calculated boldness" failed to materialize. The summit's communiqué called for restoring growth and jobs, strengthening financial supervision and regulation, funding and re-forming international financial institutions, resisting protectionism, promoting global trade and investment, and ensuring a fair and sustainable recovery for all. But the Americans failed to get the Europeans to agree to a robust stimulus program, and the Europeans failed to get the Americans to agree to a robust international regulatory regime. Yet regulation — presumably by different nations — is to be extended to many kinds of financial institutions, such as hedge funds not regulated before, and previously hidden tax havens.

Most notable were the expectations placed on the as-yet unreformed International Monetary Fund (IMF) to help fuel the global recovery and in particular to extend newly appropriated aid to developing nations. IMF resources for these purposes were increased to 750 billion. Yet no immediate changes in the IMF's assumptions and modes of operation seem to have been mandated. Up to now, nations of the global South have had little reason to trust that the IMF grasps the true nature of their needs and interests. The emerging economies represented in the G-20 did extract *promises* of re-forms from the IMF and the World Bank that would diminish a bias toward European and North American policies in favor of more responsibility to global interests. The full nature of these needed transformations seems not yet to have been worked out. Nor do the protests issuing from Belem seem to have focused on defining what these changes should be. Replacement rather than repair seems to be the message coming from the global South. But replacement with what?[74]

74. At the 2012 annual WEF meeting at Davos, attended by about 2600 people, twenty protesters of the worldwide Occupy WEF Movement were allowed to attend, but were limited to a guarded parking lot surrounded by barbed wire and piles of snow. Eager to discuss the

Belem: The World Social Forum

Meanwhile, the simultaneous and consciously countervailing WSF meeting in Belem marked a sharp contrast to the well-tailored, well-fed, but anxious Davos and London meetings. From its founding in 2001, its Charter of Principles announced that "[t]he World Social Forum is an open meeting place for reflective thinking, democratic debate of ideas, formulation of proposals, free exchange of experiences and interlinking for effective action, by groups and movements of civil society that are opposed to neoliberalism and to domination of the world by capital and any form of imperialism, and are committed to building a planetary society directed towards fruitful relationships among Mankind and between it and the Earth."[75] In 2009, more than 120,000 people gathered in Belem, a sweltering, rainy gateway to Amazonia. Unlike the invitational Davos event, the WSF is typically a come-one-come-all jamboree (described this time by younger participants as a second Woodstock) aimed at gathering representatives of hundreds of extremely diverse social movements of the global South, variously seeking social change for the benefit of the world's poor. One observer saw Belem as "a carnival of alternatives," without any single organizing agenda. Yet, if the word "justice" or the thought of it seemed rare at Davos, Belem's participants continually flogged this theme, in a multitude of variations.

---

discrepancy of global incomes, they objected that the forum's official motto, "Committed to improving the state of the world," meant making the world a better place only for profit-driven capitalists. VIPs at Davos focused on the issue of debt versus growth, especially in Europe. Despite the scheduled discussion of the future of capitalism and the "art and science of happiness," no new wider vision had a hearing. Eric Pfanner, "Outside the Forum, Impassioned Debates on Global Economics," *New York Times*, DealBook, 28 January 2012. The WEF's 2013 meeting, despite clashes between bank officials and the IMF about remaining dangers in banking operations and criticism of an excessively large financial system, evidently discussed only the usual business topics and no visionary statements of change. Jack Ewing, "At Davos, Financial Leaders Debate Reform and Monetary Policy," *New York Times*, DealBook, 23 January 2013. — *Ed.*

75. In 2012, the WSF met in Porto Alegre, Brazil, 24-30 January, as usual concurrent with the WEF meeting in Davos. http://www.fsm2009amazonia.org.br/what-the-wsf-is. Economics professor Nancy Folbre writes, "[WSF] is designed and implemented from the bottom up rather than the top down, in opposition to both authoritarian state planning and capitalist profit maximization. . . . One could say, therefore, that another economics is now under way. Still, it seems fragmentary and incomplete and not yet adequate to the task of institutional design. We still don't know how best to organize cooperative efforts or how to mobilize the capital necessary to support them on a large scale. Like the better world it could help deliver, another economics remains merely possible but profoundly necessary." Nancy Folbre, "Is Another Economics Possible?" *New York Times*, Business Day, 19 July 2010. See also note 101. — *Ed.*

This 2009 WSF meeting attracted five Latin American heads of state, including Luiz Inacio Lula da Silva of Brazil and Hugo Chavez of Venezuela. A significant delegation was present from the World Council of Churches. If Davos agonized unsuccessfully over how to repair the global economic order, many, if not most, Belem participants seemed bent on somehow replacing it. The new world (or at least Caribbean) system, Hugo Chavez proclaimed, would be socialistic in principle. Belem participants tended to see the world's bankers, corporate titans, and politicians as incapable of bringing a just social order into being, indeed as incapable of grasping what that might mean, given the ideological limitations of their thought.

At its close, the WSF issued a list of generalized demands addressed to the global North, calling attention to the impact of global recession upon the already poor. There will be follow-up events from this gathering too.[76] But rather than attempting to formulate a Schwab-like "global redesign" out of many diverse causes, these efforts will likely continue to feature street demonstrations outside the halls of power. A round of such demonstrations was promised for London at the G-20 meeting on April 2. The result on that day was about as expected. Thousands of people marched, carrying signs with a multitude of demands and slogans. Competence in the streets on the issues was combined with instances of misbehavior by some demonstrators and by the police. Selective and dismissive treatment by the media repeatedly focused on actually rare acts of violence. There was little serious analysis seeking to ascertain the demonstrators' central message. At this distance, one can validly say that the message was generalized populist anger flowing into a great variety of specific and highly idealistic slogans and agendas.

History suggests that when such populist anger is prolonged without significant satisfaction, agendas tend to coalesce around much more pointed programs and anger begins to take on specific political shape. This generally happens when some person or party manipulates the fury to use it politically. The political exploitation of popular anger is generally accompanied by the emergence of a rationale that lends strategic sense or world-historical meaning to the struggle. In the midst of the French Revolution, Diderot emerged with the Declaration of the Rights of Man and of the Citizen. In the Russian and Chinese revolutions, Leninist and Maoist versions respectively came forward.

A coalescence of the many social movements represented at Belem into a significant global movement could turn out to depend on three things:

76. Regional WSF meetings are also regularly convened. — *Ed.*

(1) the rise of a leader, (2) a precipitating event or series of events, and (3) an understandable and compelling philosophical rationale waiting in the wings to find its moment on the historical stage. If these three conditions should coincide, the result will be global, not merely regional or national. And what of the philosophical rationale? Most assume it would be some version of Marx — not the whole bag of tricks but a simplified and updated version. What else could it be?

Yet none of these scenarios can guarantee that the lives of human beings would be made better in the revolutionary process or in its outcome. There would be the heady feeling of being on the march toward an inevitable apotheosis of humankind, but a destruction of economic institutions would leave everybody poorer. Human beings would continue having the same basic acquisitive nature. They would soon sort themselves into large classes of violent small-time oppressive thugs in the service of the regime and smaller groups of financial and political oligarchs. The latter would quickly learn how to milk personal profit from that state of affairs. In short, it is difficult to believe that any conceivable new social system will alter the givens of human nature. Avarice and the pursuit of self-interest, often by fraudulent means when the opportunity presents itself, will always be present. Idealism about the liberating effects of a neo-Marxist world revolution is likely to be disappointed. Ideological purity, either of the left or of the right, can be the enemy of human well-being.

Possibilities for Real Change? Tipping-Point Scenarios

What, then, are the possibilities for real change stemming from future meetings like these? The Davos and Belem events both heard from dynamic political figures, Putin and Chavez,[77] who are capable of, and possibly positioned for, leadership toward some alternative economic world. But neither event is likely now or in the future to become a place where focused initiatives toward a more just human world can take form. In each of these settings, too many diverse interests will keep that from happening.

The impression thus persists that neither the Davos and G-20 nor the Belem agendas in themselves will lead to the fundamental change we must hope for. And that change needs to be broadly spiritual in nature, understanding that the "spiritual" is embedded in the quite concrete concept of the

---

77. Mudge wrote before Chavez's death in 2013. — *Ed.*

"oikos," or household. Davos wants a return to "business as usual." Belem offers an urgently expressed but ill-defined list of vaguely socialist demands.[78] Will there come a tipping point at which justice-oriented thinking bursts out in the form of some organized sort of global movement? Will the sense of a genuine emergency in the life of human civilization then begin to penetrate the halls of power and the fields of insurgency sufficiently that these two agendas will respectively cease to be merely making the world safe once again either for bankers and their bonuses or for ideological revolutionaries and their schemes?[79] Can economic institutions of either sort become servants of human well-being rather than instruments of oppressive power?

Political potential for change on this scale seems to lie mainly in meetings between accredited governmental representatives who would hammer out agreements leading to enforceable treaties. Such meetings have been going on for some time: the "Group of Seven" (G-7, sometimes G-8), involving heads of government from major industrialized economies of the North, and the "Group of Twenty" (G-20), involving finance ministers and central bank directors from a larger list of significant economic players, both North and South.

These groups have potential force to bear indirectly on global economic justice. Here the capacity to initiate processes of change is actually present, transcending any political push likely to emerge from the scattered agendas of the WEF and WSF thought-and-talk factories. The "Bretton Woods II" extraordinary one-day G-20 meeting in Washington in November 2008, only a month following a regularly scheduled meeting of that group in Brazil, left the impression that new intergovernmental economic initiatives were now seriously on many agendas, as for example, the virtual nationalization of certain banks in the UK and possibly the same in all but name in the

78. Or, as William Saint points out, "The voices of India, China, Brazil and others are not calling for just reform. They are simply saying, 'It's our turn.'" William Saint, email to author, 15 August 2009.

79. The "Arab Spring," or "Arab Awakening," of Spring 2011 might at first have been seen as a sign of such a tipping point. This movement against oppression in the Arab world appeared to gather strength as each despot fell (Egypt and Libya) or was forced to flee (Tunisia). Neil MacFarquhar, "As Arab Autocrats Are Toppled, Their Fates Grow More Extreme," *New York Times*, 21 October 2011, p. A13. But Egypt in mid-2013 was in severe unrest, while Syria was self-destructing in civil war. If rebelling parties in each country are successful, will they champion economic justice and democratic government? In summer 2013, *The Economist* warned politicians, especially autocrats, to beware of the power of massed protesters (June 29-July 5, 2013), pp. 11-12. And protesters will need to have leaders whom they trust and then support. Establishing stable democracies becomes the basic challenge. — *Ed.*

U.S. All this may or may not lead to some grand attempt to reorder global economic priorities.

Any future "Bretton Woods" would need to be more focused on global economic justice than the first one in 1944, or later echoes of it by the WEF and WSF. Also, its representation would have to reflect the more inclusive nature of the UN and these bodies. High on its agenda would have to be an examination of the ways economic assumptions and practices produce and perpetuate poverty. The question, of course, is how such matters may become explicit, rather than implied, in such an international agenda for post-crisis reconstruction. Not every measure with serious implications for the poor is so labeled or even recognized as such until the consequences are known.

We need to identify, independently of either right or left ideology, where and how on today's financial maps there may be discernible opportunities to resist wrong paths or opportunities to support constructive change. It is not we alone who see this need, or can bring change about. It is rather a question of selective support of, or resistance to, much that is going on around us. But the emergence of such public support or resistance, making political action plausible, usually requires more than thoughtfully planned summit meetings or legislative agendas. It often requires tipping-point scenarios consisting of unique combinations of circumstances and events.

A prolonged and disastrous depression bringing misery to billions — still a distinct, even if reduced, possibility — could be such a push. So could a genuine *collapse*, not merely a weakening, of global financial institutions. A simultaneous set of catastrophes, natural and social, feeding off one another, could do it. Economists and human scientists have recently been considering the likelihood of simultaneous, mutually reinforcing, natural and social catastrophes, a combination of ecological-natural, economic, political, military, or cultural happenings. Though such a confluence is unlikely, if it occurred, the impact could be disastrous. Cormac McCarthy's bleakly chilling novel *The Road* powerfully pictures the global consequences of such a cascade of events.[80] Many readers today find this imagined prospect not at all fanciful but rather a quite believable future. One surfaces from absorption in McCarthy's book seeking reassurance that the familiar world is still out there. Then we realize that, in many ways, it is not.

In such a moment, it is small comfort to imagine a less *ultimately* menacing contingency that would leave the world intact but fundamentally changed. Some charismatic and talented leader, building on a favorable set

80. (New York: A. Knopf, 2006).

of circumstances, might succeed in organizing the economic resentments of myriad social movements as those evident at the WSF into a linked set of neo-socialist guerrilla insurgencies. As legal or illegal guest workers in the North, radicalized masses of the South could literally join forces with family members or former fellow villagers to threaten much of the present economic system until certain coordinated demands were met.

If such a guerrilla force did arise, it would not need to be violent to be effective. Nor would it need a Marxist or even socialist rationale for its coherence. Resentment alone could start and sustain it. Under such pressure, Davos types could be induced to *negotiate* with Belem supporters to reach principles of economic justice. An expanded G-20 global economic reconstruction team could take up these agreed-upon basics. This team might even be *called* "Bretton Woods II" (or an entirely new name found), but *be* something far more portentous and comprehensive. Governments could be invited by such a body, under the not-so-gentle threat of globally instigated civil disorder within their borders, to sign on by treaty to a more just economic world.

Not that any such scenario would be easy, or that it would actually take place as described. (Local and international bodies working to promote the new political economy here advocated could forestall it from happening.) But if it should, welding Belem's array of social causes into a global movement would call for the right political conditions and for leadership of towering genius and magnetism. And opposing forces in the form of large financial interests, corporations, cabinet departments, and legislatures North and South would be formidable. Violence, which could wreck everything, would constantly be close at hand. Yet with wise leadership, it could be avoided, as was accomplished by South Africa's Faith and Reconciliation Commission after apartheid ended.

The World-Changing Emergence of China

To the iconic locations of Davos and Belem, another name now needs to be added: Beijing. The London G-20 event of April 2009 marked a further change, one that was overlooked by many observers whose focus was on the roles of existing International Financial Institutions (IFIs). This meeting was the first at which the two most powerful persons present — President Obama and President Hu Jintao of China — were not "white." Furthermore, this meeting marked China's emergence as an active superpower in global financial discussions of the G-20 type. In fact, China led the emerging G-20 economies in a new game plan: to collaborate in protest against European and North American domination of the IMF and the World Bank in favor of global rather than merely North Atlantic interests. At future G-20 meetings, China will pursue its own agenda, not merely that of the South. But its management of a new global alignment also introduces a new economic model that combines political autocracy with economic freedom. That model could give the South a decidedly threatening face in the future.

Will China provide the impetus and organizing capacity that will bring Belem's interests into the Davos and G-20 discussion? Could Chinese commercial relations, say with African countries, which involve many commodities but especially weapons, hint of something like the Soviet Union's former system of satellite nations? This time it would be the global South being organized to demand specific changes in international financial institutions, rather than randomly agitating for change, Belem style. In short, could a *genuine* "Bretton Woods II" come to pass as a response to China's presence in the G-20, because it attracted to its new leadership this spectrum of less powerful voices? And would these changes reflect the true interests of China's client states or represent an imposition of China's interests on them? Would the cultural background to such reconstruction of IFIs then be Confucian or Maoist or simply pragmatically entrepreneurial with an Asian perspective?[81]

81. My friend Walter Owensby, retired head of the Washington office of the Presbyterian Church (USA), has commented: "[You] posit a dynamic alliance between China and the global South that would be more positive and helpful to the South in 'getting its act together.' My question is, why would we expect such selfless leadership from China or any global power? To presume such is an abandonment of Niebuhrian social realism. China will undoubtedly force huge changes in the global system, but it will be out of competing self-interest, not from a more benevolent attitude. In that sense, it probably represents the perfect political counterpart to the invisible hand. I think we have to position ourselves in the churches and in the broader religious community to support the positive effects of change and to be immediate critics of destructive or indifferent national self-interest. That is, I believe, the built-in perspective of [your] stakeholder analysis linked to a theology of *oikonomia*. I agree wholeheartedly that a continued ideological dispute between capitalism and socialism is irrelevant and must be replaced by a recognition that 'what matters is the way economies are run. . . .' Pragmatism thus becomes the test of change and the companion of political-economic ethics." Walter Owensby, email attachment to author, 8 August 2009. [In 2013, China's domination of key oil markets, as in Iraq, will give critics plenty of reason to comment on its "national self-interest," indifferent or not. Tom Arango and Clifford Krauss, "China Is Reaping Biggest Benefits of Iraq Oil Boom," *New York Times,* 2 June 2013, http://www.nytimes.com/2013/06/03/world/middleeast/china-reaps-biggest-benefits-of-iraq-oil-boom.html?_r=0. The hoped-for predominance of cooperation over conflict between China and the U.S., from the meeting of their two presidents in late spring 2013, could make this vital relationship determining

On the other hand, possibly the North, taking note of Chinese power and global ambitions, might by stages produce its own revolutionary economic changes through a series of *de facto* nationalizations of banks and corporations. Even if such a move were incomplete or temporary, it would undermine the market fundamentalism that has for so long dominated the West's economic thinking. The result might be a realization that Adam Smith's "Invisible Hand" is not merely the useful net result of economic actors all interactively pursuing personal gain, but rather the cultural-spiritual context in which economic activity is set and to which it is expected to conform. Smith's *Theory of Moral Sentiments* articulates the content of such a cultural context. Although emancipated from the precepts of institutionalized religion, it reflects certain ideas of religious origin reexpressed in secular form. Might we learn from the Chinese, without adopting their centralized system, that economies with similar institutions and regulations can serve quite different political, cultural, and even moral purposes?[82]

---

for a peaceful twenty-first century. "The Summit," *The Economist*, 8-14 June 2013, p. 11. This is all the more true as both countries struggle with economic problems. Neil Gough, "Cash Crunch in China as Rising Interest Rates Crimp Lending," *New York Times*, 20 June 2013, http://www.nytimes.com/2013/06/21/business/global/china-manufacturing-contracts-to-lowest-level-in-9-months.html?pagewanted=1&_r=0. At the same time as these matters were occurring, Ben Bernanke, chair of the Federal Reserve, set off an unforeseen market dive on the perception that he was announcing a tapering-off of the Fed's "qualitative easing" in the next year, but this was only on condition that the economy no longer needed it. Binyamin Appelbaum, "Optimistic Fed Outlines an End to Its Stimulus," *New York Times*, 19 June 2013, http://www.nytimes.com/2013/06/20/business/economy/fed-more-optimistic-about-economy-maintains-bond-buying.html. See also Appelbaum's "Fed Officials Try to Ease Concern of Stimulus End," *New York Times*, 27 June 2013, http://www.nytimes.com/2013/06/28/business/economy/fed-has-not-changed-commitments-official-says.html. The Chinese interest-rate hike and Bernanke's misread predictions combined to lead a global market sell-off, a clue to continuing worldwide economic fragility. David Jolly, "Markets Fall on China's Credit Squeeze and Fed's Exit Plan," *New York Times*, 20 June 2013, http://www.nytimes.com/2013/06/21/business/global/daily-stock-market-activity.html. Interest rates in China quickly lowered somewhat, but the outlook was for sustained loan tightening from fears of excessive past lending, particularly in the country's shadow banking. David Barboza, "China's Credit Squeeze Relaxes as Interest Rates Drop," *New York Times*, 21 June 2013, http://www.nytimes.com/2013/06/22/business/global/chinas-bank-lending-crunch-eases.html?_r=0

Despite this trend, China continues a two-year-old policy of becoming one of the largest investors in U.S. commercial property, largely through third parties in the U.S. Julie Creswell, "Chinese Investors Pursue U.S. Property Deals," *New York Times*, 25 June 2013, http://www.nytimes.com/2013/06/26/business/global/chinese-investors-pursue-us-real-estate-deals.html. — *Ed.*]

82. More openness may follow the greater courage of the Chinese people — the middle-

Could a realization even begin to dawn that economic processes, while dealing with material things, do not even need to be material*istic* — that they can be designed for the well-being, not just of a few but of all the world's families? This would mean revising assumptions taken for granted in today's economic world. We could begin with Klaus Schwab's pregnant phrase "all stakeholders" and give meanings to those words beyond anything the Swiss financier may have had in mind.

An Alternative Model: Universal Stakeholdership

What follows is a modest step in that direction. Business schools have for some time been teaching the analysis of "stakeholdership" as a management tool. This idea could be more comprehensively applied to mean the whole of humanity's relationship of responsibility toward the resources of the planet and their use. A "stakeholder" is anyone *impacted* by what entrepreneurs do with planetary resources. This is distinct from a "stockholder" or "shareholder" who is an owner of the venture in question. The earth's entire economic life could be conceived as a joint enterprise by, for, and on behalf of all its stakeholders, not just its stockholders. All human beings, not just owners, would then be recognized as trustees of the world's resources, therefore having an acknowledged interest in the character of their development.

---

aged as well as the young — to protest against government policies. For the foreseeable future, China's nationalistic, non-interventionist foreign policy and strong competitive economy will continue. Keith Bradsher, *New York Times* Business reporter, interview, *Charlie Rose*, PBS, 17 July 2012. Li Congjun, president of the Xinhua News Agency (official press agency of the People's Republic of China), writes that "we cannot expect neoliberalism — privatization, deregulation, free trade — to revive growth," and also that "the credit paradox is only narrowly a financial crisis — it is a crisis of faith, one that summons us to turn away from a capital-centered economy to a human-centered one." But "faith" for Li and Mudge evidently differs. Li relies upon a "human-centered" economy, while Mudge explores how the global economy could balance inevitable human self-interest with both political constraints and interfaith values. Li Congjun, "Rebalancing the Global Economy," Op-Ed, *New York Times*, 17 July 2012. Both Mudge and Gar Alperovitz, a University of Maryland professor of political economics, agree that some nationalization of U.S. business affairs is necessary when troubled corporations and banks have gotten too big. Soon after the 2008 crisis, the government became the controlling stockholder in General Motors and the insurance giant, American International Group. Alperovitz notes that the idea of emergency nationalization arose in the heartland of free enterprise, the University of Chicago's Business School, in the 1930s, well before Milton Friedman's tenure there. Gar Alperovitz, "Wall Street Is Too Big to Regulate," Op-Ed, *New York Times*, 23 July 2012, p. A21. — *Ed.*

Comprehensive moral stakeholdership in universal well-being would make the most difference if it became the center of economic reasoning. Right now, it is an externality, an item on the periphery of entrepreneurial thought. If this shift took place, however, positive practical consequences could follow.

Pope Benedict XVI's June 29, 2009, encyclical *Caritas in Veritate* hints at such a possibility. He addresses the global economic crisis in relation to "the authentic development of every person and of all humanity." He briefly alludes to the "stakeholder" concept as an instrument of such authentic development.

> 40. Today's international economic scene, marked by grave deviations and failures, requires a *profoundly new way of understanding business enterprise.* Old models are disappearing, but promising new ones are appearing on the horizon . . . the so-called outsourcing of production weakens the company's sense of responsibility towards the stakeholders — namely the workers, the suppliers, the consumers, the natural environment and broader society — in favour of the shareholders. . . . Even if the ethical considerations that currently inform debate on the social responsibility of the corporate world are not all acceptable from the perspective of the Church's social doctrine, there is nevertheless a growing conviction that *business management cannot concern itself only with the interests of the proprietors, but also must assume responsibility for all the other stakeholders who contribute to the life of the business:* the workers, the clients, the suppliers of various elements of production, the community of reference.[83]

Is the Pope suggesting that more attention to the legitimate rights of stakeholders might have mitigated the sorts of economic behavior that have brought on the crash? Not quite. The Pope is right not to claim too much at this moment. In this passage, he is making the more limited point that outsourcing and multiple business locations breed indifference to the impact of business decisions on people's lives. Stakeholders dispersed in many widely separated venues rarely manage to coordinate their expressions of similar grievances sufficiently to make their voices count. And that is indeed a legitimate concern. But might the "stakeholder" notion, more broadly interpreted, become a newly transformative element at the very heart of economic reasoning?

If the "stakeholder" emphasis is to be a major focus, then it needs con-

---

83. *Caritas in Veritate,* Encyclical Letter, 29 June 2009 (Vatican City: Libreria Editrice Vaticana, 2009).

siderable development. In current business school curricula, "stakeholder analysis"[84] establishes a purely prudential technique for managers wishing to anticipate various obstacles to commercial operations — public, governmental, and environmental. The manager needs to discern in advance what individuals or groups are likely to feel concerning their identity, location, or other circumstances. He wants them to have a stake in the company's agenda so that opposition to it will not arise in the community, media, or the courts. For management, it is crucial to spot such possible threats early and to take steps to reduce their likelihood or intensity. Such prudence does not need to be cynical. The manager *may* genuinely believe that business operations should seek, at least as a byproduct of profit, to promote the public good.

Certainly, a different economic paradigm is needed. In such a change of scene, the generation of paper wealth by blinkered oligarchies would be replaced by business using the world's resources to benefit all members of the human household, or *oikonomia*. Economic reasoning would no longer justify itself as autonomous wealth-generation by manipulating financial transactions far removed from actual goods and services. It would serve persons and the promises inherent in their lives. The issue is not whether the economy should be largely in public or in private hands. All modern economies are mixtures of the two, whose proportions vary from time to time. (When entitlement and defense spending are included, the U.S. economy is already two-thirds public.) Talk of "capitalist" and "socialist" ideologies is fast becoming passé. Whatever the ideology involved, what matters is that economies be ethical, based on the model of human household management.

Of course, stakeholdership transcends the many worlds of business. Who stakeholders are depends on the nature of the activity in question. Alumni of a university are usually not literally shareholders, but they are certainly stakeholders with an interest in their university's success and reputation. Annual giving programs count on this. And so are the enterprises that depend on universities to produce graduates with research and management skills. Citizens are not literally shareholders in their public schools, but they have a stake — the well-being of the next generation — in their educational effectiveness. Hospitals may or may not be privately held corporations, but

---

84. For an enlightened business-school approach to stakeholdership, see Edward R. Freeman, *Strategic Management: A Stakeholder Approach* (Boston: Pittman, 1984). For ethically aware uses pointing toward change, see Marjorie Kelly, *The Divine Right of Capital: Dethroning the Corporate Aristocracy* (San Francisco: Berrett-Koehler, 2001), and Minu Hemmati et al., *Multi-stakeholder Processes for Governance and Sustainability: Beyond Deadlock and Conflict* (London: Earthscan, 2002).

their stakeholders are the whole human population around them whose health depends on their services.

Such fields of application can easily be multiplied to the whole human community. Every human being can be considered a "stakeholder" in all the earth's resources — air, water, food, fuel, plants, minerals, etc. — and therefore also in all enterprises that seek both to develop and protect these resources for the common good. Clearly, "common good" may be variously defined, depending on one's culture and interests. No notion of the human whole, even an incremental one of the sort just sketched, can or should be imposed on everyone. Rather many voices need to articulate not only their identities but their understandings of what we have called "stakeholder-ship." They may call this something else with different cultural-metaphorical connections. Will all these notions even coalesce into a coherent (Kantian) "regulative idea" of "the human"? Philosophical reflection on this and other questions is certainly worthwhile, but beyond my compass here.

The notion of "all humankind" has a simple empirical reference, that is, "all these people." Given efficient reporting mechanisms, a constantly up-dated computer file of all human beings alive at any given moment on earth, listed by name (with other relevant data), is well within our present capabil-ity. But we need agreement about what such a manifold "is" or "means" in any larger scheme of things. Here an *oikonomic* (economic) or householding metaphor is very useful. We humans make up "all earth's families" (Gen. 12:3), the universal household; therefore, we have a say in its operation. On this basis, we may participate in what I have called a "covenantal humanism."

Examples toward opening a door to this universal voice are already underway in the UK. There, the New Economics Foundation (NEF) has produced a "Happy Planet Index," a way of assessing human fulfillment that doesn't assume that the aims of economic growth are necessarily helpful to humanity's long-term good. From surveys of ordinary people, the NEF has gleaned opinions about what they need or already have that makes them happy and fulfilled. Their resulting index shows Britain at 71 on a list in which Costa Rica is first and the U.S. is in the 140s.[85] In addition, the Brit-

---

85. Other studies report different rankings. The NEH's pamphlet "Are You Happy?" de-scribes its four main programs: Global Interdependence, Thriving Communities, Well-Being, and Future Economy. info@neweconomics.org. Martin Conway to the author, email attach-ment, 6 August 2009. [The royal government of Bhutan has long held as its Buddhist-inspired official motto: "Gross National Happiness" (GNH). Its 2010 survey of 1 percent of its 700,000 citizens indicates how fully the country is advancing toward this goal; Karma Ura et al., "A Short Guide to Gross National Happiness Index," Centre for Bhutan Studies, Thimphu, Bhutan,

ish government under Tony Blair with the former chair of Friends of the Earth, Jonathon Porritt, established a Sustainable Development Commission (SDC) and the Forum for the Future. Under Porritt, the SDC has published a downloadable study, *Prosperity Without Growth?*, on transitioning to a sustainable economy.[86]

If a worldwide stakeholdership took hold, it could go beyond being recognized as a given fact. It could also found a legally defined *human right, and obligation:* to represent the interests of the planet itself where these are threatened by business or governmental operations. People would "buy in" to this stakeholdership not by purchasing stock but by simply devoting the earthly resources they themselves represent[87] and on which they depend for life itself, to activities that together constitute a common global undertaking. Such an undertaking must embody values that reflect who we think we are.

What might such stakeholder status concretely mean? If it were defined as a fundamental *right*, a certain legal "standing"[88] to prosecute individual or collective claims would be assumed. At the present time, legal actions are generally between competing claims of ownership or interest calculated in economic terms. Injuries or infringements of rights lead to financial settle-

---

www.grossnationalhappiness.com. Bhutan introduced its concept of GNH to the UN forty years ago. On April 2, 2012, six hundred governmental and social leaders attended a UN-sponsored conference in New York on the subject. Raja Murthy, "Bhutan's happiness index goes global," www.atimes.com/atimes/South_Asia/ND12Df02.htm. By consensus on 28 June 2012, the UN General Assembly declared March 20 — the equinox, when the sun is at the earth's equator, making day and night equal North and South — hereafter to be an International Day of Happiness. "United Nations Adopts International Day of Happiness," 28 June 2012, http://www.prweb.com/releases/Internationaldayof/happiness/prweb9652737.htm. — *Ed.*]

86. A two-page sheet summarizes this report, "Recession Must Make Us Question 'Relentless Pursuit of Growth,'" 30 March 2009. See rhian.thomas@sd-commission.org.uk. Also, Jonathon Porritt, *Living Within Our Means — Avoiding the Ultimate Recession* (London: Forum for the Future), info@forumforthefuture.org, persuasively unites various aspects of our economic crisis.

87. See n. 56 for the theory of measuring human capabilities as an alternative way to calculate gross domestic product (GDP), developed by Amartya Sen and Martha Nussbaum. As an inherent human capability to participate in concrete household relationships, universal stakeholdership could be added to Nussbaum's list of capabilities.

88. "Standing" legally means that one has a legitimate interest to appear before a court as party to a case, usually because the interest in question is capable of being *defined* for legal purposes in financial terms and the case can therefore be settled with a financial judgment. My idea of stakeholdership gives the stakeholder "standing" of a moral kind, above any monetary or even legal sort. Stakeholder claims based on human presence cannot be "paid off." They must be recognized in terms of whether they amend, or benefit, life itself.

ments. Whole lives are reduced to estimates of lost future earning capacity, as they were after 9/11. In contrast, the category of stakeholdership would not be expressed in monetary terms, but rather in terms of moral recognition. We have rights to be heard, simply because we exist as human beings. We have a stake in this or that business not because we own shares in it but because we live in, and are impacted by, the same household in which the company operates. Emmanuel Levinas makes the claims of this presence the basis of morality: I am here. Do not kill me. Do not hurt me.[89]

Stakeholders may thus represent the claims of the environment in ways that shareholders or owners cannot. The earth cannot make claims when it is damaged. It receives no "payoff." But stakeholders in the earth can *represent* its claims. No monetary judgment in favor of the elements can possibly compensate earth, water, or air. But through its stakeholders, nature could *become* a party to litigation. As evolutionary products of the planet's resources, we are persons through whom the planet may become conscious of itself. We may speak *for* the earth to defend it. That is stakeholdership. By encompassing this wide and deep sense of caring for the environment, health, and life itself, the term far surpasses any common understanding of the word "shareholder."

With this sort of understanding, entrepreneurs who intend to "add value" would see that their stewardship of the earth's resources would be answerable to their stakeholders. In annual reports, companies would need to account for their practices, just as they now do for stockholders, or owners. Global regulatory agencies would be needed to study these reports, conduct investigations, and discipline companies judged to have failed in these planetary responsibilities.

Could clearly defined and enforceable accounting rules be devised for this purpose? One suggestion is to put in place a "triple bottom line" standard for "profit," "people," and "planet." Annual reports would assign numbers to these three categories of value rather than the usual single focus on profit. Obviously, balance sheets for profit exist, but the other two values are also quantifiable. Reportable numbers measure the well-being of "people": infant mortality, household income, life expectancy, educational levels, happiness quotients, and more. As for "planet," statistics keep records of the sustainable usage of resources, pollution levels, rates of global warming, weather disasters, and others. Accounting for each corporation's operations in these arenas, either in absolute terms or in relation to other corporations,

89. Levinas, *Totality and Infinity,* p. 198.

would be the major problem. Also, assigning such numbers would involve inferences as well as measurements and in addition, some subjectivity by judges. But behind the numbers could be corporate achievement narratives with outside evaluations by accrediting teams. These teams would function like accreditors of educational institutions.

"Developers" of resources rightfully belonging to all stakeholders of the planet's riches would have the right to reasonable personal rewards for successful work, but such compensation in all its forms should be capped. John Rawls's principle might be invoked: that differences of compensation are only justified if they result in corresponding advantages for the stakeholders, especially the poorest among them.[90] Using resources held in trust for all stakeholders would also require total transparency of operations. Such an overall economic philosophy would not entail government ownership of "the means of production" (Marx), although it could mean an expectation that malfeasance, gross inefficiency, fraudulent or intentionally misleading transactions, or misuse of resources could result in temporary forms of nationalization.

Universal stakeholdership should not be seen as a political "system" to be installed by revolutionary upheaval or action by the UN General Assembly, as if the latter were possible. It is rather a set of attitudes and practices gradually built into business and political ethics, in some cases as the upshot of many diverse legislative moves and international treaties addressed to various issues. Certain minimum standards would need to be drafted, adopted by treaty, and upheld within nations' domestic legal systems.

Such a proposal need not follow the dictates of any ideology or "ism." It borrows and modifies themes from both "socialism" and "capitalism" without using these words. It attempts to reexpress rhetorics of justice for the world's people in terms explicitly challenging to today's financial and business worlds. Patient translation would help make negotiations between differing mindsets more feasible for those who believe such communication

---

90. There could be another parallel here with the thought of John Rawls. His "original position," reached behind the "veil of ignorance," is purely a heuristic construct, but something approaching that state of affairs may actually exist under today's economic conditions in which people have few ideas about how to actualize the interests they have. We are not *ignorant* of our identities and interests, but today's economic complexities render us too confused to pursue these interests with confidence. We are not sure what policies will further the interests we know we possess, and to that degree we function behind a *de facto* "veil of ignorance." But many of us have concluded that unbridled greed leads to eventual collapse and that altruism promotes our true interests in the long term.

ideologically impossible. But the success of any such negotiation would call for overcoming distrust, for changing minds on both sides, and for skill in devising the sorts of just national and global institutions needed to make such a thing work. The possibility of reaching a fundamentally new conception of entrepreneurial responsibility toward all resources and all human beings as franchised stakeholders of the global economy could give such negotiation an energizing focus.

Finally, is there a practical application of theology to the idea of stakeholdership? Religious institutions, while not free of survival interests of their own, generally have a better chance than others of hearing and faithfully relaying the voices of structurally disadvantaged stakeholders. (I have been reminded that the Protestant ethic is famously epitomized in the words of the eighteenth-century Methodist John Wesley, "Earn all you can, save all you can, give all you can.")[91] As for the Abrahamic faiths, they at least have rich experience with the conditions that need to be fulfilled for genuine caring in the culture, especially the concept of covenant. Comprehensive stakeholdership of all the world's resources, including humanity, arises from the idea of "covenantal humanism."[92] By definition, each stakeholder stands for every other stakeholder, and by extension, the values and ties that, by covenant, bind them together.

Stating these values and ties naturally involves the seemingly insoluble "common morality" problem.[93] It is vital that those who become agents for the earth's stakeholders do not fall into the trap of assuming they know, out of their own cultures, what is good for all others. Among followers of the Abrahamic faiths, covenantal humanism does not exist apart from its members' myriad traditions of life, religious and otherwise. It is only by working *through* these traditions and cultures that an interactive contextual process may be started in exploring the "common good." One is not just a covenantal humanist *per se*. One is a Presbyterian, or an Orthodox Jew, or a Shi'a Muslim. Likewise, one is either structurally privileged or disadvantaged. All need to temper their speaking with listening. Taking into account this diversity, practical theologians are well placed to foster an inclusive stakeholdership in the planet's possibilities. Sponsoring stakeholdership requires this sort of commitment in transforming it from a vision to an effective cultural and legal principle.

91. Donald and Peggy Shriver, email attachment to author, 17 August 2009.

92. See Chapter 1 for a fuller discussion of covenantal humanism; also *Gift*, especially pp. 18-20, 279-96. — Ed.

93. See the dissection of this issue in John H. Reeder and Gene Outka, *Prospects for a Common Morality* (Princeton: Princeton University Press, 1991).

A Role for Religious Communities, Particularly the Abrahamic Faiths

Let us not overplay the potential role of religious communities in such an evolution of economic consciousness toward a principle of stakeholdership that represents the earth's *noosphere* (a sphere of consciousness or mind). The cynical, perhaps correct view, is that most religious bodies would not be at the head of the procession but somewhere near the back. Yet it is worth sketching ways in which it could be otherwise.

As things still stand, the economic disciplines — along with other such prominent fields as law, medicine, and the different natural sciences — proclaim autonomy from traditional belief systems and ethics left behind in the eighteenth century. However, decoupled from their original religious moorings and left to their own operating systems and programming codes, as we have seen, these enterprises as run by fallible humans can malfunction. Economics, in particular, needs to recognize the comprehensive moral matrix represented by *all of its stakeholders*. The challenge, however, is to define this ethical womb, as it were — coextensive with life itself — and explain what it may mean in both spiritual and practical terms. By spiritual, I refer to those who see money as an extension of human spirit. By practical, I refer to a large swath of the world's population who are computer-literate and expect technology to be the handmaiden of economics. This is where churches and other religious communities, with self-understandings and longstanding theological anthropologies, may make a contribution.

This work does not mean a return to pre-Enlightenment "tutelage." Rather, religious communities need to find new ways to persuade economists to see humanity as a fundamental moral community that exists to be served, not dominated. In this pursuit, one must begin with a simple definition of "the human." It can mean the totality of *Homo sapiens* alive at any moment and informed by the spiritual legacies of all who have ever lived. Already that definition touches on value issues. Then add the idea of "the good" or "the common good" to the equation, and immediately that is recognized as a cultural variable. One can universalize it only in the form of an ongoing conversation of different interpretations of the good: a conversation with sufficient mutual suspicion of each party's hidden interests in what they say is "good." And, many voices need to be heard before any of us can begin to grasp the fullness of human experience.

Humanity's comprehensive well-being is a transcendental idea in the

Kantian sense: it presides over — gives conceptual coherence to — the ever-changing multitude of particular lives in search of fulfillment. It is thus also a spiritual idea graspable in the various sorts of moral narratives generated in the world's great religious traditions. The world's faiths — and particularly the Abrahamic ones — need to give alternative ways to symbolize humanity's spiritual reality. As mentioned in my introduction (Chapter 1), to redefine ourselves as *Homo oeconomicus* — men and women first formed by households and homes — is to connect our earthy actions with our spiritual sensitivity. Doing so, we revalue cash as an extension of our spiritual selves. If the world of households is equated to a universal community of stakeholders, they become a moral context for all economic activity. This sense of the human whole may come via Jewish, Christian, or Islamic symbols, or may include those from other faiths. We human beings are of the earth, "earthy." But we are also capable of reflection. And we ask, "If we are becoming more conscious of ourselves in the evolution of the cosmos, what may we do to improve all of our lives?"

Religious communities preserve a legacy of the "common good" through their narratives. For some time now, many of these "stories" are being read critically with an awareness of the time- and place-bound character of their specific expressions. Treating religious texts in this way reflects the adoption of Enlightenment thinking that may be a way to start the needed conversation with economics about adopting human well-being as a true goal. To this end, we give new meaning to a salient sense of the church, and may extend it to the Abrahamic faiths. In 1966, Vatican II in *Lumen Gentium* issued the following sentence, much quoted at the time: "By her relationship with Christ, the Church is a kind of sacrament or sign of intimate union with God and of the unity of all humankind. She is also an instrument for the achievement of such union and unity."[94]

The church expresses "the unity of all humankind" in a symbolic way that mere statistical references cannot do. It renders the idea of a human whole as a theological or value concept. But as a Christian body, it does so as one sectarian or particular perspective among many. If we are going to speak of "all humankind" as stakeholders of the global economy, then an inter-Abrahamic range of perspectives is needed, and eventually beyond

---

94. *The Documents of Vatican II,* trans. Joseph Gallagher, ed. Walter M. Abbott, SJ (New York: Guild Press, American Press, Association Press, 1966), p. 15. See my discussion of this and other "people of God" passages in *The Sense of a People: Toward a Church for the Human Future* (Philadelphia: Trinity Press International, 1992), pp. 40-45.

to other religious groups. This sense of global peoplehood then becomes a covenantal humanism. To repeat, this term does not refer to a communally organized godlessness but rather, a religiously diverse human community united in mutual forgiveness, trust, and solidarity.

With their feet in human misery and their heads in macroeconomics, Abrahamic believers in the U.S. and the North in general now experiencing this recession are brushing up against the sort of economic deprivation long familiar to the South. They have something more in common: they are well established, geographically and mentally, in both territories. In fact, the Abrahamic faiths predominate throughout the world.[95] So they become natural first venues for needed negotiations to be held, where their nonviolent techniques would offer possibilities not readily available elsewhere.

The common experience of deprivation in North and South could lead to a much stronger sense of inter-hemispheric solidarity, not only among interfaith people but among sufferers near and far. Possibilities include setting up legal or strategy clinics for persons — eligible under expanding government programs for food stamps, foreclosure relief, job creation, or otherwise — who are bewildered by different bureaucracies or who may not know what they are entitled to. In addition, congregations may join municipalities as parties to the growing number of lawsuits against mortgage lenders who resist federal pressures to modify their practices, whose acts of foreclosure force neighboring property values still lower and spread blight and crime. Or they may, with careful thought, join groups urging foreclosed families to remain in their homes or commit acts of civil disobedience by joining groups committed to physically blocking evictions and making sure that the TV cameras are on the scene to turn such acts into parables. Moves of this kind could indicate readiness to make common cause with organized movements of resentment linking peoples of the South with their family members in the North.

Once faith communities know what the economic crisis is truly about in human terms, they need to closely follow conversations going on at the highest levels to help put justice on national and international economic

---

95. Of approximately 3.4 billion followers of the Abrahamic faiths — over half of the world's worshipers — Christianity is the most numerous (2,000–2,200 million), Islam (1,300–1,650 million), Judaism (14-18 million), and Baha'i Faith (7.6–7.9 million). 19 July 2012. http://en.wikipedia.org/wiki/Major_religious_groups. The Pew Research Center's Forum on Religion and Public Life supports these figures. It also estimates that as of 2010 there were 5.8 billion religiously affiliated adults and children globally, or 84 percent of the world population of 6.9 billion. http://www.pewforum.org/global-religious-landscape.aspx. — *Ed.*

agendas. This calls for analyzing governmental proposals or work agendas, e.g., those of the G-20, to see what their implications for justice are, even if the term "justice" is seldom mentioned in the official documents. Above all, such careful following of conversations already going on, combined with firsthand knowledge of human misery, could help religious bodies to hammer out a common platform detailing the fruits of global economic justice. These goals would be expressed in terms readily understood by politicians and economists, and to which they should be held accountable.

A critic and friend, Walter Owensby, retired head of the Washington office of the Presbyterian Church (USA), has proposed a reality check on the world's recognition of the job ahead for religious bodies: "The hard part will be to get beyond exhortation and into the realm of helping to design and encourage an alternative to economic accumulation as a way of valuing human activity and achievement. Society (including faith communities) knows how to recognize economic success — high income and accumulated wealth. Yet most people would acknowledge that income and wealth beyond some amount is less about consumption than it is about scorekeeping. Unless human ego and national pride may be repealed, we are confronted with the question of what we, or society, can offer as a moral/social-benefit scale that is as concrete as salary or net worth on the economic side. How do we recognize and reward, concretely, serving the *'oikos'* and the *'oikonomia'*? I hope that documents from the faith community will increasingly turn to this underlying issue of alternative scales of valuing human activity." I could not agree more with Owensby. As a beginning, private funds might be found to honor such work internationally, as with the Nobel and Kluge prizes. Alongside them, government awards could be established, with or without monetary rewards.

Of course, proper structures are essential in the attempt to bestow prestige on stakeholder advocates in a global household. Unfortunately, as Owensby rightly points out, the world is firmly fixated on nationalism. He quotes Einstein's observation: "Nationalism is the measles of mankind," and continues: "The UN, the IMF, and the World Bank are allowed to exist only at the sufferance of the powerful states." This is presently true. But as I see it, a new paradigm could come into being at a great Bretton Woods-like event, with a new title to distinguish it. Or it could be the sum of specific moves in many places, all eventually adding up to something new.

On the church level, referring to Presbyterians, Owensby rightly points out, "There is no existing office capable of such broad monitoring of the political economy." This is undoubtedly true for other faith communities as well. Yet he goes on, "Religious faiths and institutions that are worldwide in scope, inter-generational in outlook, and planetary in stewardship have a unique opportunity to foster an *oikonomia* of stakeholders. The question is whether our churches and other religious communities are willing to be captured by such a faith-vision." He suggests, "It would be possible to mobilize a broad-based body of persons, largely volunteers, with the requisite specialized skills to focus on specific areas or problems."[96] Clearly, such volunteers are needed, and from the beginning, could include professionals. And as I mentioned above, they could meet in many settings, local and international as well as secular and religious. In fact, nascent groups, pledged to interfaith exploration, already dot the globe on every continent. So they are in place, growing, and ready to be mobilized. This book is written with the hope that they will be at the forefront of implementing an alternative world household energized by the concept of covenantal humanism.

The principle of universal stakeholdership by all people will never come to a vote as such. The idea is too upstream for that. But many different sorts of national and international legislation can act as *expressions* of the principle, as *concrete carriers* of the insight into the details of a new economic household. Religious communities can make it their business to identify such legislative *carriers* of the stakeholder principle as they emerge, to help amend and clarify them through public comment, and to support their passage. The following is a very partial list of financial and fiscal measures, government regulations, and ethical/social programs that point in the direction of desirable change, if their details are the right ones.[97] They begin in the U.S. but extend to the UN. They are also for discussion in the WEF and WSF (among other bodies), within and between NGOs and the Abrahamic faiths, as well as among other interested parties.

1. Take steps to reduce the overall size and influence of the financial services empire (Wall Street and the banks primarily and their parallel institutions in other nations) in the world's total economy. These institutions are ostensibly designed for service, not as centers of enormous power and profit. Question the ability of former Wall Street financiers to quell an economic crisis they have done so much to cause. Observe

---

96. Walter Owensby's comments in this and preceding paragraphs are from his email attachment to the author, 8 August 2009. — *Ed.*

97. Julio de Santa Ana, former directory of the Ecumenical Institute, Bossey, Switzerland, suggested the ordering of this list, email attachment to author, 21 July 2009.

as evidence that they have learned little given the return of salaries and bonuses for 2009-10 to levels approaching what they were before the crash.[98]

2. Place statutory limitations on degrees of "leveraging" (for example, buying financial instruments such as derivatives with borrowed assets) by which banks generate "money" with face value greatly exceeding the value of original investment representing actual goods and services. Such regulation reduces the gap between values in the "real economy" and values in the imaginary or Faustian economy.[99]

3. Link executive compensation to actual "value added" to the common human patrimony (GDP) by business operations, rather than to paper profits based on trading operations and leveraging. Establish legal ratios between lowest and highest compensation levels in the different industries. Again, bring the economy of financial institutions into line with the real economy.[100]

98. Executive compensation is only increasing since the recession, despite moves linking pay to long-term performance. In 2011, the median pay raise of the country's two hundred top-earning CEOs was $14.5M, up 5 percent from 2010. This increase is simultaneous with high unemployment and with the assets of average Americans still in decline. Eleanor Bloxham, chief executive of Value Alliance, an Ohio firm that consults on executive pay, says that corporate pay practices are changing, but insufficiently: "There is too much hype and too little substance." Nathaniel Popper, "C.E.O. Pay Is Rising Despite the Din," http://www.nytimes.com/2012/06/17/business/executive-pay-still-climbing-despite-a-shareholder-din.html?pagewanted=all. See also note 100. — Ed.

99. Derivatives, which are actually loans, did not die out with the notorious Enron scandal of 2001. Over a decade later, they still cover up negative balance sheets and allow evasion of taxes and accounting rules. Nor have their parallel in the insurance industry, credit default swaps, disappeared. Floyd Norris, "Wielding Derivatives as a Tool for Deceit," *New York Times,* 27 June 2013, http://www.nytimes.com/2013/06/28/business/deception-by-derivative.html?pagewanted=1&_r=0. Five years after the meltdown, JP Morgan Chase is one of the few banks receiving justice for such practices. Ben Protess and Jessica Silver-Greenberg, "JPMorgan Agrees to Pay $920 Million in Fines Over Trading Loss," *New York Times,* 19 September 2013, http://dealbook.nytimes.com/2013/09/19/jpmorgan-chase-agrees-to-pay-920-million-in-fines-over-trading-loss/. In October 2013, the Justice Department reached a possible $13 billion settlement with JP Morgan over mismanagement involved in the 2008 mortgage crisis and afterward. See p. 27, note 6. — Ed.

100. From 2011 to 2012, the median CEO pay package (cash plus stock and grant options) increased 16 percent. The highest paid CEO was Oracle's Lawrence J. Ellison at $96.2 million, a 24 percent increase from the previous year. But his shareholder returns were a negative 22 percent for the company's fiscal year, ending in May 2012. Gretchen Morgenson, "An Unstoppable Climb in C.E.O. Pay," *New York Times,* 29 June 2013, http://www.nytimes.com/2013/06/30/business/an-unstoppable-climb-in-ceo-pay.html?_r=0. — Ed.

4. Place narcotics (perhaps not marijuana) and arms (including nuclear materials) trades under international control based on detailed knowledge of the dynamics that drive such markets. At present these are shadow or parallel economies that do great damage to mainstream economies and bring untold human misery.

5. Bring into being a new international "reserve currency" as a means of securing stable, shared denomination of all cross-border financial transactions among national central banks. At the moment this reserve currency is the U.S. dollar, whose exchange value fluctuations (and possible manipulation) raise resentment and impose burdens on the treasuries of other nations.[101]

6. Further promote the mitigation of international indebtedness that continues to burden developing countries. Earlier efforts were successful but many debt burdens remain.[102]

7. Establish global accounting rules that require corporations to report the full public (for example, environmental) costs of conducting their businesses and compensating the human community — represented by governments and their taxpayers — for the uses of these resources in which all human beings (not just the putative "owners" of mines, oil leases, forests, etc.) are viewed as stakeholders.

8. Make purely financial transactions subject to a "Tobin Tax"[103] that not only helps track the movement of money between financial institutions

---

101. The idea of a global rebalancing of debt linked to an IMF-administered new global currency is one of several major proposals in the New America Foundation's paper, "The Way Forward: Moving from the Post-Bubble, Post-Bust Economy to Renewed Growth and Competitiveness." Joe Nocera, "This Time, It Really Is Different," Op-Ed, *New York Times*, 11 October 2011, p. A23. — *Ed.*

102. At the annual conference of central bankers in Jackson Hole, Wyoming, 27-28 August 2011, Christine Lagarde, the then new IMF head, announced several measures to forestall a double-dip recession. One of her anti-austerity proposals was to rebalance global trade by stimulating demand in developing countries with big export surpluses. "Christine Lagarde's Tough Message," Editorial, *New York Times*, 31 August 2011. In June 2012, Ms. Lagarde strongly recommended that the euro area move swiftly toward "a fiscal union including issuance of joint euro zone debt and said the viability of the currency was being questioned." "Christine Lagarde," Times Topics, *New York Times*, 21 July 2012; see also James Kanter, "I.M.F. Urges Europe's Strongest to Shoulder Burdens of Currency Bloc," *New York Times*, 22 June 2012, p. B3. — *Ed.*

103. A Tobin Tax is an excise tax on cross-border currency transactions. Originally defined by Nobel laureate economist James Tobin as a tax on all spot conversions of one currency into another, this tax is intended to put a penalty on short-term financial round-trip excursions into another currency. www.wikipedia.org/wiki/Tobin_tax. — *Ed.*

and across national borders but helps restrain the sheer amount of speculative activity in the system.

9. Establish, in advance of need, policies and procedures for periods of government ownership and management of financial institutions when the need arises, with clear statutory limitations.

10. Devise global environmental regulation, keyed to accompany regulation within individual nations, aimed not only at cutting carbon emissions from established industrial technologies but also at giving incentives to "green" technologies. Developing nations that insist on enjoying their own centuries of industrial pollution because the West did so first need to be shown that this will give the West a huge advantage in producing green technologies that it can eventually sell for profit.

11. Support legislation and regulation bringing greater rationality into global food production, transportation, and marketing, remembering the recent ruinous spike in food prices. Oppose the privatization and politicization of water supplies. Question the business models of giant agricultural firms.

12. Render national regulatory structures open to the establishment by treaty of international regulatory schemes that are in turn sensitive to the different economic cultures and their varying uses of the world's resources. Such regulations need to curtail corporations from shopping around for unregulated operational venues or for tax havens that will let them escape social responsibility. Requirements for responsibility to all persons as stakeholders need to be translated into regulatory principles, acknowledging that it will not be easy to conceive the right way to do this.

13. Set up improved social safety nets in nations (like the U.S.) that lag in this regard: nets that not only do justice to the most impacted but cushion whole economies in times of downturn. Where pensions, healthcare, and other such benefits are partially or wholly privatized, nations must now bail out insolvent banks and corporations just in order to care for their structurally disadvantaged citizens: an extremely expensive way of going about it. (At the G-20 in London in April 2009, it became evident that countries like Germany, France, and Spain, with superior publicly financed social safety nets in place, felt far less moral — or financial, or any other sort of — pressure to pour bailout funds into private institutions and thus far more able to limit debts for future generations to pay.)[104]

104. In hindsight and strengthening Mudge's point, safety nets in the U.S. kept poverty from increasing more than it did during the worst of the recession. Jared Bernstein,

14. Devise policies by which the IMF and other sources of aid to developing or distressed economies actually help the structurally disadvantaged citizens of these countries by investing in social safety nets rather than squeezing them, as IMF "structural readjustment" policies have done in the past. Respect universal stakeholdership instead of enriching local oligarchies.

15. Support current proposals for an agency protecting users of consumer financial services.[105]

16. Support some sort of government-managed and -funded public health program in competition with private plans as a consumer option.[106]

This short list of projects is but a beginning toward institutionalizing economic justice by religious and secular bodies. Faith communities are a good starting place. It is their business to be aware that human passions embodied in enterprising spirits may make the world go, but that such spirits may also pollute it through hubris and greed. As front-line instruments for promoting economic change, religious groups do not do so merely on the basis of revolutionary principles of the sort pushed by the liberationist left. Rather, their ethical insights give businesses and government agencies freshly reconsidered traditional concepts and values on which to act, beginning in the West and extending to parts of the world in which political disorder and corruption work massive injustice on their people.

I hope that this book gains a reputation for a visionary sort of realism, based upon the state of the world economy today and on historic wisdom

---

"Lessons of the Great Recession: How the Safety Net Performed," *New York Times*, 24 June 2013, http://economix.blogs.nytimes.com/2013/06/24/lessons-of-the-great-recession-how-the -safety-net-performed/?_r=0. — *Ed.*

105. Mudge was writing before passage of the Wall Street Reform and Consumer Protection Act — the Dodd-Frank Act — in 2010. But only in 2012 was the Consumer Financial Protection Bureau's director, Richard Cordray, able to begin activating consumer protections. See note 8. — *Ed.*

106. Again, Mudge wrote before President Obama signed the Patient Protection and Affordable Care Act (PPACA) on 23 March 2010, intended to enshrine, in his words, "the core principle that everybody should have some basic security when it comes to their health care." From the start, the law was vehemently opposed, largely by Republicans. Nevertheless, on 28 June 2012, the Supreme Court supported the act's key requirement that most Americans buy health insurance or pay a penalty, on the basis of the congressional power to tax. (The Obama administration had argued on the basis of Congress's power to regulate interstate commerce.) But the Court also greatly limited Medicaid. Adam Liptak, "Justices, By 5-4, Uphold Health Care Law, Roberts in Majority, Victory for Obama," *New York Times*, 29 June 2012, p. A1. — *Ed.*

about the nature of human beings, their desires and fallibilities. Since all of us who work in religious or economic institutions share this common mix of potentials and limitations, together we may become equally anxious to envision, and vigilant to promote, the kind of human household we need, if our species is to survive and thrive.[107]

107. From its start in mid-September 2011, the Occupy Wall Street (OWS) movement spread to over nine hundred cities in more than eighty countries. "Protests: Not Quite Together," *The Economist*, 22-28 October 2011, pp. 73-75. The protesters in New York and OWS's website describe followers as a "leaderless resistance movement with people of many colors, genders, and political persuasions. The one thing we all have in common is that we are the 99 percent that will no longer tolerate the greed and corruption of the 1 percent." "Occupy Wall Street, Times Topics," *New York Times*, 3 October 2011; also "Occupy the Midwest Conference: Detroit, Aug. 23-26," 21 July 2012, http://occupywallst.org. One New York protester, William Buster, affirms that the movement is "not anti-business," but seeks a way around the legislative logjam in Washington that is preventing reform. Interview, *Charlie Rose*, PBS, 12 October 2011. Nicholas Kristof also asserts that the OWSers wish to save capitalism from its abusers. "Crony Capitalism Comes Home," Op-Ed, *New York Times*, 27 October 2011. Paul Krugman called this protest, joined by unions and increasing numbers of Democrats, "an important event that just might even eventually be seen as a turning point." He asked politicians to provide the specific policy demands that the protesters, on principle, are not. "Confronting the Malefactors," *New York Times*, 7 October 2011, p. A23. David Harvey, professor of geography at the City University of New York and author of the book *Rebel Cities*, welcomes the novel challenge of the OWS to the control of public spaces by the power elite, arguing that such spaces are needed as forums for political debate. And Richard D. Wolff, visiting professor of economics at the New School University, New York, and author of *Occupy the Economy*, observes that the OWS was more effective by going straight to Wall Street and not to Washington. He sees its challenge to the taboo of criticizing capitalism giving the country "a quantum leap forward." Interviews, *Charlie Rose*, PBS, 26 July 2012. Occupy continued to emphasize its collaborative aim above its activist goals in directly aiding Hurricane Sandy victims. Jeffrey Lawrence and Luis Moreno-Caballud, "In Hurricane Sandy Relief, a Reminder of Occupy's Original Spirit," *Yes! Magazine*, 29 November 2012, http://www.nationofchange.org/hurricane-sandy-relief-reminder-occupy-s-original-spirit-1354181886. In addition, Occupy collaborated with churches in aiding Sandy's victims and the churches themselves, thereby winning over former skeptics, even enemies, as it strengthened its spiritual reason for being. Nathan Schneider, "How Occupy Wall Street Got Religion," *Nation of Change*, 21 December 2012, pp. 1-2, http://www.nationofchange.org/how-occupy-wall-street-got-religion-1356104826. In September 2013, that spirit continues in the form of public pressure to prioritize economic equality. See Richard Eskow of Campaign for America's Future, "Memo to Washington: The Occupy Movement Lives," *Nation of Change*, 19 September 2013, http://www.nationofchange.org/memo-washington-occupy-movement-lives-1379598826. — *Ed.*

CHAPTER 3

Outline for My Unfinished Book, 9/11/2009

Foreword: This book developed as an independent personal offshoot along-side a report on the global economy that was being developed by the Advisory Committee on Social Action Policy of the Presbyterian Church (USA), an elected committee on which I was serving. This structure allowed for an indispensable dialogue on the subject that both aided, and eventually stymied, my own thinking. Better said, the committee stimulated me to think for my church in ways it seems not yet ready to think. I nevertheless continue to affirm my membership in this community of faith as I also in particular invite Jews and Muslims to join me, as co-descendants of Abraham, and others to bring their wisdom to bear on how we may shape the economy of the future.

Introduction: My 2008 book *The Gift of Responsibility* concludes with a discussion of "covenantal humanism." This "humanism" is not godlessness. It's a shared understanding of our gift of responsibility, handed down through Abraham's covenant with God, to be a blessing to all humanity. The ongoing recession demands that the focus of that blessing be to secure our mutual economic, or householding, natures. The best sources for this job may be encountered *through* any one of the Abrahamic faiths: Jewish, Christian, and Muslim. Here are living historic religious communities based on rich spiritual and concrete economic wisdom expressed in particular symbols and practices. Independently, they have made households or "homes of meaning" for their congregations, and potentially, for others. Stretched to include "all the families of the earth" (Gen. 12:3), such households are potential centers for covenantal humanism in action that are an opportunity to restore us from the economic irresponsibility of our present global crisis.

There are two interacting perspectives from which I write this book.

First, it is time for economics to return to its humanistic roots from having developed into a mathematical discipline dedicated to the maximization of profit. I argue for taking up again the ancient idea of *political economy,* the economy of the *polis,* of the public human household. Second, we need to meet the challenge of our present crisis by deepening the reach of the human spirit — *what we do with our collective capacities.* The crisis then becomes an opportunity to reexamine our economic assumptions before the severe downturn we're undergoing may become a full collapse.

This book offers six fresh arguments:

1. I examine economic justice not simply as it is now practiced — things as they are — but rather I reassess our economic system from a new view of human nature as a species that values and is valued. I attempt to display the crisis in its truest relevance: a set of urgent symptoms of dysfunction in our social organism whose roots lie deeper, in disorders of the spirit. In that light, I ask, what may we do to make things right?

2. I affirm that it is all humanity's job, from economists to theologians, to ask this question, because all of us are impacted by a system that profoundly affects our habitats, our homes, and whether we may continue to live in them. The family is a microcosm of the social-global household. Therefore, I begin with the notion of *Homo oeconomicus,* humanity defined by the kind of household generated by our basic wish to exist and desire to be.

3. I argue that we have a great capacity for self-delusion about the meaning of what we have done in bringing about our global recession. We generate ideological worlds that justify what we do. We explain ourselves to ourselves with high-sounding principles that justify our self-interested behavior. And we maintain our ideologies in power by power.

4. I seek to embed economics once again in culture, in the ongoing question of humanity's nature and value, or in Reinhold Niebuhr's words, its "nature and destiny." At present, a self-justified cultural reality based on disproportionate wealth has taken on repressive aspects. The thrust of life into culture has produced uneven results, favorable to some, unjust toward many. Those favored produce justifying symbols. Those disfavored produce revolutionary ones.

5. I locate our nature and destiny within an evolutionary perspective. How can humanity as an economic animal have arisen within evolution as we know or imagine it? Throughout this process, Spirit gets played out in the form of economic assumptions and systems. In this light, economics

becomes a story — from cuneiform financial records on clay tablets to computer spreadsheets. In that story, the arising of division of labor undergirds the start of gender discrimination.

6. I argue that as we seek to make human life-together truly just, we need to go deep and explore a new vision of humanity and its many households. Only then, may we gain the perspective we need to make our economic institutions more attuned to the whole world's needs and to structure our systems of exchange more fairly.

Part I

Chapter 1: The "Lay of the Land" sets forth the situation, my approach, and what I will attempt to do. I explain why this book's spinal column is an *economic* argument. The modern world sees the need for a new understanding of what is meant by the human. Writers speak of the "post-human" situation that challenges our sense of identity as a species. The present global economic meltdown newly calls attention to this question in concrete examples that are anything but theoretical. Now that I've lost my job, who am I? People can understand the emergency, because they profoundly experience it. Some may also sense that the crisis destabilizes our human identity by threatening our co-responsibility for one another as members of a "commonwealth," or household. The Enlightenment valued individual autonomy as the essence of the human. Since then, this autonomy has steadily degenerated into irresponsibility toward one another, leading to the economic meltdown. Therefore, to address the crisis at its center is also to think about what kind of human community we are called to be, and that leads back to who we are as a species. From the perspective of God's providence, human nature must be expressed as mutual responsibility.

Many economists and economic analysts claim today that economics is a closed system of reasoning called "rational choice theory." They also claim that its intricate, intrinsic (that is, not influenced by the "extrinsic") principles are fully grasped only by economists. They argue that if we want prosperity, we can only reason and behave in one way. Hence economics is thought to be impervious to "noneconomic" conditions, intentions, or "externalities." But no. Economics is one of the expressions of human spirit, of our identity as human beings. It, too, is human spirit objectified. Economics is an ensemble of many "sources of the self," defined by the kind of interactive global household that we make for ourselves.

Chapter 2: "Toward a New Genealogy of Morals" examines the divine purpose as seen in evolutionary terms. How does our moral sense arise? Is it all hard-wired? Today, we have differing scientific, mostly reductionistic, explanations of the origins of "morality." Philip Hefner's *The Human Factor* takes a different view; and likewise does Viktor Frankl. Our very survival depends on meaning. From organic evolution to the dawn of culture, or shared human life, moral narratives have revealed such meaning. There have been many of these primordial narratives. How do they arise? What do they say?

Chapter 3: "From Habitat to Household" brings together organic evolution with the "phenomenology of Spirit" in our present stage of the history of culture. We may now understand ourselves as having a "human nature" and "value" because we are members of a universal household in which we profoundly take one another into account. In the context of a "covenantal humanism," our nature is to live in a network of mutual responsibility for the maintenance of a divinely given, world "household" of "stakeholders." This is a global enterprise in which we are all "players." How then do we generate expressions of its meaning and put that meaning into play?

Many earlier and different expressions of "objective spirit" (Hegel) took for granted slavery and other oppressive systems. Escape from such economic oppression has generated "identity politics." Can the offspring and continuing beneficiaries of slaveholders legitimately speak of a universal human household? How do we deal with the problem of moral universalism? Who can speak for all? No one? Yet a global morality may be constructed not as a set of precepts or concepts, but in action. Since the most concrete, pragmatic expression of ties that join all human beings together lies in the economic or householding realm, the most useful answer takes the form of "household rules," that is, how the house is set up and managed in the economic sense. Simultaneously, we are responsible for maintaining the earth's whole substance or resources. In addition, we have an investment in adding value to the cosmic gift.

Otherwise put, this chapter's underlying notion is that economics — how we conceive, organize, and manage it — is, along with art, music, literature, and architecture — an expression of the human spirit, that is, of our true identity. Who we are in the wake of the recession is most problematic. The world's economic turmoil challenges us to redefine ourselves. We do this with our innate human spirit made visible — "objective spirit" — with our breath, with our minds, with our hands! It appears as spoken, written, sculpted, painted, built, acted out, and other forms of tangible "cultural artifacts." The kind of "household" we make out of our "habitat" — the earth

— is such an objectified spirit. Household is the global ensemble of people turning resources into meanings at the family dinner table, Passover, the Lord's Supper, or breaking fast after Ramadan. Our households are transformed into moral spaces for our collective spirit.

Part II: Religious Traditions in the Oikonomic Dialogue

Chapter 4: "What Can Religious Perspectives Contribute?" interprets Christian sources offered alongside of, and with responsibility toward, parallel efforts among Christians differing from myself and among the two other Abrahamic faiths that are also taking stock in this economic crisis. There are no real walls between us, but I cannot speak *for* any of them. Rather I acknowledge their instruction and challenge to my own thoughts. In short, I attempt to show a multi-Christian and interfaith context of a wide and differing range — the "many voices" within and between each faith — that have influenced me, while also remaining authentic to my religious heritage. Among other sources, I will refer to the eighth-century prophets, the "Jubilee" tradition in Leviticus, Jesus' parables, and passages from the Qur'an.

Further comment: Possibly the "knowledge of good and evil" in Genesis 3 really means the capacity to see in advance what will be either a blessing or a curse. Yet this kind of knowledge is only for the gods. It is denied human beings. Thus we always live in anxiety, uncertain of what will come of our decisions. We try various ways of escaping from, or insulating ourselves against, this basic unknown. One is to control the future through aspiration to absolute power, and another, to armor ourselves with authority and status, seeking such honor and reputation that no one can undermine us. Or we define ourselves ideologically by adopting inflexible fundamentalisms: a "market fundamentalism" relying on alleged sureties about certain economic "facts," or a theological fundamentalism trying to seal out doubt by affirming rigid beliefs.

Chapter 5: "The Christian Contribution Rethought for Our Present Situation" draws upon Christology and the concept of the Holy Spirit to speak of an "economic Trinity." This economic Trinity is Spirit ramifying itself through evolution and the histories of culture. Jesus' remembered presence and his message "rise" into the world-historical array of *oikonomia,* or households, lifting them up. He gives a human face to this Spirit, which, if it dwells in the ways people live together, brings blessing rather than curse.

Further explained: What does it mean to say that the things we invest with meaning as households reflect "Spirit"? And how, if at all, does this Spirit relate to the notion of "Holy Spirit"? In what I am calling the "economic Trinity," the Third Person (Holy Spirit) extends Jesus' presence in the world throughout the history of institutions and culture. Such Spirit is not only an inward personal force. It becomes actual in instances of real justice, healing, and blessing by the influence and impact of Christ's prayers, parables, actions, and sacraments. I believe even Orthodox Christians would agree with this "theological economy." I go a bit further, linking this "economic Trinity" with "economics" as literal "household rules" that regulate and transform our mere global habitats into homes.

Chapter 6: "The Role of the Reformed Tradition" explores economic justice in the dawn, development, and aftermath of the "modern age," including the contemporary work of the World Alliance of Reformed Churches.[1]

From the Reformers' first sixteenth-century debates to today's differing slants on their legacy, multiple voices have searched the Bible to answer the same question: What *kind* of responsibility do we owe the world? I understand the organic growth of commentary on such matters in the same way as does Catholic writer Alasdair MacIntyre: a theological tradition doesn't develop any single idea but is rather a recognizable argument among many related ideas and practices extended over time. As I see it, then, Reformed thinking follows an identifiable continuity, in the midst of obvious plurality, about the nature of humanity's response to God's promises.

Calvin's discussion of Christian public responsibility in his *Institutes of the Christian Religion* (1559) launches the issue by exploring the interaction of law and grace. For him, grace is approached through the work of the clergy but also by public magistrates, both administering laws based on the Torah and "natural law." But grace is also at work within redeemed individual sinners, defining a "third use" for the law: to motivate us into action as concerned citizens in the world. Calvin argued, "We are not our own," but are inspired to enlarge the grace we have received for the common good. That sense of grace, repeated in the Presbyterian Westminster Confession of Faith (1646), further developed in the seventeenth and eighteenth centuries to influence both political philosophy (Locke) and Enlightenment thinking about "civil society." In the twentieth century, the notion of "common grace" arose within Dutch Reformed Protestantism

1. In June 2010, WARC merged with the Reformed Ecumenical Council (REC), forming the World Communion of Reformed Churches (WCRC) at a uniting General Council held in Grand Rapids, Michigan. — *Ed.*

to recognize that, as Georges Bernanos ends his novel *Diary of a Country Priest,* "Grace is everywhere." God is at work in ordinary human goodness wherever that may be found.

The World Alliance of Reformed Churches (WARC) at its councils in Debrecen (1997) and Accra (2004) sought to shift the Reformed tradition's sense of responsibility from its middle-class roots in Calvin's Geneva to a more universal locus. Its councils encouraged members to recognize that, perhaps unwittingly, they have supported a global "empire" of military, po-litical, and economic exploitation of those without the capacity to defend themselves. The Reformed tradition is today far less an establishment tradi-tion than it was in Calvin's time and throughout much of its history. Socially located on the margins of power, it may now better grasp the meaning of solidarity with the poor, suffering, oppressed, or excluded.

Without abandoning WARC's denunciation of global imperial econom-ics, I think we should look again at what mid-twentieth-century Calvinists (including Anglican Calvinists like J. H. Oldham) meant by "responsible society." What is now bringing curse on the world is not mere oppression by financial empires. Rather, it's the institutional irresponsibility, fueled by greed, of banking and business moguls themselves. And as the empire col-lapses, the poor may well suffer even more.

Part III: Reconsecrating the Global Household as "Theater of God's Glory"

"And behold, God saw that it was good."

Chapter 7: "Stakeholdership as a Theory to Meet the Household's Disorder" begins by noting that the recession has revealed not only a breakdown of our economic system, but also its eclipse of basic household values. Economics as "rational choice theory" has become impervious to moral considerations in principle. Sources of help are not to be found in the simple reiteration of either "capitalist" or "socialist" values. Rather, we need a new and larger perspective for reconstructing the economy.

In the notion of "global stakeholdership," I propose that stockholders would morph into stakeholders by becoming recognized as the universal and ultimate "owners" of enterprises. In principle if not actually, stakehold-ers would then be responsible for the nature and purpose of all business activity. Every inhabitant on earth — their voices regularly accessible in this widely digital age from the humblest hut to urban apartments — would be acknowledged, thus valued, as a stakeholder in developing the planet's use. That would include everyone's own use, or virtue, as evolutionary products of the earth. Such self-beneficial responsibility would encourage stakeholders to become consciously moral persons, if they were not already, thus justifying their place as the first and final touchstones for "added value" entrepreneurship.

In this way, stakeholdership would take the need to embed economics in spiritual-cultural meanings into an open and flexible kind of economic theory. By involving the totality of the world's people, stakeholdership would restructure our present economic institutions to be more inclusive and just. And stakeholders would be highly motivated to transform the roles of former stockholders. They would be responsible not to petroleum-bearing rock or atmospheric chemistry as such, nor to the mere profits that would continue to be gained from them. Their principal responsibility would be to the ways in which these resources and gains from them were used to benefit the earth and its people — namely everyone. In the hands of stakeholders — persons whose future flourishing depended on nature's preservation — raw materials would become better protected and efficiently rationed to serve the end goal: making the places where we live truly just and loving households.

Chapter 8: "Examining Possibilities" will explore the dimensions of religious resistance as well as congregational and community up-building. It will present situation analyses of householding criteria in their many forms. From congregations of all three Abrahamic faiths and from public witness, examples of eco-justice and household reordering will be described as the potential for turning curse into blessing. Each study will emphasize a practical bent to answer the question: What can be done about disorder in the household?

Justice — and its corollaries, respect and compassion — is not defined abstractly as a noun referring to a "thing" that is present. It is an action arising from a type of reasoning that itself may be "just" or not, in this case, scriptural-traditional reasoning. Therefore, it is an attribute of action, an adjective, as in an institution that operates *justly*.[2]

The Abrahamic traditions derive from lived illustrations of moral argument, often in the form of narratives. With a focus on what justice arguments

2. Paul Ricoeur, *The Just*, trans. David Pellauer (Chicago: University of Chicago Press, 2000).

originally meant and continue to mean — asking in what forms are these questions alive today? — I will take the following slices into each tradition's materials:

1. *The ownership and management of the land.* What did/does justice demand in the world of land tenure? Examples: the eighth-century prophets and contemporary Israeli settlements in the West Bank.
2. *The ethics of financial services.* What was/is just in lending and interest-taking activities, and how was/is a just price reached? Examples: ancient, medieval, and early modern practices to international agencies today.
3. *The formation of capital.* What was/is the just means of sharing risks in pledging communal wealth to private enterprises? Examples: from each of the Abrahamic scriptures and contemporary practices, particularly Islamic (Sharia) banking principles.
4. *The meaning and rights of labor.* What was/is the Abrahamic concept of work and work in a world of universal stakeholdership?

I will borrow some aspects of the 1950s-60s "responsible society" theory (clearly neither the "white man's burden" nor colonialist thinking), as well as "middle axiom" analysis.[3] This exploration, hardly establishing utopia, simply attempts to take humanity forward one more step.

3. Both "middle axiom" and "responsible society" analyses arose within the Christian ecumenical movement just before and after World War II. At Oxford in 1937, Scottish missionary and ecumenical pioneer J. H. Oldham introduced the "middle axioms" approach to doing social ethics. The World Council of Churches adopted "responsible society" at its First Assembly in Amsterdam in 1948. The term assumed that freedom was fundamental to responsible action. Paul Abrecht, "Ecumenical Social Thought and Action," in *History of the Ecumenical Movement: The Ecumenical Advance, 1948-1968,* ed. Ruth Rouse, Stephen C. Neill, and Harold E. Fey (Geneva: World Council of Churches, 1993), vol. 2, pp. 238-39, 241-42. "Middle axioms" are temporary guideposts derived from Christian ethics about what must be done next. They are useful nonpermanent ways to forward the slow process of implementing justice inspired by love. Oldham described them as "an attempt to define the directions in which, in a particular state of society, Christian faith must express itself. They are not binding for all time, but are provisional definitions of the type of behavior required of Christians at a given period and in given circumstances." W. A. Visser 't Hooft and J. H. Oldham, *The Church and Its Function in Society* (Chicago: Willett, Clark & Co., 1937), p. 194. John C. Bennett, in *Christian Ethics and Social Policy* (New York: Scribner's, 1946), points to examples of middle axioms: the need of international collaboration in the United Nations, the maintenance of balance between free enterprise and government control of economic power, the removal of racial segregation in the churches, and its progressive elimination in society. Georgia Harkness, "Christian Ethics," www.religion-online.org/showchapter.asp?title=802&C=1085. — *Ed.*

Coda: A Vision of Interfaith Work

This book seeks to show how religious communities whose traditions bear multiple meanings can once again speak to today's dominant contexts of power, or "empire." I have sketched an outline of a human household on a global scale, the starting point of my hope for a new planetary political economy. To implement this vision requires the joint work of prophetic critiques and the doing of justice, precisely what religious communities are meant to do. Present in the world, they ask questions of it, and provide space for all sorts of inquiry in which everyone may engage, not just their members. Faith groups probe basic issues, prime among them: the nature of the human family. As a lifetime member of such a group, I suggest that a touchstone for greater understanding could be what I've called "covenantal humanism," defined in *Gift* as "a lived *interpretation*" of one or another of the Abrahamic faiths.

It would be helpful if, like these traditions, we might find a contemporary panhuman symbol for this project. (Here I draw upon a classic idea of *Homo symbolicus* developed by Paul Tillich.)[4] Each Abrahamic faith's widely recognized symbol — Judaism's Star of David, Christianity's Cross, and Islam's Crescent Moon and Star — points to a concrete past and practice. Certain familiar emblems today — the peace symbol, for example — are useful to be sure, but they lack the resonance (the height and depth) of plural and idiosyncratic religious symbols. Arising from particular histories, these symbols cannot be expressed in universal terms. For now, the sapling of common understanding that is growing from Abrahamic roots up toward a tree of some stature — a tree of covenantal humanism — needs to use nodes of deeper awareness and spaces for profound questioning that could one day leaf into such a locus of meaning.

In this recession, faith groups have at least two duties: (1) to help their members and institutions faithfully and creatively meet the economic challenge, and (2) to think together about the kind of global household they want to see after this crisis ends. How may this come about? In Oakland, California, a "Faith Trio" composed of participants from Jewish, Muslim, and Christian communities is an ongoing, successful example of interreligious engagement.[5] In the wake of 9/11, it has been meeting monthly to form

---

4. Paul Tillich, "The Meaning and Justification of Religious Symbols," in *Religious Experience and Truth*, ed. Sydney Hook (New York: New York University Press, 1961), pp. 3-11. — *Ed.*

5. The congregations represented in the Faith Trio of Oakland are the Islamic Cultural

friendships, exchange information about each faith, and have joint programs. As a participant, I have watched this Trio's far-reaching activities that, not surprisingly, have spawned greater understanding of each tradition's link to Abraham in fact and in spirit. I hope that this sort of open and ongoing discussion could come to include other faiths and secular people as well.

In fact, faith communities are by nature an excellent avenue for enlisting secularists. That's because their members, unlike clergy, are already in and of the world. They can be addressed just as the world is addressed. In fact, each week the rabbi, pastor, or imam has the opportunity to remind congregants of their double role in and outside of worship. Since all are worldly, what deeply speaks to people of faith, especially on economic matters, could be appealing to open-minded secularists.

But can the ancient stories of covenants made along the very human paths of striving, desire, and preeminence engage the larger human scene? Can that arena be brought into the struggle to overcome alienation in the streets and corruption in marketplaces and halls of power? The answer lies in another question: May we reconsider ourselves as *Homo oeconomicus* in the sense I've been arguing in these pages? If so, then searching for a new world household or political economy, which takes us back to religious traditions, will tell much about who we might become as a species.

This possibility brings to mind a musical analogy: the majestic opening chords of Beethoven's stirring overture, "The Consecration of the House." In the same way that music and drama manifest the human spirit, economics could embody that spirit in a world of stakeholder-based households. Beethoven's "House" celebrated and consecrated a new theater's first performance in Vienna in 1822.[6] Theaters have always been sites of meaning-bearing action where humanity's heights and depths are on full display by *the quality of their actors' performances.* So stakeholdership would be another sort of "overture" to the rest of the human story. I imagine the curtain opening to reveal all the earth's people — the audience as actors (Kierkegaard)! The conductor would then lead the audience in singing a song consecrating a world of true and just human habitation. What would be the music for

---

Center of Northern California, Kehilla Community Synagogue, and Montclair Presbyterian Church. Mudge was well aware that nationally and internationally similar groups have formed, or are forming. — *Ed.*

6. The theater's director commissioned this overture, Beethoven's Opus 124. http://www .musicwithease.com/consecration-house.htlm; http://cn.wikipedia.org/wiki/Consecration_of _the_House_Overture. — *Ed.*

that? Would people know the words? There would be many different scores and librettos. Only the future will tell us.

We're supremely cautious about what we consecrate, because consecration signifies that the human spirit has become suffused with, or been taken up into, a beneficial Higher Spirit. What is required for us to consecrate? To recognize and connect with the deeper meanings between human spirit and Spirit? One thing is certain. The act is always provisional and carries degrees of force. Emily Dickinson's slant on her sometimes stormy household could yet reach moments of unconditional apex. "Home," she once wrote a friend, "is the definition of God."

Let us consider that the "consecration of the house of humanity" specifically refers to how we might live together with a fair distribution of the world's goods among all of its households, and to the earth's benefit. We'd then be approaching a "theater of God's glory" (Calvin). Such meaning requires us to capitalize "house" when we say, "Bless this House, O Lord, we pray!"

CHAPTER 4

Responses from a Jew, a Christian, and a Muslim

"To Work It and Preserve It": A Jewish Response to Mudge's Covenantal Humanism and Stakeholdership

ELLIOT N. DORFF

I am writing this when the memory of the world's financial meltdown of 2008 is still painfully fresh and when economies throughout the world are being sorely tested. The European Union is faced with supporting bankrupt governments in Greece, Spain, Portugal, Ireland, and possibly Italy. During the last two weeks riots have plagued many English cities, as the disaffected and unemployed have looted and burned businesses. The United States Congress seems incapable of agreeing on a plan to rein in deficit budgets and to begin to pay off the national debt. In the summer of 2011 in Israel, demonstrators numbering into the hundreds of thousands and in cities all across the nation protested the structure of the economy that makes renting an apartment out of reach for most Israelis and in which government money has been spent so heavily on defense that the infrastructure and the educational system are crumbling.

These conditions make it ever more important and even urgent that people of faith bring to bear the insights of their traditions to economic activity in general and to business in particular. Lewis Mudge has done this admirably in his previous work and in this book. I have been asked briefly to articulate a Jewish approach to two themes to which he so eloquently speaks from his own Christian tradition — namely, covenantal humanism and stakeholdership.

The Relevance of Religion to Economics and Business

Many people, including some religious ones, think of business and religion as two isolated realms, each with little or no relevance to the other. Why, then, should people in business be interested in what religion has to say about their profession in the first place?

Religions depict the ways in which we are linked to each other, to the environment, and to God. The very word "religion" means this. The "lig" in that word comes from the Latin root meaning to connect, the same root from which we get the English word "ligament." Religions describe our linkages, as our ligaments tie the various elements of our body to each other.

One's religion is therefore important in a discussion of business because religions help us to put all our activities *in context*. In describing its particular picture of reality and of the ideal person and society, each religion defines the role of business within that picture. That helps to determine the goals of business and the values and rules by which it must operate in order to achieve those goals. It helps to make business not just a source of livelihood, but part of a meaningful life. Mudge stresses this linkage between religion and economics when he says that "[c]ovenantal humanism, the humanism of blessing in Hebrew scripture, focuses in a significant degree on economic questions."

Fundamental Concepts

1. God as the Owner of All Creation

"Mark, the heavens to their uttermost reaches belong to the Lord your God, the earth and all that is on it" (Deut. 10:14). "To the Lord belong the earth and all that it holds, the world and all those who inhabit it" (Ps. 24:1). These biblical verses bespeak the underlying assumption of all Jewish assessments of business. Ultimately, God owns the world. We enjoy the right to use it and to make our living on it only at God's behest, and only when we abide by the rules God has set for such activity.

In the Torah (the Five Books of Moses), that has an immediate effect on the profits we may make through the use of God's property. Chapter 25 of Leviticus, the third book of the Torah, delineates a number of ways in which landowners must provide for the poor. This includes not only outright gifts, but also loans so that the poor can ultimately free themselves of their need for support. In specifying these rules, the Torah explains why we must obey them: ". . . for the land is Mine; you are but strangers resident with Me" (Lev. 25:23). We are, after all, tenants on God's land, and we therefore may use it only under the conditions that the Owner has set.[1]

God, however, is depicted in Judaism not as disparaging human economic activity, but as encouraging it. In direct contrast to the Prometheus myth, which depicts man as stealing fire from the gods, the Rabbis say that when Adam and Eve were expelled from the Garden of Eden, they were both cold and afraid when night fell. God gave them two sticks and showed them how to make fire with them.[2] Thus the human ability to make fire, the very symbol of human hubris in the Greek tradition, is instead, in the Jewish tradition, a gift of God to show mankind how to reshape the world for our own economic benefit.

2. Individuals with Rights vs. Members of a Community with Duties

The contemporary Western world is largely the product of the Enlightenment, with its fundamental doctrine that we are all created as individuals "with certain unalienable rights," as the United States' Declaration of Independence asserts. If one begins with this assumption, the burden of proof is always on the one who maintains that I do *not* have the right to do *x*. As many of their laws attest, Western societies certainly impose such limitations on each person's rights, but in each case the restriction is constantly subject to challenge on the grounds that it is an unnecessary and unjustified intrusion into an area which, by rights, belongs to that individual's private judgment. The United States, in particular, is characterized by a feisty individualism.

This individualism extends even to American identity itself. In Enlightenment ideology, membership in a community is a voluntary act of the individual that can be renounced, together with its benefits and burdens, at will. Thus as an American I can decide to join a particular religious group or not, to live anywhere I want, to attend whatever school I can get into, and to pursue any legal job I wish. I may spend all of my time and energy on my own interests, or I can devote some of it to communal needs and activities.

---

1. For more on Judaism's view of, and provisions for, the poor, see Elliot N. Dorff, *To Do the Right and the Good: A Jewish Approach to Modern Social Ethics* (Philadelphia: Jewish Publication Society, 2002), ch. 6.

2. B. *Pesahim* 54a; *Genesis Rabbah* 11. In this and all following notes, B. = Babylonian Talmud (edited c. 500 CE); M.T. = Maimonides' code, the *Mishneh Torah*; and S.A. = Joseph Caro's code, the *Shulhan Arukh*.

Even American citizenship is voluntary: It is hard to become an American citizen, but as long as I have not committed a felony, I can go into any American embassy or consulate outside the United States and fill out a form to renounce my American citizenship.[3]

This American ideology has some critically important advantages. It affords Americans a degree of freedom unknown in any other time or place. In doing so, it enables people of all religions and ethnic origins to live together in peace and mutual fructification; the United States is the most pluralistic country that has ever existed on the face of the earth, and that can only happen if Americans begin with strong assumptions of individualism and freedom. Moreover, it has given people the free rein to be creative in virtually every area of human endeavor, making the United States the leader, or at least one of the leaders, in science, medicine, technology, the arts, the social sciences, and the humanities.

American ideology also, like every other ideology, has its disadvantages. Individualism can mean loneliness, and it can mean lack of care for others. This translates into, for example, the difficulty that Americans have had in creating a healthcare system that cares for us all and a thin social service network that leaves all too many people homeless and hungry. It also has meant that Americans have had difficulty creating a public school system that works well. The pragmatic strain of American ideology, while the source of American creativity, has also spawned American materialism.

Judaism begins with radically different assumptions about who we are, assumptions that bring their own burdens and benefits. The People Israel left Egypt not as individuals but as a group. Every Jew since then must, as the *Haggadah* for the Passover Seder asserts, "see himself as if he himself left Egypt" and was part of that band that received God's revelation of the Torah at Sinai and then trekked to the Promised Land. Moses similarly asserts to the second generation, to those who had not in fact been at Sinai, that they are nevertheless to see themselves as if they were there: "It is not only with our ancestors that the Lord made this Covenant, but with us, the living, every one of us who is here today."[4] Moreover, this Covenant is for future generations as well:

---

3. See http://travel.state.gov/law/citizenship/citizenship_776.html, which is the State Department website that describes the right to renounce one's U.S. citizenship as provided for in Section 349(a)(5) of the Immigration and Naturalization Act and the ways in which it must be done — specifically, by (1) appearing in person before a U.S. consular or diplomatic officer, (2) in a foreign country (normally at a U.S. embassy or consulate); and (3) signing an oath of renunciation.

4. Deuteronomy 5:3.

> I make this covenant, with its sanctions, not with you alone, but both with those who are standing here with us this day before the Lord our God and with those who are not with us here this day. . . . Take to heart all the words with which I have warned you this day. Enjoin them upon your children, that they may observe faithfully all the terms of this Teaching. For this is not a trifling thing for you: it is your very life. . . .[5]

Jews begin, then, not as individuals with rights, but as members of a community with duties.

This communal identity is not voluntary; it is organic. In the traditional, Jewish way of seeing things, those born Jewish (that is, according to traditional Jewish law, born to a Jewish woman) are part of the community for life, whether they like it or not. Adults who convert to Judaism do so, of course, of their own free will. The very rites of conversion, though, symbolize their rebirth into the Jewish community, and so once converted they too lose all rights to leave the fold. Even those Jews who during their lives convert to another faith become, in Jewish religious law, not members of another community, but apostate Jews. Such people lose many of the benefits of their Jewish identity (e.g., to be married or buried as a Jew, to count in a prayer quorum, etc.), but retain all the obligations![6]

There are clear disadvantages in seeing oneself this way. They are, in sum, that one may lose the strengths of American ideology. If you are a member of a tightly knit community, privacy can be hard to come by, for your business is everyone else's, and vice versa. Moreover, communities can stifle individualism, freedom, and creativity.

On the other hand, there are real benefits in seeing oneself through these communitarian lenses. As the first-century sage, Hillel, said, "If I am here, everyone is here,"[7] a graphic expression of the tenet that, in the Jewish view of the world, the entire Jewish community, past, present, and future, here and abroad, is part of you even when you are physically isolated. You are, therefore, never alone; you are part of an extended family and community throughout time and the world over. Moreover, as that Talmud says,

---

5. Deuteronomy 29:13-14; 32:46-47.

6. In the Brother Daniel case, the Israeli Supreme Court was determining the criteria for Jewish identity under Israel's Law of Return and not under Jewish religious law, but the court's response was the same as that of Jewish religious law — namely, that Brother Daniel could *not* claim citizenship as a Jew because that is a privilege that he lost when he converted to Christianity.

7. B. *Sukkah* 53a.

"All Israelites are responsible for each other."[8] This attitude prompts Jews to provide a strong safety net for the vulnerable within — and, as we shall see — even outside the community. This gives one a mission in life — to fix the world *(tikkun olam)*, and working toward that goal can give a strong sense of meaning to life.[9]

These differences should not be exaggerated. As President Obama has elegantly articulated, American individualism is accompanied with strong ties to one's family, community, and nation.[10] Conversely, the Torah's doctrine that each human being is created in the image of God has meant that Jewish law takes great pains to protect the interests of individuals. Furthermore, Jews love to assert their own opinions in arguments — following in the footsteps of Abraham, Moses, Isaiah, and Job, all of whom argued with God, and the classical Rabbis who argue with each other on virtually every page of the Talmud. Judaism is definitely not a tradition that encourages passive reception of whatever one is told; it instead asks people to question and evaluate every belief and proposed action, and it makes each and every Jew responsible for learning more about Judaism on a lifelong basis and for carrying out the Jewish mission to improve humanity's lot in the world. Individualism thus definitely exists in the Jewish way of thinking and acting. Even with these important caveats, however, it is nevertheless true that Americans begin from a foundation of individual rights, and Jews think of themselves first and foremost as members of a community with duties.

3. Expectations of Others in One's Community

One's view of the nature of communal ties has direct implications for the expectations that each of us can legitimately have of ourselves and of each other. In Enlightenment ideology, I can expect you to fulfill the obligations that we have mutually agreed upon as part of the social contract, but only those. Otherwise, I must assume and respect your freedom and privacy. I might contribute to the poor or take part in a social action project, but if

8. B. *Shevu'ot* 39a.

9. See Elliot N. Dorff, *The Way into Tikkun Olam (Repairing the World)* (Woodstock, VT: Jewish Lights, 2005), and Elliot N. Dorff with Reverend Cory Willson, *The Jewish Approach to Repairing the World (Tikkun Olam): A Brief Introduction for Christians* (Woodstock, VT: Jewish Lights, 2008).

10. Barack Obama, *The Audacity of Hope: Thoughts on Reclaiming the American Dream* (New York: Crown, 2006), p. 55.

I do so I am going beyond what can be legitimately expected of me. I am engaged in an act of charity.

In the Jewish view of community, by contrast, we are all members of a people with mutual obligations toward each other. That is the default status of each one of us. Therefore, I can expect you not only to fulfill the requirements of Jewish law, which demands considerably more than American law does in caring for the other, but, indeed, to go beyond the law in doing so.[11]

Even the words used in each tradition for helping others bespeak these different assumptions. In English, when I extend myself to help others, I am doing an act of "charity," from the Latin *caritas,* meaning caring. This connotes that I am an especially good person. The Hebrew word for these exact same acts is *tzadakah,* from the Hebrew root *tzedek,* meaning justice. In other words, when I go out of my way to help others, from a Jewish perspective I am simply doing what is expected of me in fulfilling the demands of justice.

One example will make this distinction clear. If I see a person drowning or accosted by robbers, in all American states except four I have no obligation to try to save him or her or even to seek help in doing so. On the contrary, if I try to do that and in the process unintentionally cause the drowning or robbed person harm, until recently, when most states passed "Good Samaritan" laws, I could actually be sued for negligence or even assault.[12] In Jewish law I have a positive duty to save the drowning

---

11. This concept, *lifnim m'shurat ha'din,* going beyond the letter of the law, along with other moral duties that complement the duties embedded in Jewish law, are explained and explored in my article, "The Interaction of Jewish Law with Morality," *Judaism* 26, no. 4 (Fall 1977): 455-66.

12. *Sifra,* Kedoshim 4:8 (on Lev. 19:16); B. *Sanhedrin* 73a. Minnesota Stat. Ann. Par. 604A.01 (West 2000); Rhode Island General Laws, par. 11-56-1 (2002); Vermont Statutes, Title 12, par. 519 (2002); Wisconsin Criminal Statutes 940.34, "Duty to Aid Victim or Report Crime." For more on this, see Elliot N. Dorff, *For the Love of God and People: A Philosophy of Jewish Law* (Philadelphia: Jewish Publication Society, 2007), pp. 5-8 and note 18 on pp. 38-39. Even in these four states, though, failing to seek aid to save someone's life is a misdemeanor, punishable by a small fine (in Vermont the fine cannot be more than $100). Typical for American legal theory, this positive obligation, limited as it is, is justified as a protection against an abuse of the rights of the person in distress (since s/he has a right to life), not a moral duty that now has legal consequences. See Lon T. McClintock, "Duty to Aid the Endangered Act: The Impact and Potential of the Vermont Approach," *Vermont Law Review* 7, no 1 (Spring 1982): 143-83; Samuel Freeman, "Criminal Liability and the Duty to Aid the Distressed," *University of Pennsylvania Law Review* 142, no. 5 (May 1994): 1455-92; and Mitchell McInnes, "Protecting the Good Samaritan: Defences for the Rescuer in Anglo-Canadian Criminal Law," *Criminal Law Quarterly* 36, no. 3 (May 1994): 331-71. On the duty to rescue in Jewish law generally,

person or the one being robbed, if I can, or to get help, if I cannot. The Talmud bases this obligation on the Torah's demand, "Do not stand idly by the blood of your brother" (Lev. 19:16). Later Jewish sources take this to mean that God demands of us that we care for each other not only in life-threatening situations, but also in advising others against making bad business deals.[13]

4. Relationships to Those outside One's Community

American ideology, on one hand, asserts that the American people have the duties announced in the Declaration of Independence and the Preamble of the Constitution only to fellow American citizens. In American law, legal residents have lesser duties and therefore lesser rights and benefits, and visitors and undocumented aliens have even fewer duties and benefits. Because we do not live in the world by ourselves, Americans from the very founding of the United States have found it prudent to make agreements with other nations for a variety of practical ends, especially military and commercial — and modern means of transportation and communication have made such agreements even more important today. Although that is all that Americans feel that they really must do by right, Americans have in recent history been enormously generous to other nations, most graphically illustrated, perhaps, in how we helped Germany and Japan — our enemies in a devastating war — rebuild themselves under the Marshall Plan after World War II. Some aid that the United States now gives to other countries is motivated by our own best interests, but some of our donations to this day are humanitarian acts of charity.

If the community is the primary reality for Judaism rather than the

---

together with some comparisons to Western law, see Anne Cucchiara Besser and Kalman J. Kaplan, "The Good Samaritan: Jewish and American Legal Perspectives," *The Journal of Law and Religion* 10, no. 1 (Winter 1994): 193-219; Ben Zion Eliash, "To Leave or Not to Leave: The Good Samaritan in Jewish Law," *Saint Louis University Law Journal* 38, no. 3 (Spring 1994): 619-28; and Aaron Kirschenbaum, "The Bystander's Duty to Rescue in Jewish Law," *Journal of Religious Ethics* 8 (1980): 204-26. I would like to thank Professors Martin Golding and Arthur Rosett for these references.

13. The Hafez Hayyim (Rabbi Israel Meir Ha-Kohen, Poland, 1838-1933) takes Leviticus 19:16 to mean that when "A" knows that "B" is about to enter into a partnership relationship with "C," and "A" is certain that the venture will prove harmful, then, under carefully constructed conditions, "A" must warn "B." Zelig Pliskin, *Guard Your Tongue* (based on the Hafez Hayyim) (Jerusalem: Aish Ha-Torah, 1975), p. 164.

individual, what is the status of those outside the Jewish community? The chauvinism that might emerge from communitarian doctrines embedded in Judaism is counteracted by a number of features of Jewish theology and law. For example, the Torah's theological doctrine that every person is created in the image of God attributes divine status to non-Jews no less than to Jews.[14] One implication of this is that every person, according to Jewish tradition, is bound by God to the Covenant of the Children of Noah, which consists of seven laws: prohibitions of murder, incest/adultery, idolatry, tearing a limb from a living animal, blasphemy, and theft, and the positive obligation to establish a system of justice.[15] In a typically Jewish way, people are honored and loved by being subject to rules![16]

Conversely, while the full gamut of protections within Jewish law applies only to Jews, who are obligated to take on the reciprocal duties,[17] many of the most important duties to others apply to the relationships between Jews and non-Jews as well. For example, according to Jewish law, a Jew is duty-bound to save the lives of non-Jews and to care for their sick and bury their dead if non-Jews need assistance in carrying out these tasks.[18] Ultimately, the Rabbis

---

14. Genesis 1:27; 5:1. The meaning of that doctrine in the Torah apparently refers to the fact that human beings are like God in being able to know the difference between right and wrong and to choose between them (see Gen. 3:22). It may also, though, refer to human beings' ability to speak and name things (Gen. 2:20), like God (Gen. 1:3, 5, etc.), although not with the same creative force; or, as Maimonides claimed, to the human ability to think (see his *Guide for the Perplexed*, part 1, ch. 1).

15. The doctrine of the Seven Noahide Laws appears in several different orders and slightly different wording, but the laws are the same in each version: Tosefta, *Avodah Zarah* 8:4; B. *Sanhedrin* 56a-56b; *Genesis Rabbah* 16:6, 34:8; *Canticles Rabbah* 1:16; *Pesiqta d'Rav Kahana*, "Bahodesh," pars. 202-3. For more on this doctrine, see David Novak, *The Image of the Non-Jew in Judaism* (Lewiston, NY: Edwin Mellen, 1983).

16. Probably the most poignant expression of this is in the prayers said morning and evening just before reciting the *Shema*. The evening version, the shorter one, says this: "With constancy You have loved Your people Israel, teaching us Torah [instruction] and mitzvot [commandments], statutes and laws. Therefore, Lord our God, when we lie down to sleep and when we rise, we shall think of Your laws and speak of them, rejoicing in Your Torah and commandments always. For they are our life and the length of our days; we will meditate on them day and night. Never take away Your love from us. Praised are You, Lord, who loves His people Israel."

17. For a description of at least some of the positions within Jewish sources about exactly who is included in the Jewish duties to "your neighbor" — i.e., to fellow Jews — see Ernst Simon, "The Neighbor *(Re'a)* Whom We Shall Love," in *Modern Jewish Ethics*, ed. Marvin Fox (Columbus: Ohio State University Press, 1975), pp. 29-56, and the response of Harold Fisch, pp. 57-61.

18. B. *Gittin* 61a. The codes based on that passage with regard to sustaining non-Jewish

assert that the righteous of the non-Jewish world merit a place in the World to Come, for they have done all that God expects of them.[19] Indeed, although Conservative and Reform rabbis no longer do this, historically rabbis have discouraged conversion to Judaism, arguing that becoming Jewish would be more of a burden than a benefit for potential converts: after all, those born to other faiths need only obey the seven laws given to all descendants of Noah in order to fulfill what God wants of them and merit salvation, while Jews must obey all of the Torah's 613 commandments, together with their Rabbinic expansions, and then endure anti-Semitism and persecutions at the hands of non-Jews.[20] Still, conversion to Judaism is possible. Moreover, by the Talmud's count, the Torah insists a full thirty-six times that Jews not only treat non-Jews within their midst fairly, but that they actually love the stranger, "for you were strangers in the land of Egypt."[21]

Because no human community lives in isolation from others, what one community thinks and does critically affects all humanity. Thus, very much in agreement with these ancient Jewish sources proclaiming the duties of Jews to care for others and to recognize the legitimacy of their faith traditions for them, Mudge's doctrine of covenantal humanism stresses a pluralistic approach to religion and to its economic implications. As he says, "In the case of Abrahamic faiths, this means responsibility to a covenantal promise of blessing, of the sort described in Genesis 12:1-3, with its scriptural echoes and parallels. Members of each of the three faiths living in mutual relationships are able to recognize such a gift of responsibility to covenant in the lives and traditions of those other faiths."

---

poor: M.T. *Laws of Gifts to the Poor* 7:7; M.T. *Laws of Idolatry* 10:5; M.T. *Laws of Kings* 10:12; S.A. *Yoreh De'ah* 151:12. With regard to visiting non-Jewish sick people: M.T. *Laws of Kings* 10:12; M.T. *Laws of Mourning* 14:12; S.A. *Yoreh De'ah* 335:9. With regard to burying the non-Jewish dead: M.T. *Laws of Kings* 10:12; M.T. *Laws of Mourning* 14:12; S.A. *Yoreh De'ah* 367:1.

19. *Sifra* on Leviticus 19:18.

20. The traditional stance of discouraging conversion to Judaism: B. *Yevamot* 47a: "In our days, when a proselyte comes to be converted, we say to him: 'What is your objective? Is it not known to you that today the people of Israel are wretched, driven about, exiled, and in constant suffering?'" Despite such warnings, in some periods, proselytes were accepted easily, while in other times and places it was all but impossible to convert to Judaism. See "Proselytes," *Encyclopedia Judaica* 13:1182-93. For more general Jewish reflections on the relationship of Judaism to Christianity, see Rabbi Leon Klenicki, ed., *Toward a Theological Encounter: Jewish Understandings of Christianity* (New York: Paulist, 1991).

21. E.g., Exodus 22:20; 23:9; Leviticus 19:34. The count of 36 times in the Torah prohibiting oppression of the stranger ("and some say 46"!): B. *Bava Mezia* 59b.

5. Our Relationship with the Environment

In the opening chapters of Genesis, God tells Adam and Eve that they were put into the Garden of Eden "to work it and to preserve it" (Gen. 2:15). In other words, we have not only a right, but a duty, to use the land to support ourselves and to enhance human life, but we concurrently have the duty to preserve the environment as we do so. This sets the stage for later Jewish business law that demands preventive and curative measures to be taken against air and water pollution.[22]

This, of course, is exactly Mudge's idea of "stakeholdership." He defines a "stakeholder" as follows:

> A "stakeholder" is anyone impacted by what entrepreneurs do with planetary resources. This is distinct from a "stockholder" or "shareholder" who is an owner of the venture in question. The earth's economic life could be conceived as a joint enterprise by, for, and on behalf of all its stakeholders. . . .

Jewish assertions that God owns the world and humans must both "work it and preserve it" are precisely the vision that Mudge wants us to see. Vis-à-vis other human beings, I may own something, and I therefore have certain rights to keep it and to use it. Even in that human frame, though, I may not harm others through my use of what I own. Furthermore, countries are increasingly legislating and enforcing laws to protect the environment from uses that some human beings want to make of it, and there have been some attempts at international standards to protect the environment. Vis-à-vis God, though, none of us is an owner of anything in the world; God owns everything. In that frame, we have a right to use the world only on God's terms, and God gives us the right to use the world on a fiduciary basis, where we are entrusted to preserve it for all the stakeholders who also inhabit God's world. This imposes duties on us of taking care of those who cannot support themselves — the poor, the disabled, the elderly — and simultaneously to preserve the environment.

---

22. For summaries of Jewish environmental beliefs and laws, see, in chronological order of publication, Ellen Bernstein, *Ecology and the Jewish Spirit* (Woodstock, VT: Jewish Lights, 1998); Arthur Waskow, ed., *Torah of the Earth: Exploring 4,000 Years of Ecology in Jewish Thought*, 2 vols. (Woodstock, VT: Jewish Lights, 2000); and Jeremy Benstein, *The Way into Judaism and the Environment* (Woodstock, VT: Jewish Lights, 2006).

6. Jewish Anthropology

Our duty to preserve the environment, however, is balanced with our duty "to work it." This derives not only from God's command to Adam and Eve, but from Judaism's underlying concept of the human being.

The Torah asserts that "the inclination of human being is evil from his youth" (Gen. 8:21). In Christianity, this and other sources led to the doctrine of Original Sin, from which only a supernatural intercessor, Jesus, could redeem us. The Rabbis, however, maintained that human beings are born with two inclinations, one to do evil *(yetzer ha-ra)* and one to do good *(yetzer ha-tov)*. The *yetzer ha-ra*, although that term is correctly translated as "the evil inclination," is not always morally evil. It is the self-centered inclination, which is the source of our drive toward ego enhancement, greed, and selfishness, and it can lead a person to idolatry and to acting immorally toward others. It is also, however, the source of some very important activities in life, as the following Rabbinic statement makes clear:

> The evil inclination is sometimes called very good. How can this be? Were it not for the evil impulse, a man would not build a house, marry a wife, beget children, or conduct business affairs.[23]

During the first thirteen years of life, the Rabbis say, the self-centered inclination is dominant (think of how infants care only for themselves), and that is how the Rabbis understand the verse from Genesis cited above. Gradually, though, children learn to care about others as well; they build their superego, Freud would say, and integrate it into their ego. When a girl reaches the age of twelve and a boy thirteen, the two inclinations are equally powerful.[24] The child is then legally responsible for her or his actions, for Judaism presumes that at that time the child both knows right from wrong and has the power to act on that knowledge. For the rest of one's life, one must balance the *yetzer ha-ra* and the *yetzer ha-tov*, blending self-regarding activities with other-regarding ones. This is the nature of human moral struggles, and all of us who are not psychopaths are fully capable — and therefore fully responsible — to carry on that struggle throughout our lives. We will get it wrong sometimes — in theological terms, we will sin, sometimes intentionally and sometimes not — and hence Jewish liturgy has us ask for God's forgiveness three times each day. But we do not need a supernatural intercessor to carry

23. *Genesis Rabbah* 9:7.
24. *Ecclesiastes Rabbah* on Ecclesiastes 4:13; *Avot D'Rabbi Natan* 16.

on this struggle: God has given us the faculty to discern what is right and the power to do it, and God has given us the ability to atone for what we have done wrong.

This means that the self-promotion and competition inherent in business are not necessarily bad. Whether those urges are bad or good depends completely on how they are expressed. Inevitably, one person's success in business will sometimes harm competitors or even customers, and law is therefore needed to regulate business to avoid these effects as much as possible. If people follow the rules laid down by Jewish law, however, their efforts may benefit not only the people in the business and their shareholders, if any, but society as a whole. This is what God created us to do, to "work the land." "Six days shall you work" is just as much of a commandment as the end of that verse, "and on the seventh day you shall desist" (Exod. 23:12). On the other hand, if we use these entrepreneurial urges to help ourselves but harm others, then we have engaged in business badly.

This also means that Judaism does not presume socialism or communism. In line with its conception of a closely knit community, it bids us create a thick safety net for the poor and vulnerable, but Jewish law presumes free enterprise and capitalism — albeit with substantial protections for the downtrodden.

These fundamental Jewish concepts that delineate our relationship to God, to other humans, and to the environment and that describe Judaism's view of who we are as human beings and the role of business in God's plan for us, then, serve as the grounds for a Jewish view of business. They provide the broad picture of the role of business in life, as Judaism understands it, and they explain and motivate the specific norms that Judaism asserts for business through its laws and ethics. They are remarkably close to what Lewis Mudge calls for in the covenant he bids us to recognize that we all have with each other, with the environment, and with God.

A Christian Response to Mudge's Thesis

JOHN C. KNAPP

In his preface to this volume, Lew Mudge recalls the resistance he encountered while presenting many of these ideas to his colleagues on a national committee of the Presbyterian Church (USA). Some challenged his notion of *responsibility* as a vestige of a paternalistic theology that historically marginalized and disempowered the oppressed. Others objected to his premise that Abraham was "blessed to be a blessing," arguing that the patriarch of three major faiths ought to be best remembered for his unjust treatment of Sarah and Hagar who had no opportunity to tell their own stories to posterity.

These debates continued over many months as Mudge listened, took careful notes, and responded to criticism with his characteristic patience and kindness. As a member of the committee, it was my privilege to collaborate with him as he weighed these critiques and refined several drafts. Throughout the process he modeled his own ideal of "moral hospitality," which he describes in *The Church as Moral Community* as "the offering of a kind of space for deeper reflection to fellow human beings of all sorts."[25] He once remarked that interfaith dialogue is sometimes easier than debate within one's own church.

Responsibility and *Oikoumene*

A central theme of the present book resounds through much of Mudge's recent work: The notion that God's gift of responsibility can be the cornerstone of an alternative *oikoumene*. He finds the seeds of this idea in the work of H. Richard Niebuhr who writes, "The first element in the theory of responsibility is the idea of *response*."[26] Mudge emphasizes that we are blessed with moral capacities to respond to others as co-equals in the global household, and that in doing so we are actually responding to God's action upon us. Adopting the language of stakeholder theory, he helps us visualize how all people share an interest in the well-being of the human community.

25. Lewis S. Mudge, *The Church as Moral Community: Ecclesiology and Ethics in Ecumenical Debate* (New York: Continuum, 1998), p. 107.

26. H. Richard Niebuhr, *The Responsible Self* (New York: Harper & Row, 1963), p. 61.

This theory, originally conceived as a play on the word "stockholder," is more often used in the literature of business and economics as a wider lens for examining the relationship between businesses and those whom they may affect or be affected by. By viewing organizations as "open systems" that function interdependently within a larger ecology of relationships, stakeholder theory seeks to open the possibility of mutual benefit by strengthening relationships and trust among disaffected or even adversarial groups.[27] Mudge's innovation shows how this concept may be equally useful for broadening our thinking in the theological context.

The pages of this volume build on the ideas of his previous book, *The Gift of Responsibility*, by further exploring the potential of dialogue among Christians, Jews, and Muslims — traditions with a common ancestor and shared stakeholdership in the human household. I was recently in a retreat near Geneva, Switzerland, where scholars representing the three Abrahamic faiths devoted several days to learning from each other and contrasting their traditions' perspectives on economic life with the ideology of self-interest that helped precipitate a collapse of credit markets and a worldwide recession.

Our dialogue began with a necessary acknowledgment of serious and substantive differences in belief, as we agreed not to expect theological consensus, but simply to seek resonances among the three faiths' teachings relevant to economics. In essence, we engaged in what Mudge calls "a parallel-interactive hermeneutics of responsibility," which he describes as "a certain kind of together-doing that constitutes an interpretation of what it means to grasp the nature of the opportunity to help modernity save itself . . . [and] actually to take on together the responsibility for helping do this."[28] It was this sense of communal responsibility that animated our dialogue and led to the interfaith "Mountain House Statement," published subsequently by the Caux Round Table, the international consortium that convened the meeting. A few excerpted paragraphs capture the spirit and tone of the dialogue:

> While encouraging marketplace innovation and growth, these [Abrahamic] traditions acknowledge the devastating human impact of hubris and vanity that often accompanies — and eventually undermines — marketplace power and success. These faith traditions also understand that fear, uncertainty, and vulnerability often accompany ambitious human

27. See Edward R. Freeman, *Strategic Management: A Stakeholder Approach* (Boston: Pittman, 1984).

28. Lewis S. Mudge, *The Gift of Responsibility: The Promise of Dialogue Among Christians, Jews, and Muslims* (New York: Continuum, 2008), p. 131.

endeavors, and that they can lead to destructive behaviors. Yet these traditions simultaneously point to the folly of those who seek personal consolation in these market opportunities by imputing a salvific role to markets and other human institutions. Such idolatry compounds our difficulties by diverting us from a proper understanding of how best to use our creative capacities. . . .

Our traditions insist that there is an inherent social dimension to the human experience of life. We should, therefore, construe those circles of community expansively and generously. Our traditions also caution that, within community, we serve God's aspirations as well as one another. Therefore, our undertakings cannot be reduced merely to strategic or instrumental manipulations of opportunity. The voices of the Prophets have long called all our communities to heed the overlooked voices of the powerless and the disadvantaged, and the too-often ignored voice of God.

Our task, essentially, is to understand our calling as human persons so that we look upon both people and things — both our work and our resources — as opportunities for fulfillment of our various roles in the stewardship of creation.[29]

This declaration of shared convictions may affirm the true potential of Mudge's vision of *oikoumene* as a human "household" of stakeholders.

Biblical Perspectives and Christianity

This statement represents a degree of consensus among those present, but would it be acceptable to all Christians, Jews, and Muslims? Certainly not. We would be mistaken to think there is broad agreement about matters of economics within any of these religious groups. One need only read the policy statements of major Protestant denominations and the Roman Catholic Church to see the diversity of thought among Christians regarding globalization, economic justice, and the like.[30] At one end of the Christian spectrum

29. "Mountain House Statement," Caux Round Table, 2010, accessed online at http://www.cauxroundtable.org.

30. Examples include: *Vocation and Work* (Louisville: Advisory Committee on Social Witness Policy, Presbyterian Church USA, 1990); *Caritas in Veritate,* Encyclical Letter of Pope Benedict XVI (Vatican City: Libreria Editrice Vaticana, 2009); *Centesimus annus,* Encyclical Letter of Pope John Paul II (Vatican City: Libreria Editrice Vaticana, 1991); *Economic Justice for All,* Pastoral Letter of the National Conference of Catholic Bishops (Washington, DC: U.S. Catholic Conference, 1986); *Christian Faith and Economic Life* (New York: United Church

we find the Marxist critic of capitalism who embraces the ideals of liberation theology, while at the other extreme, we find the proponent of a "prosperity gospel" who equates the accumulation of individual wealth with God's favor and blessing. These differences are reflective of widely different traditions and interpretations of the church's historical struggle to apply the lessons of scripture to the challenges of economic life.

In the Old Testament, individual and national wealth are often seen as signs of divine favor or rewards from God. Abraham was blessed with great riches and his son "Isaac sowed seed in that land, and in the same year reaped a hundredfold. The Lord blessed him, and the man became rich; he prospered more and more until he became very wealthy" (Gen. 26:12-13). Yet we also read of material blessings being withheld from the righteous and are reminded that all wealth belongs to a God whose purposes we do not understand. "The Lord makes poor and makes rich; he brings low, he also exalts" (1 Sam. 2:7). God permits some to gain wealth, but the Old Testament often warns against desiring money or property for oneself. Reminders that wealth comes from God alone stand in contrast to the modern ideal of the "self-made" person. "Do not say to yourself, 'My power and the might of my own hand have gotten me this wealth.' But remember the Lord your God, for it is he who gives you power to get wealth . . ." (Deut. 8:17-18).

The desire for wealth is seen as a futile quest for self-sufficiency. "The wealth of the rich is their strong city; in their imagination it is like a high wall. Before destruction one's heart is haughty, but humility goes before honor" (Prov. 18:11-12). Believers are to pray, "give me neither poverty nor riches; feed me with the food that I need, or I shall be full, and deny you, and say, 'Who is the Lord?' or I shall be poor, and steal, and profane the name of my God" (Prov. 30:8-9). How many preachers would invite their congregations to pray *not* to be rich on Sunday morning in America?

Just as challenging are early Hebrew laws prohibiting landowners from maximizing profits and requiring them to leave a portion of their crops in their fields, orchards, or vineyards to be eaten by the poor. "When you reap the harvest of your land, you shall not reap to the very edges of your field, or gather the gleanings of your harvest. You shall not strip your vineyard bare, or gather the fallen grapes of your vineyard; you shall leave them for the poor and the alien: I am the Lord your God" (Lev. 19:9-10).

Three economic principles run throughout the Old Testament: (1) all

---

Board for World Ministries, United Church of Christ, 1987); "The Oxford Declaration on Christian Faith and Economics," *Transformation* 7, no. 2 (April-June 1990): 7-18.

wealth belongs to the sovereign God who is concerned with justice in all human relationships; (2) an unrestrained desire for wealth leads both individuals and nations to lose sight of their proper dependence on God; and (3) economic prosperity may be a blessing, but this is always a test of one's willingness to share with those less fortunate.

The economic teachings of the New Testament are even more difficult for contemporary Christians, for they offer no indication that God is pleased to make us rich. Warnings about the love of wealth are even more pointed. "No one can serve two masters; for a slave will either hate the one and love the other, or be devoted to the one and despise the other. You cannot serve God and wealth" (Matt. 6:24). Christians have long debated how seriously to take the admonition that to love wealth is to *despise* God. Other texts (e.g., Matt. 18:21-35; Mark 10:21-25; Luke 12:14; 1 Tim. 6:10; 1 Peter 5:2; Heb. 13:15) reiterate the principle that we are to place our trust in God alone, for mammon is not merely a neutral resource to be used for good or for ill; it is a false deity that threatens to use us for purposes that violate God's will.

What are Christians to do with such teachings? Should it surprise us that the twenty-first-century church is so inarticulate in relating scripture to the complex milieu of global economics?

Not a New Challenge

These are daunting questions, to be sure, but they are not altogether new. Even as the early church began to spread through the Roman Empire, leaders wrestled with questions of money and economics. In the second century, Clement of Alexandria taught that the rich may receive salvation, but not without difficulty. But growth brought the church increasing numbers of affluent members, and by the time of Constantine's edict of Milan in the fourth century, the church rolls not only included the wealthy, but the emperor and political elite as well. At about this time, the influential teacher Lactantius argued that wealth is not a problem, *per se,* but only when used irresponsibly. This softening of earlier biblical interpretations became common in church teachings thereafter.

Doctrinal battles flared frequently as the church's ideas about money and economics evolved to accommodate the wealthy establishment. When Augustine of Hippo emerged near the turn of the fifth century as the most influential Christian thinker since the New Testament writers, he sought to distinguish between needs and wants, urging believers to give to the poor and reminding them that earthly riches are of no use in the next life. On other economic questions, he was less consistent, on one hand insisting that money lending is sinful, while on the other condemning a public rebellion of debtors against usury. His teaching helped frame a growing consensus, which persists today, that Christians should be detached emotionally, but not literally, from wealth, provided they can keep their priorities straight.

As church institutions diversified throughout the Middle Ages, fewer official teachings called for sacrificial generosity or warned of the dangers of mammon. Long-held restrictions on money lending were eased and wealth was no longer seen as a sign of refusal to share with the poor. In the thirteenth century, Thomas Aquinas defended private property ownership but urged Christians to use only what they truly needed to support themselves and their families, arguing that all goods should be used to meet the needs of all. He approved of investing for profit, yet warned that profit should not be the investor's principal motivation. He also discouraged individuals from charging interest to borrowers (even though the medieval church itself was both a borrower and a lender).

Up to this time, the church's teachings were concerned almost exclusively with what we now refer to as microeconomics. It had not yet developed a theology relevant to macroeconomics, the arena where the church was then a major player.

With the Reformation, economic issues came to the fore in theological debates about church financial corruption and the selling of indulgences, which Martin Luther decried as a distortion of the doctrine of salvation. Other reformers, especially John Calvin, shared these concerns and sought to adapt theology to the economic realities of an expanding mercantile economy. They saw that a growing economy could benefit the poor even more than almsgiving and cautioned that charity could deprive the poor of the opportunity to work.

Both Luther and Calvin also contributed to a new understanding of vocation, where many occupations — not the clergy alone — were viewed as serving God's purposes in the world. As Calvin saw it, profits earned by Christians could make it possible to serve even more people; therefore, he approved investments in business ventures so long as investors' aims were not the accumulation of personal wealth. Our contemporary "Protestant work ethic" and the rise of capitalism are often attributed to Calvin, but it is clear that he would object to lifestyles of unrestrained consumption. By clearing the way for the private ownership of profit-making businesses, he was a catalyst for production-oriented capitalism, writes Cameron Murchison. "While it is true that certain [of Calvin's] theological claims sponsor habits and practices that can lead to capital accumulation — thus supporting production-oriented capitalism; other equally important theological claims sponsor habits and practices that tend to curb material acquisition due to the communal obligation to use excess wealth not for self-satisfaction but for needs of others — thus contending with a version of consumer-oriented capitalism that relentlessly attends only to consumer demand."[31]

Reformation thinkers were among the first to apply theological insights to macroeconomics, but they could not have foreseen that their ideas would contribute to the development of the economic rationalism of the Enlightenment, which freed individuals from restraints on private economic initiative and rendered the church's ideas about a just economy passé. Pursuing one's financial self-interest was deemed a social good as long as one refrained from preventing others from doing likewise. The rising tide of modernity diminished the church's influence in economic life, despite its continuing contributions to public debate (for example, the ecumenical Social Creed of 1908 that called attention to injustices in the industrial economy).

By the late twentieth century the *Homo oeconomicus* assumptions of neoliberal economists like Milton Friedman had permeated Wall Street, corporate America, and much of popular culture. With theories that reduced human aspirations to self-interest maximization based on economic criteria, this movement left little room for love of neighbor or for Mudge's more expansive vision of the human household. A business culture steeped in this ideology inevitably came to see other-regarding actions, especially those that may entail a cost to oneself, as alien and not justifiable under the rationalistic logic of so-called management science.

Much of the political and economic establishment continues to labor under an unquestioning allegiance to these ideas. Thus, the single-minded pursuit of self-interest in the form of profit maximization continues unchecked, despite an economic recession that may be attributed in large measure to the narrow, short-term priorities of the world's financial markets. General prosperity, some still argue, can be achieved only if private financial interests are free to pursue as much profit as possible, by any means the market will permit. Mudge argues that the broader purposes of human beings and society are obscured and ill-served by this constricted conception of economics.

31. Cameron Murchison, "Reformed Resources for Practical Theology: The Christian Life and Consumer Capitalism," unpublished paper, January 12, 2005.

A Necessary Voice

In the early twenty-first century, much of the world asks what, if anything, Christianity has to offer a globalized economic system that is assumed to operate by objective, rational principles. This uncertainty, which is even common within the church, tends to relegate much religious discourse to the private sphere of life. Yet Christians have always believed the gospel must be made relevant not just to individuals but to the world in which their lives must be lived. Mudge finds his own Reformed theology especially well suited to this task as he grapples with the larger questions facing society. He insists that economic activity, as an indispensable dimension of human relationships, must be taken seriously by any who would bring theology to bear in matters of human well-being.

Mudge describes the narrow assumptions of neoliberal economics as "self-delusional," pointing out that such thinking facilitated the widespread moral blindness that led to the global meltdown that began in 2008. He offers a more robust alternative, inviting us to envision economics as the responsible management of the human household, where the needs of all stakeholders are weighed, while attending to the voices and interests of the powerless. In this way, economic activity in business and politics might be informed by universal human values rather than the indifference of self-interest. The voice of the faith community in the global discussion must insist that economics not be divorced from moral considerations and notions of human flourishing. Christians have a responsibility to place the big questions on the table: What counts as good? Who is my neighbor? What are my responsibilities to future generations? What is God's will for creation (our habitat)?

In Christian theology, human nature and purpose are always understood in light of the relationship between God and humanity. Thus, all anthropology must be approached as what Karl Barth memorably called theological anthropology, a recognition of the depth of human sinfulness and the promise of human potential.[32] This is the inescapable tension in a theological anthropology — that we are at once finite and infinite, sinful yet bearing God's own image.

Barth and some of his contemporaries were responding to the post-Enlightenment influence of theological rationalism, a close relative of the

---

32. Karl Barth, *The Humanity of God*, trans. John Newton Thomas and Thomas Weiser (Richmond, VA: John Knox Press, 1960), p. 11.

Cartesian philosophical claim that human reason is the sole source of pure knowledge, and of the empiricist belief (from John Locke and David Hume) that knowledge derives exclusively from science and concrete human experience. Indeed, Charles Taylor shows how theology actually played a part in the formation of the rationalist, secularized ontology that is "perhaps the dominant outlook of modern Western technological society." This ontology arises from a fusion of Cartesian philosophy with ideas of freedom and individuality drawn from the reformers (mostly through Francis Bacon): ". . . they shared common opponents in the defenders of the older, hierarchical views of order, and came together in endorsing the instrumental stance to the self and world."[33] As this worldview took hold, the primacy of reason and individualism transformed traditional conceptions of God and of self, a shift that Taylor credits primarily to Locke. We come to God because it is the *rational* thing to do; and we do so freely as a result of our self-responsible autonomy. Locke's fateful step moved theology from the reformers' notion of living *worshipfully* for God toward an ideal of living *rationally.* Both God and the human self become objects of instrumental, disengaged knowledge, such that there is little room for the mystery of a God who is "wholly other" or a creature whose very being depends upon such a God.

As Reinhold Niebuhr demonstrates, this is the point where the distinction between Creator and creature begins to disappear, as "rationalism practically identifies rational man (who is essential man) with the divine; for reason is, as the creative principle, identical with God."[34] The "curious compound of classical, Christian and distinctively modern conceptions of human nature, involved in modern anthropology" has profoundly influenced theological thought, giving rise to the idealistic inclination to "protest against Christian humility" and to dismiss the idea of human sinfulness.[35]

> Modern man has an essentially easy conscience; and nothing gives the diverse and discordant notes of modern culture so much harmony as the unanimous opposition to the sinfulness of man. The idea that man is sinful at the very centre of his personality, that is in his will, is universally rejected. It is this rejection which has seemed to make the Christian gospel simply irrelevant to modern man. . . . If modern culture conceives

33. Charles Taylor, *Sources of the Self: The Making of the Modern Identity* (Cambridge, MA: Harvard University Press, 1989), p. 234.

34. Reinhold Niebuhr, *The Nature and Destiny of Man,* vol. 1 (New York: Charles Scribner's Sons, 1941), p. 7.

35. Niebuhr, *The Nature and Destiny of Man,* pp. 18-19.

man primarily in terms of the uniqueness of his rational faculties, it finds the root of his evil in his involvement in natural impulses and natural necessities from which it hopes to free him by the increase of his rational faculties.[36]

Barth concurs, noting that the theology of the eighteenth and nineteenth centuries frequently "ascribed a normative character to the ideas of its environment," especially philosophical and psychological ones.[37] In accepting the Enlightenment notion that the human being is the measure of all things, including God, theology fell into the "the old error that one can speak of man without first, and very concretely, having spoken of the living God."[38]

> . . . When the Christian gospel was changed into a statement, a religion, about Christian self-awareness, the God was lost sight of who in His sovereignty confronts man, calling him to account, and dealing with him as Lord. This loss also blurred the sight horizontally. The Christian was condemned to uncritical and irresponsible subservience to the patterns, forces, and movements of human history and civilization. Man's inner experience did not provide a firm enough ground for resistance to these phenomena.[39]

This has never been so evident as in our own time, but it would be a mistake to read these theologians' critiques of rationalism as a rejection of rationality, or of human reason. Indeed, Niebuhr holds that it is the "force of reason" (but not reason alone, "as the educator and social scientist usually believes") that encourages individuals to restrain self-interest for the common good of society, and enables society to "analyse the pretensions made by the powerful and privileged groups" in order to overcome its uncritical acceptance of injustice. He even sees potential in rational suasion for helping "destroy the morale of dominant groups by making them more conscious of the hollowness of their pretensions, so that they will be unable to assert their interests and protect their special privileges with the same degree of self-deception."[40] In the end, however, Niebuhr cautions strongly against the "understandable *naiveté* of rationalists" who attribute too much power

36. Niebuhr, *The Nature and Destiny of Man*, p. 23.
37. Barth, *The Humanity of God*, p. 19.
38. Barth, *The Humanity of God*, p. 57.
39. Barth, *The Humanity of God*, p. 27.
40. Reinhold Niebuhr, *Moral Man and Immoral Society* (New York: Charles Scribner's Sons, 1932), p. 31.

to reason, for human beings "will not cease to be dishonest, merely because their dishonesties have been revealed or because they have discovered their own deceptions."[41] This is certainly evident today in the economic sphere.

His brother, H. Richard Niebuhr, attempts to show the inadequacies of both extremes, offering another possibility: "Our ultimate question in this existential situation of dependent freedom is not whether we will choose in accordance with reason or by faith, but whether we will choose with reasoning faithlessness or reasoning faith."[42] Theologically understood, the relational alternative to the rationally conceived self is the self created in God's image. Some theologians see a model of this relationality in the I-Thou-We doctrine of the trinity. Daniel L. Migliore explains: "[T]he trinitarian selves have their personal identity in relationship" and provide a model of the human self that contradicts "modern theories that equate personal existence with absolute autonomy and isolated self-consciousness." With God, human selves are "relational realities that are defined by intersubjectivity, shared consciousness, faithful relationships, and the mutual giving and receiving of love."[43] Through the selfhood, humanity, and suffering of Christ, we learn of a God who accompanies creatures and shares their pain. "The God of free grace does not will to act alone and does not will that the creatures should suffer alone."[44]

With his final book, Lew Mudge leaves us with a reminder of his lasting contributions to theological and social thought. As we contemplate his vision of a more abundant life together in the global household, let us recall again his spirit of openness and generosity in inviting others to join him in a much-needed conversation.

41. Niebuhr, *Moral Man and Immoral Society,* p. 34.

42. H. Richard Niebuhr, *Christ and Culture* (New York: Harper & Row, 1951), pp. 110-13.

43. Daniel L. Migliore, *Faith Seeking Understanding* (Grand Rapids: Eerdmans, 1991), p. 68.

44. Migliore, *Faith Seeking Understanding,* p. 117.

An Islamic Perspective on Covenantal Humanism

DJAMEL EDDINE LAOUISSET

Introduction

The primary belief around which the Islamic faith revolves is that Allah (S.W.T.) has created man and appointed him as His vicegerent on Earth to fulfill His mission and obey His commands in every life aspect. Nevertheless, Islam has left to man's own rational judgment most areas of social and economic activities provided that decision making abides by strict moral and ethical principles.[45]

Applying moral and ethical principles to economics is considered by most neoliberal spokespersons an oxymoron. Whenever asked about how social interest would be served — when all socioeconomic actors have unlimited freedom to pursue their self-interest — these secular and materialist apologists would reply that market and competitive forces will keep self-interest under check.[46] Islam, for its part, emphasizes that both freedom and the pursuit of self-interest need to be toned down by moral values and good governance to ensure that general well-being is realized and that social harmony is not hurt in the process. This ideal of social harmony for humankind is theoretically the cornerstone of the intended strategy of all the Abrahamic faiths, but on the ground, it unfortunately mirrors a deformed realized strategy.

Unquestionably, local intrafaith social harmony cannot subsist without global interfaith social harmony. Muslims, Christians, and Jews all over the globe should once and for all — before it is too late — lobby for positive responsibility and empowerment for active roles in a critically endangered world.

Economic and political ploys for a permanent interfaith "clash of civilizations"[47] or "clash of ignorance,"[48] Islamophobic media crusades, or reactive jihad are not an appropriate "win-win," nonzero-sum game strategy. Such ploys

---

45. Tjalling C. Koopmans, *Three Essays on the State of Economic Science* (New York: McGraw-Hill, 1968), p. 70.

46. Milton Friedman, *Capitalism and Freedom* (Chicago: University of Chicago Press, 1962), p. 22.

47. Samuel P. Huntington, *The Clash of Civilizations and the Remaking of World Order* (New York: Simon & Schuster, 2002), p. 21.

48. Edward Said, "The Clash of Ignorance," *The Nation* (October 2001).

can only generate escalating, destructive boomerang effects and hence fuel global hatred and disastrous global conflicts. The Abrahamic faiths' collective responsibility, moral hospitality, and covenantal humanism are the only inescapable paths for a sustainable global village of justice, peace, and prosperity.[49]

Islamic vs. Neoliberal Economics

The fundamental difference between capitalist and Islamic economics resides in the fact that in secular capitalism, the profit motive and private ownership are given unbridled power and sovereignty to make economic decisions. Islam recognizes private ownership, the profit motive, and market forces, but it nevertheless places certain "divine" restrictions in areas of decision making, such as resource allocation and government regulation, so as to warrant a social and economic justice-based general equilibrium.[50]

Obviously, this is not Islam-specific. There are huge commonalities between revealed religions due to the continuity and similarity in the value systems of such religions. As a matter of fact, the Qur'an clearly states that "[n]othing has been said to you [Muhammad] that was not said to the Messengers before you."[51] Thus, the role of value judgments and good governance in the efficient and equitable allocation and distribution of resources can be considered a common heritage of revealed religions.[52]

There is no doubt that the market system led to a long period of economic growth in Western market-oriented economies. However, all this growth did not lead to an economic development in conformity with the Judeo-Christian value system. Inequalities of income and wealth, economic instability, and unemployment indicate that both efficiency and equity have remained elusive in spite of this rapid growth and rise in the wealth of nations.[53] Consequently, there has been persistent criticism of self-interested "laissez-faire" economics by a number of writers in England (Charles Dick-

---

49. Lewis S. Mudge, *The Gift of Responsibility* (New York: Continuum, 2008), p. 279.

50. Joseph J. Spengler, "Economic Thought of Islam: Ibn Khaldun," *Comparative Studies in Society and History* 6, no. 3 (1964): 268-306; Jean David C. Boulakia, "Ibn Khaldûn: A Fourteenth-Century Economist," *Journal of Political Economy* 79 (1971): 1105-18.

51. Qur'an, 41:43.

52. Louis Baeck, *The Mediterranean Tradition in Economic Thought* (New York: Routledge, 1994), p. 80.

53. Adam Smith, *An Inquiry into the Nature and Causes of the Wealth of Nations* [1776] (Chicago: University of Chicago Press, 1977), p. 447.

ens, 1854; John Ruskin, 1862) and in America (Henry George, 1879). As early as 1843, Thomas Carlyle labeled "laissez-faire" economics a "dismal science." In the late twentieth century, well before more recent cyclical economic and financial crises, others commented on the misalignment of business with ethics, rejecting the idea that free and uncontrolled private interests would work in harmony and further public welfare.[54]

More recent cyclical economic and financial crises have again brought back these issues. In 1987, Amartya Sen noted the divide between business and ethics, arguing that "the distancing of economics from ethics has impoverished welfare economics and also weakened the basis of a good deal of descriptive and predictive economics." In addition, he noted that economics "can be made more productive by paying greater and more explicit attention to ethical considerations that shape human behavior and judgment."[55]

While conventional economics is now widely questioned in terms of effectiveness, Islamic economics has never been applied anywhere so far, hence it never got engaged in the debate as one of the alternatives to the dominant secular and materialist worldview. Islam recognizes the role of market forces in the efficient allocation of resources, but does not find competition to be sufficient to safeguard social interest. Islam promotes, above all, human brotherhood, socioeconomic justice, and the well-being of all through the integrated role of moral values, market mechanisms, and good governance.[56] Without complementing the market system with morally based value judgments, we may end up perpetuating inequities in spite of our good intentions through inaction, nonchoice, and drifting.[57]

From the above, one may easily confirm existing similarities between revealed religions in terms of allocation and distribution of resources, fulfillment of material needs, and fulfillment of spiritual needs. While all revealed

54. Charles Dickens, "Hard Times: For These Times" (a weekly serial in *Household Words*, 1 April 1854 to 12 August 1854). John Ruskin, "Munera Pulveris: Six Essays on the Elements of Political Economy," *Fraser's Magazine*, 1862-63 (published in book form, 1872), in *The Works of John Ruskin*, vol. 17 (Cambridge: Cambridge University Press, 2010); Henry George, *Progress and Poverty* [1879] (reprint, London: Kegan Paul, Tench & Co., 1886), pp. 283-84; Thomas Carlyle, *Past and Present*, Project Gutenberg (1843), p. 50; Peter Jay and Margaret Jay, economic editorials, *The Times* (London, 1986).

55. Amartya Sen, *On Ethics and Economics* (Oxford: Blackwell, 1987), p. 50.

56. C. Brockleman, "Al-Mawardi," *The Encyclopedia of Islam*, 2nd ed. (Leiden: Brill, 1960-2005), vol. 6, p. 869.

57. Robert A. Solo, "Values and Judgments in the Discourse of the Sciences," in *Value Judgment and Income Distribution*, ed. Robert Al Solo and Charles A. Anderson (New York: Praeger, 1981), pp. 9-40.

religions recognize the important role of market mechanisms in the allocation and distribution of resources, they all agree that the market by itself is unable to fulfill the material needs of all human beings. All revealed religions acknowledge that human beings are not always trying to serve their self-interest, and even if they do, the concept of self-interest is not confined to this world, but it extends to the afterlife. Humans are also altruistic and are willing to make sacrifices for the well-being of others. All this serves to provide a motivating mechanism for sacrifice for the well-being of others that conventional rational positive economics fails to provide. The innate goodness of human beings along with the long-run perspective given to self-interest has the potential of inducing a person to be not only efficient but also equitable and caring.

Muslim *Homo oeconomicus*

While there is hardly anyone opposed to the need for rationality in human behavior, there are differences of opinion in defining rationality.[58] Whenever rationality is defined in terms of overall individual as well as social well-being, then rational behavior can only be that which helps us realize that goal. Conventional economists, social-Darwinists, and utilitarians equate rationality with the serving of self-interest through the maximization of wealth and want satisfaction. Within this framework, society is conceptualized as a mere collection of individuals united through ties of self-interest.

In contrast, the Islamic economic model sees that since all resources at the disposal of human beings are a trust from God, and human beings are accountable before Him, there is no other option but to use them in keeping with the main terms of the trust, which is comprehensive justice and human brotherhood. Islamic comprehensive justice, as Al-Mawardi wrote in 1058, "inculcates mutual love and affection, obedience to the law, development of the country, expansion of wealth, growth of progeny, and security of the sovereign."[59] According to Ibn Taymiyyah in 1328, justice "towards everything and everyone is an imperative for everyone, and injustice is prohibited to everything and everyone. Injustice is absolutely not permissible irrespective of whether it is to a Muslim or a non-Muslim or even to an unjust person."[60]

58. Sen, *On Ethics and Economics*.

59. Brockleman, "Al-Mawardi."

60. Ibn Taymiyyah, *Majmuʿ Fatawa Shaykh al-Islam Ahmad Ibn Taymiyyah*, ed. ʿAbd al-Rahman al-ʿAsimi (Riyadh: Matabiʿ al-Riyad, 1963), p. 33.

Muslim State Interventionism

It is the duty of the state to restrain all socially and economically harmful behavior such as injustice, fraud, and the nonfulfillment of contracts and other obligations. The Prophet Muhammad once said: "God restrains through the sovereign more than what He restrains through the Qur'an."[61] This emphasis on the role of the state has been reflected in the writings of all leading Muslim scholars throughout history. An effective government is indispensable for preventing injustice and wrongdoing.[62] However, regimentation or the owning and operating of a substantial part of the economy by the state is not recommended. Several classical Muslim scholars (Al-Dimashqi in 1175 and Ibn Khaldun in 1406)[63] clearly expressed their disapproval of the state becoming directly involved in the economy. The state should not resort to a high degree of regimentation; it should be welfare-oriented, moderate in its spending, respect property rights, and avoid onerous taxation.

Many classical Muslim scholars (Avicenna in 1037; Averroes, 1198; Abu Yusuf, 798; Al-Mawardi, 1058; Ibn Hazm, 1064; Al-Sarakhsi, 1090; Al-Tusi, 1093; Al-Ghazali, 1111; Al-Dimashqi, 1175; Ibn Rushd, 1187; Ibn Taymiyyah, 1328; Ibn al-Ukhuwwah, 1329; Ibn al-Qayyim, 1350; Al-Shatibi, 1388; Ibn Khaldun, 1406; Al-Maqrizi, 1442; Al-Dawwani, 1501; and Shah Waliyullah, 1762)[64] have made valuable contributions to modern economic theory. But as Todd Lowry has rightly observed, "the character and sophistication of Arabian writings" have generally been ignored.[65]

One of the most important contributions of Muslim economists was the adoption of a multidisciplinary dynamic approach. They considered overall human well-being to be the end product of interaction above economic, moral, social, political, demographic, and historical factors. Because neoclassical economics ignores this multidisciplinary dynamic approach, it seems to be "an inappropriate tool to analyze and prescribe policies that will induce development."[66]

---

61. Brockleman, "Al-Mawardi."

62. Brockleman, "Al-Mawardi."

63. Ibn Khaldun, *Muqaddimah* (Cairo: Al-Maktabah al-Tijariyyah al-Kubra, 1950), p. 30.

64. A. Azim Islahi, *History of Economic Thought in Islam* (Aligharh, India: Department of Economics, Aligharh Muslim University, 1996), p. 70.

65. Todd Lowry, foreword to S. M. Ghazanfar, *Medieval Islamic Economic Thought* (London: Routledge, 2004), p. xi; see also Joseph Pifer, "Scholasticism," *Encyclopaedia Britannica*, 1978, pp. 352-55.

66. Douglas C. North, "Economic Performance through Time," *American Economic Review* (June 1994): 359-68.

Islam and Global Financial Issues

Islamic economics has much to offer for growing a more just and stable market system that encourages real wealth creation and limits market fluctuations. To build a sustainable system, debt must increase in tandem with real wealth and leverage must be capped by productivity potentials. Heavy reliance on debt intensifies economic instability, hence human insecurity, and generates significant negative economy-wide externalities. For its part, the Islamic banking alternative has shown much resilience in the current crisis and hence may provide lessons for Western conventional banks.

The issue of corporate governance and search for optimal governance structure has also recently received considerable attention in conventional economic literature and public policy debates. The traditional shareholder, value-centered view of corporate governance is being questioned in favor of a corporate governance structure extended to a wide circle of stakeholders and incorporating each stakeholder's claims, rights, and obligations. All revealed religions would agree that the governance model should be a stakeholder-oriented model where governance structure and process, at the system and firm levels, protect the rights of stakeholders.

Whereas the Western conventional system is struggling with finding convincing arguments to justify stakeholders' participation in governance, the foundation of a stakeholder model is found in Islam's principles of property rights, of commitment to explicit and implicit contractual agreements, and to the implementation of an effective incentive system. The design of a system of governance in Islam can be best understood in light of the principles governing the rights of the individual, society, and state; the laws governing property ownership; and the framework of contracts.

Islam's recognition and protection of rights is not limited only to human beings but encompasses all forms of life as well as the environment. Each element of the creation of Allah (S.W.T.) has been endowed with certain rights and duties. Human rights are bundled with the responsibilities for which humans are held accountable. The importance of being conscious and mindful of the rights of others (of all stakeholders, human or nonhuman) and the significance of discharging the responsibilities associated with such rights is reflected by the following saying of the Prophet (P.B.U.H.): "So give to everyone who possesses a right *(kull dhi haq)* his right."

The first axiom of property rights in Islam is that Allah (S.W.T.) — the real owner, creator, and benefactor — reserves the right to prescribe for man (His vicegerent, recipient, and possessor) — the rules of property ownership, while it is in the temporal possession of man. Ownership rights in Islam originate from the concept of *Khilafah* (stewardship) as the Qur'an and *Sunnah* clearly and explicitly state: Allah (S.W.T.) is the sole owner of property and that man as vicegerent of Allah (S.W.T.) is merely trustee and custodian. This relationship implies that man has the right to use and manage his "private property" in a manner similar to that of a custodian and trustee. Property is not an end in itself, but a means to discharge effectively man's responsibilities as the vicegerent of Allah (S.W.T.).

Whereas the conventional stakeholders' theory is searching for sound arguments to incorporate implicit contracts into the theory of a business firm, the rights of and obligations to stakeholders are taken for granted in Islam. Principles of property rights in Islam clearly justify inclusion of stakeholders in the decision-making process.

The Islamic economic system is an incentive system based on the rules of *Shariah* with the ultimate goal of maintaining a just and harmonious social order. In Islam, the expected behavior of a firm would not be any different from the expected behavior of any other member of the society. In other words, the economic and moral behavior of a business is shaped by managers acting on behalf of owners; hence it becomes their fiduciary duty to manage the firm as a trust for all stakeholders and not for the owners alone. Consequently, it will be incumbent upon managers to ensure that the behavior of the firm conforms to the principles and the rules of *Shariah*.

The design of corporate governance in an Islamic economic system entails implementation of a rule-based incentive system such that compliance with the rules ensures efficient governance to preserve social justice and order among all members of society. This would imply the design of institutions and rules that induce or, if needed, compel managers to internalize the welfare of all stakeholders. In an Islamic system, the observance of rules of behavior guarantees an internalization of stakeholder rights, and no other institutional structure is needed. It is the duty of the Islamic administration to specify the appropriate corporate governance structure, "incorporating all stakeholders' rights into fiduciary duties of managers" of the firm on behalf of secondary stakeholders.

Conclusion

Our mother planet is desperately requesting our help. It deserves to be considered as a precious gift to look after and care for, a precious legacy to transmit safe and sane to guest generations to come and with a wiser "owners' manual." To this end, Islam, Christianity, and Judaism must now, more than ever, coordinate and use all their resources to repel any globally destructive economic and political forces. Our common human condition calls for crafting a shared sacred vision and mission that necessitate building a much stronger operational interfaith relational praxis, hence translating our common responsibility toward global peace for our respective societies and future generations.[67]

67. Mudge, *The Gift of Responsibility.*

Author's Profile:
Lewis Seymour Mudge Jr. (1929-2009)

Lewis Seymour Mudge, son and grandson of Presbyterian ministers, seems destined to have become a "rooted cosmopolitan"[1] with a strong interfaith global perspective and concern. His father, Lewis Seymour Mudge Sr., was Stated Clerk (or CEO) of the Presbyterian Church (1920-38), and participated in international conferences sponsored by the nascent ecumenical movement of pre–World War II. In 1937, Mudge Sr. took his seven-year-old son to the second of such meetings in Oxford, convened to focus on the churches' role in world society. Years later, in Oxford again as a Rhodes Scholar (1951-54), Mudge Jr. began adult life among a host of fellow international scholars. The following year, he graduated from Princeton Theological Seminary and was ordained a Presbyterian minister. Two years later, in process of earning his Ph.D. from the Department of Religion at Princeton University, he became the first theological secretary for the World Alliance of Reformed Churches (WARC), in Geneva, Switzerland, with offices adjacent to those of the World Council of Churches. The two organizations regularly shared ideas and personnel. In this capacity for five years (1957-62), Mudge traveled widely to participate in conferences throughout Europe and in India, Brazil, and Africa.

At Amherst College from 1962 to 1976, Mudge was Minister to the College and professor of philosophy and religion. Besides courses in Old and New Testament, he taught in an interdisciplinary program, "Problems of Inquiry," and co-led a seminar on Marxism. During these years, he and his

---

1. Kwame Appiah uses this phrase in *Cosmopolitanism: Ethics in a World of Strangers* (New York: W. W. Norton, 2006), as Mudge acknowledges in *The Gift of Responsibility*, p. 47. — Ed.

family lived in the former home of Emily Dickinson, owned by the college, becoming familiar with the work of that world-renowned poet. When racial and gender issues swept the college in the 1960s, Mudge led groups of student activists to the South for voter registration, tutoring, and civil rights marches. Primed by his church to the issue of gender-exclusive language, he persuaded his colleagues to substitute terms, as in "chairperson" for "chairman," to better suit increasing numbers of women faculty.

Mudge's openness to fresh ideas derived from a number of disciplines: philosophy and theology dominated, but also ethics, social theory, history, and more recently, economics. During a sabbatical year in Paris (1973-74), he studied with Paul Ricoeur, the French philosopher of anthropology (via existential phenomenology and hermeneutics). This contact led to Mudge's editing a collection of Ricoeur's essays illustrating his biblical analysis.[2] Also central to Mudge's thinking were the theological ethics of Reinhold and H. Richard Niebuhr and the seminal ideas of Hannah Arendt. During the late 1970s and '80s, while Dean at McCormick Theological Seminary in Chicago, Mudge represented the Reformed Churches in a series of bilateral dialogues between WARC and the Papacy. This responsibility continued when Mudge became Dean at San Francisco Theological Seminary and a core professor at the Graduate Theological Union (GTU), Berkeley, in 1987. Naturally, he had kept up with the U.S. Bishops' pastoral on American economic life in 1984 and several Vatican encyclicals on economic values.[3] Mudge continued to teach ecumenical ethics at the GTU until his death in 2009. Two months later, the National Council of the Churches of Christ in the USA and Church World Service posthumously honored him with the Joseph Cardinal Bernardin Award for Ecumenical Service.

2. Paul Ricoeur, *Essays on Biblical Interpretation,* ed. Lewis S. Mudge (Philadelphia: Fortress Press, 1980). [Mudge also wrote an essay recommending Ricoeur for the prestigious Kluge Prize, subsequently awarded him by the Library of Congress in 2004. — *Ed.*]

3. "Catholic Social Teaching and the U.S. Economy," *Origins* 14 (15 November 1984).

Contributors' Profiles

John C. Bogle is the longest-serving leader in the U.S. mutual fund industry. After graduating from Princeton University in 1951 with an A.B. degree in economics, *magna cum laude,* he entered the mutual fund industry. In 1974, he founded the Vanguard Group, serving as chief executive and then senior chairman through 1999, and since then as President of its Bogle Financial Markets Research Center. In 1975, he also founded the world's first index mutual fund. With current assets totaling more than $2 trillion, Vanguard is the largest mutual fund organization in the world. In 1999, *Fortune* magazine named Mr. Bogle one of the investment industry's four "Giants of the 20th Century," and in 2004, *Time* magazine named Mr. Bogle one of the hundred "Most Influential People in the World." A prolific writer and speaker, Mr. Bogle has written ten books. The most recent are: *The Clash of the Culture: Investment vs. Speculation* (2012), *Don't Count on It!* (2011), *Enough.* (2008), and *The Little Book of Common Sense Investing* (2007).

Elliot N. Dorff is currently Rector and Distinguished Professor of Philosophy at the American Jewish University (formerly, the University of Judaism), Los Angeles. Earlier, he directed the university's rabbinical and master's programs. He was ordained a conservative rabbi by the Jewish Theological Seminary of America in 1970 and earned his Ph.D. in philosophy from Columbia University in 1971 with a dissertation in moral theory. For over thirty years, as a Visiting Professor at UCLA School of Law, he has taught a course on Jewish law. Dorff has received the *Journal of Law and Religion*'s Lifetime Achievement Award, and holds three honorary doctoral degrees. He is a past president of Jewish Family Service, and is a member of the ethics committee at U.C.L.A. Medical Center and the Jewish Homes for the Aged. He serves as co-chair of the Priest-Rabbi Dialogue of the Los Angeles Archdiocese and the Board of Rabbis of Southern California, and he is immediate past president of the Academy for Jewish, Christian, and Muslim Studies centered at UCLA. Dorff's publications include over two hundred articles on Jewish thought, law, and ethics, together with twenty books, among them *Jewish Choices, Jewish Voices: Money* (edited with Louis E. Newman, 2008) and *The Jewish Approach to Repairing the World (Tikkun Olam): A Brief Introduction for Christians* (with Cory Willson) (2008).

John C. Knapp, Ph.D., is President and Professor at Hope College, a national liberal arts college in Holland, Michigan. Prior to this appointment he was University Professor and founding director of the Frances Marlin Mann Center for Ethics and Leadership at Samford University, Birmingham, Alabama, where he supported teaching and research across the university's eight schools and served as a resource to professional communities. Earlier, he was professor of ethics at Georgia State University's J. Mack Robinson College of Business and founding director of the Center for Ethics and Corporate Responsibility, as well as adjunct professor of Christian ethics at Columbia Theological Seminary. His books include *How the Church Fails Businesspeople (and What Can Be Done About It)* (Eerdmans, 2011); *For the Common Good: The Ethics of Leadership in the 21st Century* (Praeger, 2007); *Leaders on Ethics: Real-World Perspectives on Today's Business Challenges* (Praeger, 2007); and *The Business of Higher Education* (ABC-CLIO, 2009). Internationally known as a speaker and seminar leader, he chairs the Oxford Conclave on Global Higher Education and is a fellow of the Caux Round Table. He earned the Doctor of Philosophy degree at the University of Wales, United Kingdom; the Master of Arts at Columbia Theological Seminary; and the Bachelor of Science at Georgia State University.

Djamel Eddine Laouisset, Ph.D., is Professor of Management at Alhosn University Faculty of Business, Abu Dhabi, United Arab Emirates (UAE). His past positions include Expert at the Center for Research and Studies (UAE), Expert and Advisor to the United Arab Emirates' Minister of Economy (UAE), University Vice Chancellor for Graduate Studies, Research and External Relations (Algeria), Director of Studies and Research at the National Institute for Global Strategic Studies (Algeria), Advisor to the CEO of the Algerian Development Bank (Algeria), and Expert-Trainer at the Arab Iron and Steel Union (Arab League-Algeria). He taught at the Universities of Constantine and Annaba (Algeria), Tunis (Tunisia), Tripoli (Libya), Ajman and Dubai (UAE). He holds a bachelor's degree from the University of Algiers (Algeria) and two master's degrees and a doctorate from the University of Miami (USA). Professor Laouisset was a Member of the National Scientific and Technology Research Council (Algeria). As a professor at Hamdan Bin Mohammed e-University (Dubai), he initiated the Distinguished Visiting Professorship (DVP) Program as well as the Leadership and Advancement Program (LEAP). He was Vice-President of Business and Training at Alhosn University Center for Research and Consulting (Abu Dhabi). Currently, he is the Middle East Representative for the Africa Academy of Management. His specialties are International Business, Organizational Behavior, Strategic Management, and Islamic Management.

Bibliography

Books and Journal Articles

Abrecht, Paul. "The Development of Ecumenical Social Thought and Action." In *History of the Ecumenical Movement: The Ecumenical Advance, 1948-1968,* vol. 2, edited by Ruth Rouse, Stephen C. Neill, and Harold E. Fey. Geneva: World Council of Churches, 1993.

Akerlof, George, and Robert J. Shiller. *Animal Spirits: How Human Psychology Drives the Economy and Why It Matters for Global Capitalism.* Princeton: Princeton University Press, 2008.

Albrecht, Gloria. "Detroit: Still the 'Other' America," *Journal of the Society of Christian Ethics* 29, no. 1 (Spring/Summer 2009): 3-24.

Alpert, Daniel, Robert Hockett, and Nouriel Roubini. "The Way Forward: Moving from the Post-Bubble, Post-Bust Economy to Renewed Growth and Competitiveness," New America Foundation Policy Paper, 10 October 2011.

The Accra Confession: Covenanting for Justice in the Economy of the Earth. Geneva: The World Alliance of Reformed Churches, 2004.

Baeck, Louis. *The Mediterranean Tradition in Economic Thought.* New York: Routledge, 1994.

Barth, Karl. *The Humanity of God.* Translated by John Newton Thomas and Thomas Weiser. Richmond, VA: John Knox Press, 1960.

Becker, Carl L. *The Heavenly City of the Eighteenth-Century Philosophers.* New Haven: Yale University Press, 1932.

Becker, Gary. *The Economic Approach to Human Behavior.* Chicago: University of Chicago Press, 1976.

Benstein, Jeremy. *The Way into Judaism and the Environment.* Woodstock, VT: Jewish Lights, 2006.

Bernstein, Ellen. *Ecology and the Jewish Spirit.* Woodstock, VT: Jewish Lights, 1998.

144

Binswanger, Hans Christoph. *Money and Magic: A Critique of the Modern Economy in the Light of Goethe's Faust.* Chicago: University of Chicago Press, 1994.

Bouwsma, William J. *John Calvin: A Sixteenth-Century Portrait.* New York: Oxford University Press, 1988.

Brown, Gordon. *Beyond the Crash: Overcoming the First Crisis of Globalization.* New York: Free Press, 2010.

Calvin, John. *Institutes of the Christian Religion,* vol. 1. Edited by John T. McNeill. Translated by Ford L. Battles. Philadelphia: Westminster, 1960.

Christian Faith and Economic Life. New York: United Church of Christ, 1987.

Carlyle, Thomas. *Past and Present.* Project Gutenberg (originally published 1843).

The Constitution of the Presbyterian Church (USA), Part I: Book of Confessions. New York and Atlanta: Office of the General Assembly, 1983.

Daly, Mary. *Gyn/Ecology: The Metaethics of Radical Feminism.* Boston: Beacon Press, 1990.

The Documents of Vatican II. Edited by Walter M. Abbott, SJ. Translated by Joseph Gallagher. New York: Guild Press, American Press, Association Press, 1966.

Dorff, Elliot N. *For the Love of God and People: A Philosophy of Jewish Law* Philadelphia: Jewish Publication Society, 2007.

———. *The Way into Tikkun Olam (Repairing the World).* Woodstock, VT: Jewish Lights, 2005.

———. *To Do the Right and the Good: A Jewish Approach to Modern Social Ethics.* Philadelphia: Jewish Publication Society, 2002.

———, with Reverend Cory Willson, *The Jewish Approach to Repairing the World (Tikkun Olam): A Brief Introduction for Christians.* Woodstock, VT: Jewish Lights, 2008.

Dorrien, Gary. "Economic Crisis, Economic Democracy, Religious Awakening," *Tikkun,* September/October 2010.

———. "Financial Collapse: Lessons from the Social Gospel," *The Christian Century,* 30 December 2008.

Economic Justice for All. Pastoral Letter of the National Conference of Catholic Bishops. Washington, DC: U.S. Catholic Conference, 1986.

Freeman, Edward R. *Strategic Management: A Stakeholder Approach.* Boston: Pittman, 1984.

Freeman, Samuel. "Criminal Liability and the Duty to Aid the Distressed," *University of Pennsylvania Law Review* 142, no. 5 (May 1994).

Friedman, Milton. *Capitalism and Freedom.* Chicago: University of Chicago Press, 1962.

George, Henry. *Progress and Poverty* [1879]. Reprint, London: Kegan Paul, Tench & Co., 1886.

Ghazanfar, S. M. *Medieval Islamic Economic Thought.* London: Routledge, 2004.

Goudzwaard, Bob, with Julio de Santa Ana. "The Modern Roots of Economic Globalization." In Julio de Santa Ana et al., *Beyond Idealism: A Way Forward for Ecumenical Social Ethics.* Grand Rapids: Eerdmans, 2006.

Habermas, Jürgen. *Theory of Communicative Action,* vol. 2. Boston: Beacon Press, 1987.

Hacker, Jacob S., and Paul Pierson. "What Krugman & Stiglitz Can Tell Us," *New York Review of Books* 59, no. 14 (September 27, 2012): 55-58.

Hadsell, Heidi. "Ecumenical Social Ethics Now." In *Beyond Idealism: A Way Forward in Ecumenical Social Ethics,* edited by Robin Gurney, Heidi Hadsell, and Lewis Mudge. Grand Rapids: Eerdmans, 2006.

Hardt, Michael, and Antonio Negri. *Empire.* Cambridge, MA: Harvard University Press, 2000.

Hemmati, Minu, et al. *Multi-stakeholder Processes for Governance and Sustainability: Beyond Deadlock and Conflict.* London: Earthscan, 2002.

Holy Bible, New Revised Standard Version. Oxford: Oxford University Press, 1989.

Huntington, Samuel P. *The Clash of Civilizations and the Remaking of World Order.* New York: Simon & Schuster, 2002.

Islahi, A. Azim. *History of Economic Thought in Islam.* Aligharh, India: Department of Economics, Aligharh Muslim University, 1996.

John Paul II, Pope. *Centesimus annus,* Encyclical Letter. Vatican City: Libreria Editrice Vaticana, 1991.

Johnson, Simon. "The Quiet Coup: How Bankers Seized America," *The Atlantic,* May 2009.

Kelly, Marjorie. *The Divine Right of Capital: Dethroning the Corporate Aristocracy.* San Francisco: Berrett-Koehler, 2001.

Khaldun, Ibn. *Muqaddimah.* Cairo: Al-Maktabah al-Tijariyyah al-Kubra, 1950.

Kinnamon, Michael, and Brian Cope, eds. *The Ecumenical Movement: An Anthology of Key Texts and Voices.* Grand Rapids: Eerdmans, 1997.

Klein, Naomi. *The Shock Doctrine: The Rise of Disaster Capitalism.* New York: Picador, 2007.

Klenicki, Rabbi Leon, ed. *Toward a Theological Encounter: Jewish Understandings of Christianity.* New York: Paulist Press, 1991.

Koopmans, Tjalling C. *Three Essays on the State of Economic Science.* New York: McGraw-Hill, 1968.

Kristof, Nicholas, and Sheryl WuDunn. *Half the Sky: Turning Oppression into Opportunity for Women Worldwide.* New York: A. Knopf, 2009.

Levinas, Emmanuel. *Totality and Infinity.* Pittsburgh: Duquesne University Press, 1962.

Locke, John. "An Essay Concerning the True Original, Extent and End of Civil Government." In *Social Contract: Essays by Locke, Hume and Rousseau,* edited by Ernst Barker. New York: Oxford University Press, 1960.

McCarthy, Cormac. *The Road.* New York: A. Knopf, 2006.

Migliore, Daniel L. *Faith Seeking Understanding.* Grand Rapids: Eerdmans, 1991.

Mittleman, Alan R. "The Modern Jewish Condition," *First Things* (October 1994).

Morgenson, Gretchen, and Joshua Rosner. *Reckless Engagement: How Outsized Ambition, Greed and Corruption Led to Economic Armageddon.* New York: New York Times Books/Henry Holt & Co., 2011.

Mudge, Lewis S. "Ecumenical Social Thought." In *History of the Ecumenical Movement, 1968-2000,* vol. 3, edited by John Briggs, Mercy A. Oduyoye, and George Tsetsis. Geneva: World Council of Churches, 2004.

———, ed. *Essays on Biblical Interpretation,* by Paul Ricoeur. Philadelphia: Fortress Press, 1980.

———. *The Church as Moral Community: Ecclesiology and Ethics in Ecumenical Debate.* New York: Continuum, 1998.

———. *The Gift of Responsibility: The Promise of Dialogue Among Christians, Jews, and Muslims.* New York: Continuum, 2008.

———. *The Sense of a People: Toward a Church for the Human Future.* Philadelphia: Trinity Press International, 1992.

Niebuhr, H. Richard. *Christ and Culture.* New York: Harper & Row, 1951.

———. *The Responsible Self.* New York: Harper & Row, 1963.

Niebuhr, Reinhold. *The Nature and Destiny of Man,* vol. 1. New York: Charles Scribner's Sons, 1941.

———. *Moral Man and Immoral Society.* New York: Charles Scribner's Sons, 1932.

Novak, David. *The Image of the Non-Jew in Judaism.* Lewiston, NY: Edwin Mellen, 1983.

Nussbaum, Martha. *Women and Human Development: The Capabilities Approach.* Cambridge: Cambridge University Press, 2011.

Obama, Barack. *The Audacity of Hope: Thoughts on Reclaiming the American Dream.* New York: Crown, 2006.

"The Oxford Declaration on Christian Faith and Economics," *Transformation* 7, no. 2 (April-June 1990).

Pliskin, Zelig. *Guard Your Tongue.* Jerusalem: Aish Ha-Torah, 1975.

Rasmussen, Larry. *Moral Fragments and Moral Community.* Minneapolis: Fortress Press, 1993.

Reeder, John H., and Gene Outka. *Prospects for a Common Morality.* Princeton: Princeton University Press, 1991.

A Reformed Understanding of Usury for the Twenty-first Century, Report of the Advisory Committee for Social Witness Policy, 217th General Assembly of the Presbyterian Church (USA). Louisville: Office of the General Assembly, 2006.

Ricoeur, Paul. *Figuring the Sacred: Religion, Narrative and Imagination.* Edited by Mark I. Wallace. Translated by David Pellauer. Minneapolis: Augsburg Fortress Press, 1995.

————. *Freud and Philosophy: An Essay in Interpretation.* New Haven: Yale University Press, 1970.

————. *The Just.* Translated by David Pellauer. Chicago: University of Chicago Press, 2000.

Ruether, Rosemary Radford. *Integrating Ecofeminism, Globalization, and World Religions.* Lanham, MD: Rowman & Littlefield, 2005.

Sacks, Jonathan. *The Dignity of Difference.* New York: Continuum, 2002.

Seligman, Adam B. *The Idea of Civil Society.* New York: Free Press, 1992.

Sen, Amartya. *Development as Freedom.* New York: A. Knopf, 2001.

————. *On Ethics & Economics.* Oxford: Blackwell, 1987.

Simon, Ernst. "The Neighbor *(Re'a)* Whom We Shall Love." In *Modern Jewish Ethics,* edited by Marvin Fox. Columbus: Ohio State University Press, 1975.

Smith, Adam. *An Inquiry into the Nature and Causes of the Wealth of Nations* [1776]. Chicago: University of Chicago Press, 1977.

Solo, Robert A. "Values and Judgments in the Discourse of the Sciences." In *Value Judgment and Income Distribution,* edited by Robert Al Solo and Charles A. Anderson. New York: Praeger, 1981.

Taylor, Charles. *Sources of the Self: The Making of the Modern Identity.* Cambridge, MA: Harvard University Press, 1989.

Tillich, Paul. "The Meaning and Justification of Religious Symbols." In *Religious Experience and Truth,* edited by Sydney Hook. New York: New York University Press, 1961.

Visser 't Hooft, W. A., and J. H. Oldham. *The Church and Its Function in Society.* Chicago: Willett, Clark & Co., 1937.

Vocation and Work. Louisville: Office of the General Assembly, Presbyterian Church (USA), 1990.

Wallis, Jim. *Rediscovering Values: On Wall Street, Main Street and Your Street.* New York: Howard Books, 2010.

Walzer, Michael. *The Revolution of the Saints.* Cambridge, MA: Harvard University Press, 1982.

Waskow, Arthur, ed. *Torah of the Earth: Exploring 4,000 Years of Ecology in Jewish Thought,* 2 vols. Woodstock, VT: Jewish Lights, 2000.

Wickeri, Philip L. "The Political Economy of Christian Mission," unpublished essay presented in Lew Mudge's class on "Globalization, Ecumenism and Ethics," Graduate Theological Union, Berkeley, California, October 2008.

Wolterstorff, Nicholas. "Has the Cloak Become a Cage? Charity, Justice, and Economic Activity." In *Rethinking Materialism,* edited by Robert Wuthnow. Grand Rapids: Eerdmans, 1995.

"The Summit," *The Economist,* 8-14 June 2013, p. 11.

"The World Economy: Semi-Rational Exuberance," *The Economist,* 26 January–1 February 2013.

Newspaper and Online Articles; PBS Television Broadcasts

Alden, William. "Returns at Hedge Funds Run by Women Beat the Industry, Report Says," http://dealbook.nytimes.com/2013/01/10/returns-at-hedge-funds-run-by-women-beat-the-industry-report-says/.

Alperovitz, Gar. "Wall Street Is Too Big to Regulate," Op-Ed, *New York Times*, 23 July 2012, p. A21.

Angelides, Phil. "On the Anniversary of Dodd-Frank: Wall Street Fights Back and American Families Fight to Survive," *Huffington Post*, 21 July 2011, http://www.huffingtonpost.com/phil-angelides/dodd-frank-anniversary.

Appelbaum, Binyamin. "Fed Extends Stimulus as Growth Fails," *New York Times*, 31 October 2013, http://www.nytimes.com/2013/10/31/business/economy/fed-maintains-stimulus-awaiting-sustainable-growth.html?page wanted=1&_r=0.

―――. "Fed Officials Try to Ease Concern of Stimulus End," *New York Times*, 27 June 2013, http://www.nytimes.com/2013/06/28/business/economy/fed-has-not-changed-commitments-official-says.html.

―――. "Optimistic Fed Outlines an End to Its Stimulus," *New York Times*, 19 June 2013, http://www.nytimes.com/2013/06/20/business/economy/fed-more-optimistic-about-economy-maintains-bond-buying.html.

Arango, Tom, and Clifford Krauss. "China Is Reaping Biggest Benefits of Iraq Oil Boom," *New York Times*, 2 June 2013, http://www.nytimes.com/2013/06/03/world/middleeast/china-reaps-biggest-benefits-of-iraq-oil-boom.html?_r=0. *(Ed.)*

Associated Press. "Reports Signal Lift in U.S. Economy," *New York Times*, 27 November 2012, http://www.nytimes.com/2012/11/28/business/economy/report-signals-lift-in-business-spending.html.

Baker, Dean. "California Gold Rush? Righting Underwater Mortgages," www.nationofchange.org, 17 July 2012.

Barboza, David. "China's Credit Squeeze Relaxes as Interest Rates Drop," *New York Times*, 21 June 2013, http://www.nytimes.com/2013/06/22/business/global/chinas-bank-lending-crunch-eases.html?_r=0.

"Be Afraid," *The Economist*, 1 October 2011, p. 13.

Benedict XVI, Pope. *Caritas in Veritate*, Encyclical Letter, 29 June 2009. Vatican City: Libreria Editrice Vaticana, 2009.

Bernstein, Jared. "Lessons of the Great Recession: How the Safety Net Performed," *New York Times*, 24 June 2013, http://economix.blogs.nytimes.com/2013/06/24/lessons-of-the-great-recession-how-the-safety-net-performed/?_r=0.

Besser, Anne Cucchiara, and Kalman J. Kaplan. "The Good Samaritan: Jewish and American Legal Perspectives," *The Journal of Law and Religion* 10, no. 1 (Winter 1994).

Biden, Joseph R. "China's Rise Isn't Our Demise," Op-Ed, *New York Times*, 8 September 2011, p. A29.

Birger, Jon. "The Prophet of Dollars and Sense," *Brown Alumni Magazine*, May/June 2009, pp. 22-26.

Black, George. "The TINA Syndrome: Is There Life After Thatcher?" *Nation*, 8 May 2009.

Boulakia, Jean David C. "Ibn Khaldûn: A Fourteenth-Century Economist," *Journal of Political Economy* 79 (1971): 1105-18.

Bowley, Graham, and Liz Alderman. "In European Crisis, Little Hope for a Quick Fix," *New York Times*, 30 September 2011, p. A1.

Bradsher, Keith. Interview, *Charlie Rose*, PBS, 17 July 2012.

Brockleman, C. "Al-Mawardi," *The Encyclopedia of Islam*, 2nd ed. Leiden: Brill, 1960-2005.

Brooks, David. "An Economy of Faith and Trust," Op-Ed, *New York Times*, 15 January 2009, p. A29.

———. "The Lost Decade?" Op-Ed, *New York Times*, 26 September 2011, p. A27.

———. "The Planning Fallacy," Op-Ed, *New York Times*, 16 September 2011, p. A23.

Buster, William. Interview, *Charlie Rose*, PBS, 12 October 2011. www.pbs.org.

"Christine Lagarde," Times Topics, *New York Times*, 21 July 2012.

"Christine Lagarde's Tough Message," *New York Times*, 31 August 2011, p. A26.

Creswell, Julie. "Chinese Investors Pursue U.S. Property Deals," *New York Times*, 25 June 2013, http://www.nytimes.com/2013/06/26/business/global/chinese -investors-pursue-us-real-estate-deals.html.

"Databases, Tables & Calculators by Subject," Bureau of Labor Statistics, 26 June 2013, http://data.bls.gov/timeseries/LNS14000000.

Dewan, Shaila. "Needy States Use Housing Aid Cash to Plug Budgets," *New York Times*, 16 May 2012, p. A1.

———, and Louise Story. "U.S. May Back Refinance Plan for Mortgages," *New York Times*, 24 August 2011, p. A1.

Dienst, Jonathan. "FBI Arrests 2 Women in Connection with Madoff Case," 18 November 2010, www.nbcnewyork.com/news/local/Feds-Make-Another -Arrest-in-Madoff-Case-108923469.html.

Dorff, Elliot N. "The Interaction of Jewish Law with Morality," *Judaism* 26, no. 4 (Fall 1977).

Eavis, Peter. "An Enigma in the Mortgage Market That Elevates Rates," *New York Times*, DealBook, 18 September 2012.

———, and Nathaniel Popper. "Libor Scandal Shows Many Flaws in Rate-Setting," *New York Times*, DealBook, 19 July 2012.

Eliash, Ben Zion. "To Leave or Not to Leave: The Good Samaritan in Jewish Law," *Saint Louis University Law Journal* 38, no. 3 (Spring 1994).

Ewing, Jack. "At Davos, Financial Leaders Debate Reform and Monetary Policy," *New York Times*, DealBook, 23 January 2013.

————. "Lowering Forecast, European Central Bank Keeps Rate Steady," 6 June 2013, http://www.nytimes.com/2013/06/07/business/global/ecb-keeps -interest-rates-unchanged-in-hopes-for-recovery.html?_r=0.

Feldstein, Martin S. "How to Stop the Drop in Home Values," Op-Ed, *New York Times*, 13 October 2011, p. A25.

"Fight for the Housing Trust Fund," *New York Times*, 12 January 2013, http://www .nytimes.com/2013/01/13/opinion/sunday/fight-for-the-housing-trust-fund .html?_r=0.

Folbre, Nancy. "Is Another Economics Possible?" *New York Times*, Business Day, 19 July 2010.

"The Global Religious Landscape: A Report on the Size and Distribution of the World's Major Religious Groups as of 2010," December 18, 2012, http://www .pewforum.org/global-religious-landscape.aspx.

Gough, Neil. "Cash Crunch in China as Rising Interest Rates Crimp Lending," *New York Times*, 20 June 2013, http://www.nytimes.com/2013/06/21/business/ global/china-manufacturing-contracts-to-lowest-level-in-9-months.html ?pagewanted=1&_r=0.

Gopnik, Adam. "Decline, Fall, Rinse, Repeat," *The New Yorker*, 12 September 2011.

Harkness, Georgia. "Christian Ethics," www.religion-online.org/showchapter .asp?title=802&C=1085.

Isidore, Chris. "It's Official: Recession since December '07," money.cnn .com/2008/12/01/news/economy/recession/index.htm.

————, and Jennifer Liberto, "Mortgage Deal Could Bring Billions in Relief," CNNMoney, 15 February 2012.

Jay, Peter, and Margaret Jay. Economic Editorials, *The Times*. London, 1986.

Johnson, Simon. "Betrayed by Basel," *New York Times*, 10 January 2013, http:// economix.blogs.nytimes.com/2013/01/10/betrayed-by-basel.

Jolly, David. "Markets Fall on China's Credit Squeeze and Fed's Exit Plan," *New York Times*, 20 June 2013, http://www.nytimes.com/2013/06/21/business/ global/daily-stock-market-activity.html. *(Ed.)*

Joshi, Pradnya. "We Knew They Got Raises: But This?" *New York Times*, 3 July 2011, p. BU1.

Kanter, James. "I.M.F. Urges Europe's Strongest to Shoulder Burdens of Currency Bloc," *New York Times*, 22 June 2012, p. B3.

"Keynes, John Maynard (1883-1946)." The Concise Encyclopedia of Economics, http://www.econlib.org/library/Enc/bios/Keynes.html.

King, Desmond S., and Rogers M. Smith. "On Race, the Silence Is Bipartisan," Op-Ed, *New York Times*, 3 September 2011, p. A15.

Kirschenbaum, Aaron. "The Bystander's Duty to Rescue in Jewish Law," *Journal of Religious Ethics* 8 (1980).

Kristof, Nicholas D. "Crony Capitalism Comes Home," Op-Ed, *New York Times,* 27 October 2011, p. A25.

———. "She's (Rarely) the Boss," Op-Ed, *New York Times,* 26 January 2013, http://www.nytimes.com/2013/01/27/opinion/sunday/kristof-shes-rarely -the-boss.html?_r=0.

Krugman, Paul. "Confronting the Malefactors," Op-Ed, *New York Times,* 7 October 2011, p. A23.

———. "Free to Die," Op-Ed, *New York Times,* 16 September 2011, p. A23.

———. "Letting Banks Walk," Op-Ed, *New York Times,* 18 July 2011, p. A17.

———. "The Big Fail," Op-Ed, http://www.nytimes.com/2013/01/07/opinion/ krugman-the-big-fail.html?_r=0.

———. "The Social Contract," Op-Ed, *New York Times,* 23 September 2011, p. A27.

Kuttner, Robert. "The Debt We Shouldn't Pay," *The New York Review of Books,* 9 May 2013, pp. 16-18.

Lattman, Peter. "U.S. Sues Wells Fargo, Alleging Mortgage Deceit," *New York Times,* DealBook, 9 October 2012.

Lawrence, Jeffrey, and Luis Moreno-Caballud. "In Hurricane Sandy Relief, a Reminder of Occupy's Original Spirit," *Yes! Magazine,* 29 November 2012, http://www.nationofchange.org/hurricane-sandy-relief-reminder-occupy -s-original-spirit-1354181886.

Li Congjun. "Rebalancing the Global Economy," Op-Ed, *New York Times,* 17 July 2012.

"A Lifeline for Homeowners," *New York Times,* 26 August 2011, p. A26.

Liptak, Adam. "Justices, by 5-4, Uphold Health Care Law, Roberts in Majority, Victory for Obama," *New York Times,* 29 June 2012, p. A1.

Lipton, Eric, and Ben Protess. "House, Set to Vote on 2 Bills Is Seen as an Ally of Wall St.," *New York Times,* 30 October 2013, http://dealbook.nytimes.com/ 2013/10/28/house-set-to-vote-on-2-bills-is-seen-as-an-ally-of-wall-st/.

Lipton, Eric, and Ken Sack. "Fiscal Footnote: Big Senate Gift to Drug Maker," 19 January 2013, http://www.nytimes.com/2013/01/20/us/medicare-pricing -delay-is-political-win-for-amgen-drug-maker.html?pagewanted=all.

Lohr, Steve. "First Make Money. Also, Do Good," *New York Times,* 14 August 2011, p. B3.

Lowrey, Annie. "I.M.F. Lowers Its Forecast for Global Growth," *New York Times,* 9 October 2012, p. B1.

———. "I.M.F. Concedes Major Missteps in Bailout of Greece," *New York Times,* 5 June 2013, http://www.nytimes.com/2013/06/06/business/global/ imf-concedes-major-missteps-in-bailout-of-greece.html.

———. "I.M.F. Forecasts Modest Global Economic Growth, at Best," 23 January

2013, http://www.nytimes.com/2013/01/24/business/economy/imf-forecast
-global-economic-growth-modest-at-best.html.

———. "Pay Still High at Bailed-Out Companies, Report Says," *New York Times*,
28 January 2013, http://www.nytimes.com/2013/01/29/business/generous
-executive-pay-at-bailed-out-companies-treasury-watchdog-says.html.

MacFarquhar, Neil. "As Arab Autocrats Are Toppled, Their Fates Grow More
Extreme," *New York Times*, 21 October 2011, p. A13.

"The March of Protest," *The Economist*, June 29, 2013, pp. 11-12.

Marmor, Theodore R., and Jerry L. Mashaw. "How Do You Say 'Economic Security'?" Op-Ed, *New York Times*, 24 September 2011, p. A19.

"Martha Stewart Starts Prison Term," BBC News, 8 October 2004, http://news
.bbc.co.uk/2/hi/americas/3726990.stm.

Martin, Andrew. "Banks Penalized for Performance in Mortgage Modification
Program," *New York Times*, 10 June 2011, p. B4.

McInnes, Mitchel. "Protecting the Good Samaritan: Defences for the Rescuer
in Anglo-Canadian Criminal Law," *Criminal Law Quarterly* 36, no. 3 (May
1994).

"More of the Same Won't Save Europe," *New York Times*, 30 September 2011,
p. A20.

Morgenson, Gretchen. "An Unstoppable Climb in C.E.O. Pay," *New York Times*,
29 June 2013, http://www.nytimes.com/2013/06/30/business/an-unstoppable
-climb-in-ceo-pay.html?_r=0.

———. "The Rescue That Missed Main Street," *New York Times*, 28 August
2011, p. BU1.

———. Interview, "Moyers and Company," PBS, 26 May 2013.

———. Interview, "Moyers and Company," PBS, 26 October 2013.

———. "A $13 Billion Reminder of What's Wrong," *New York Times*, 27 October
2013, http://www.nytimes.com/2013/10/27/business/a-13-billion-reminder
-of-whats-wrong.html.

"Mountain House Statement," Caux Round Table, 2010, accessed online at http://
www.cauxroundtable.org.

Murchison, Cameron. "Reformed Resources for Practical Theology: The Christian Life and Consumer Capitalism," unpublished paper, January 12, 2005.

Murthy, Raja. "Bhutan's happiness index goes global," www.atimes.com/atimes/
South_Asia/ND12Df02.htm.

Mutikani, Lucia. "U.S. First-Quarter Growth Is Cut," *New York Times*, 26 June
2013, http://www.nytimes.com/reuters/2013/06/26/business/26reuters
-usa-economy.html?_r=0.

Neuman, Scott. "Is the World Ready for a New Bretton Woods?" National Public
Radio, 29 October 2008, www.npr.org.

Nocera, Joe. "Financial Scandal Scorecard," Op-Ed, *New York Times*, 21 July
2012, p. A19.

Norris, Floyd. "The Myth of Fixing the Libor," *New York Times*, 28 September 2012, http://www.nytimes.com/2012/09/28/business/the-myth-of-fixing-the-libor-high-low-finance.html?emc=eta1&_r=0.

———. "Wielding Derivatives as a Tool for Deceit," *New York Times*, 27 June 2013, http://www.nytimes.com/2013/06/28/business/deception-by-derivative.html?pagewanted=1&_r=0.

North, Douglas C. "Economic Performance through Time," *American Economic Review*, June 1994.

"Occupy the Midwest Conference: Detroit, Aug. 23-26 [2012]," 21 July 2012, http://occupywallst.org.

"Occupy Movement, Occupy Wall Street," Times Topics, *New York Times*, 17 September 2012.

Packer, George. "Don't Look Down: The New Depression Journalism," *The New Yorker*, 29 April 2013, pp. 70-75.

Palaez, Marta. Interview, *Bill Moyer's Journal*, PBS, 20 March 2009, www.pbs.org.

Pfanner, Eric. "Outside the Forum, Impassioned Debates on Global Economics," *New York Times*, DealBook, 28 January 2012.

Pifer, Joseph. "Scholasticism," *Encyclopaedia Britannica*, 1978.

Popper, Nathaniel. "Behind the Rise in House Prices, Wall Street Buyers," 3 June 2013, *New York Times*, http://dealbook.nytimes.com/2013/06/03/behind-the-rise-in-house-prices-wall-street-buyers/.

———. "Wells Fargo Posts $4.6 Billion Profit, Up 17%," *New York Times*, Investment Banking, Wall Street Earnings, 13 July 2012.

———. "C.E.O. Pay Is Rising Despite the Din," http://www.nytimes.com/2012/06/17/business/executive-pay-still-climbing-despite-a-shareholder-din.html?pagewanted=all.

Portnoy, Frank, and Jesse Eisinger. "What's Inside America's Banks?" *Atlantic* (January/February 2013), pp. 60-71.

"Poverty: Not Always with Us," *The Economist*, 1-7 June 2013, pp. 22-24.

Powell, Michael. "Bank Accused of Pushing Mortgage Deals on Blacks," *New York Times*, 7 June 2009, p. A16.

———. "Federal Judge Rejects Suit by Baltimore Against Bank," *New York Times*, 8 January 2010, p. A11.

Protess, Ben. "Court Ruling Offers Path to Challenge Dodd-Frank," *New York Times*, 18 August 2011, DealBook, p. 3.

———. "Unlike Banks, This Wall St. Group Embraces Dodd Frank," *New York Times*, 21 August 2011, www.nytimes.com/dealbook.

———, and Peter Lattman. "After a Decade, SAC Capital Blinks," *New York Times*, 4 November 2013, http://dealbook.nytimes.com/2013/11/04/after-a-decade-sac-capital-blinks/?_r=0.

———, and Jessica Silver-Greenberg. "In Its First Action, Consumer Bureau Takes Aim at Capital One," *New York Times*, Legal/Regulatory, 18 July 2012.

"Protests: Not Quite Together," *The Economist*, 22-28 October 2011, pp. 73-75.

Rampell, Catherine. "Middling Jobs Numbers Signal a Long Path to Healthy Payrolls," *New York Times*, 7 June 2013, http://www.nytimes.com/2013/06/08/business/economy/us-added-175000-jobs-in-may-jobless-rate-rises-to-7-6.html?_r=0.

————. "Weak Job Gains May Cause Delay in Action by Fed," *New York Times*, 23 October 2013, http://www.nytimes.com/2013/10/23/business/economy/us-economy-added-148000-jobs-in-september.html?_r=0.

Rank, Mark R. "Poverty in America is Mainstream," *New York Times*, 2 November 2013, http://opinionator.blogs.nytimes.com/2013/11/02/poverty-in-america-is-mainstream/?_r=0.

Reuters. "Consumer Sentiment Ended June Near a Six-Year High," *New York Times*, 28 June 2013, http://www.nytimes.com/2013/06/29/business/economy/consumer-sentiment-ended-june-near-a-six-year-high.html?_r=0.

————. "Private Hiring Slows: Consumer Inflation Stays Muted," *New York Times*, 30 October 2013, http://www.nytimes.com/reuters/2013/10/30/business/30reuters-usa-economy-employment-adp.html.

Roose, Kevin. "The Invisible Hand Behind Bonuses on Wall Street," *New York Times*, 16 January 2012, p. B1.

Ruskin, John. "Munera Pulveris: Six Essays on the Elements of Political Economy," *Fraser's Magazine*, 1862-63, in *The Works of John Ruskin*, vol. 17. Cambridge: Cambridge University Press, 2010.

Said, Edward. "The Clash of Ignorance," *The Nation*, October 2001.

Savage, Charlie. "Wells Fargo Will Settle Mortgage Bias Charges," *New York Times*, 12 July 2012, p. B3.

Schmitt, Rick. "Prophet and Loss," *Stanford*, March/April 2009.

Schneider, Nathan. "How Occupy Wall Street Got Religion," *Nation of Change*, 21 December 2012, http://www.nationofchange.org/how-occupy-wall-street-got-religion-1356104826.

Schwartz, Nelson D., and Kevin Roose, "U.S. Sues 17 Mortgage Institutions," *New York Times*, 3 September 2011, p. B1.

Schwartz, Nelson D. "U.S. Growth Revised Up, but Year-End Slowdown Is Feared," *New York Times*, 30 November 2012, http://www.nytimes.com/2012/11/30/business/economy/third-quarter-gdp-growth-is-revised-up-to-2-7.html?_r=0.

————. "Economy Contracted Unexpectedly in Fourth Quarter," *New York Times*, 31 January 2013, http://www.nytimes.com/2013/01/31/business/economy/us-economy-unexpectedly-contracted-in-fourth-quarter.html?_r=0.

Scott, Mark. "British Regulators Plan Changes to Libor Oversight," *New York Times*, DealBook, 10 August 2012.

Sen, Amartya. "Capitalism Beyond the Crisis," *New York Review of Books*, 26 March 2009.

Shiller, Robert J. "A New Housing Boom? Don't Count on It," *New York Times,* 26 January 2013, http://www.nytimes.com/2013/01/27/business/housing-mar kets-future-still-has-many-clouds.html?_r=0.

Silver-Greenberg, Jessica. "Consumer Bureau Proposes New Mortgage Disclosure Rules," *New York Times,* Legal/Regulatory, 9 July 2012.

————, and Peter Eavis. "In Deal, Bank of America Extends Retreat from Mortgages," *New York Times,* 7 January 2013, http://dealbook.nytimes .com/2013/01/07/bank-of-america-extends-retreat-from-mortgages/.

————, and Ben Protess. "US Inquiry Broadens Into JP Morgan's Asia Hiring," *New York Times,* 1 November 2013, http://dealbook.nytimes.com/2013/ 11/01/u-s-inquiry-broadens-into-banks-asia-hiring.

Singer, Natasha. "In Executive Pay, a Rich Game of Thrones: C.E.O. Pay Gains May Have Slowed, But the Numbers Are Still Numbing," *New York Times,* 7 April 2012, p. BU1.

Smith, Martin. "The Untouchables," *Frontline,* PBS, 23 January 2013; rebroadcast, 21 May 2013.

Spengler, Joseph J. "Economic Thought of Islam: Ibn Khaldun," *Comparative Studies in Society and History* 6, no. 3 (1964): 268-306.

"A Step Backward in Bank Regulations," http://www.nytimes.com/2013/01/10/ opinion/a-step-backward-in-bank-regulations.html.

Stivers, Laura. "Making a Home for All in God's Compassionate Community: A Feminist Liberation Assessment of Christian Responses to Homelessness and Housing," *Journal of the Society of Christian Ethics* 28, no. 2 (Fall/Winter 2008): 51-74.

Stolberg, Sheryl Gay, and Robert Pear. "Obama Signs Health Care Overhaul Bill, with a Flourish," *New York Times,* 23 March 2010, www.nytimes.com/ health_policy.

Surowiecki, James. "Bankers Gone Wild," *The New Yorker,* 30 July 2012, p. 25.

Tavernise, Sabrina. "Soaring Poverty Casts Spotlight on 'Lost Decade,'" *New York Times,* 14 September 2011, http://nytimes.com/2011/09/14/us/14census.htm.

Thomas, Landon Jr., "Financial Fears Gain Credence as Unrest Shakes Turkey," *New York Times,* 5 June 2013, http://www.nytimes.com/2013/06/06/world/ europe/financial-fears-as-street-unrest-shakes-turkey.html?pagewanted=1.

"To Change the World, We Need to Change the Lives of Women," International Trade Union Confederation. www.scoop.co.nz/stories/print.

"United Nations Adopts International Day of Happiness [20 March]," 28 June 2012, http://www.prweb.com/releases/Internationaldayof/happiness/ prweb9652737.htm.

Ura, Karma, et al. "A Short Guide to Gross National Happiness Index," Centre for Bhutan Studies, Thimphu, Bhutan, 2012, www.grossnationalhappiness.com.

Wolf, Martin. "How Austerity Has Failed," *The New York Review of Books,* 11 July 2013, pp. 20-21.

Wyatt, Edward. "U.S. Consumer Watchdog to Issue Mortgage Rules, http://www.nytimes.com/2013/01/10/business/consumers-win-some-mortgage-safety-in-new-rules.html?_r=0.

Zillow Report, "The U.S. Housing Crisis: Where Are Home Loans Underwater?" http://www.zillow.com/visuals/negative-equity/#4/39.98/-107.01.

General Index

Abrahamic faiths, 5, 6, 8, 9, 14, 15, 16-17, 44, 45, 63, 84, 95; books of, 5, 12, 15-16, 20-21, 32, 99; diverse economic opinions within each, 122-23; symbol for, 104; and world economy, 30-31, 41, 45, 85-94, 99, 102-3, 104-6, 121-22, 131, 137-38; world population of, 87n.95. *See also* Christianity; Covenantal Humanism; Islam; Judaism; Torah
Akerlof, George, 61

Barth, Karl, 127, 129
Becker, Carl, 47
Benedict XVI, 78
Bourdieu, Pierre, 39n.27, 51, 51n.44, 55, 58
Bretton Woods Monetary and Financial Conference (1942), 42
"Bretton Woods II," 42n.30, 43, 67, 72-73, 74, 75, 88
Brooks, David, 3n.10, 11

Calvin, John: on church corruption and the poor, 125; and *Institutes of the Christian Religion*, 34, 39, 100; on lending, 34-36; quote: "theater of God's glory," 106
Calvinism, 47, 48
Capitalism, 50, 79, 83, 101, 123, 125-26; and Islam, 132; and Judaism, 119. *See also* Economics; Globalization

China, 74-77
Christianity, 5, 15, 16, 19, 99, 127. *See also* Abrahamic faiths; Reformed Protestantism
Consumer Financial Protection Bureau (CFPB), 28n.8, 29n.10, 93n.103
Covenantal Humanism, 8, 16-17, 80, 87, 95, 98, 104, 116. *See also* Abrahamic faiths

Depression, 41, 42
Dickinson, Emily, 106
Dodd-Frank Act, 27n.8, 28n.9, 58n.58, 93n.105
Dorrien, Gary, 5n.15, 25, 37n.22

Economics: and Christian tradition, 19-22, 99-100, 124-26; critics of, 30-33, 132-33; economic reasoning, 46, 52-54, 61, 78, 79, 97; global renewal of, 43-46; historic Western ideas about, 46-55; as humanities subject, 6, 14-16, 61, 95, 97, 98; and Islamic tradition, 133, 136; and Judaic tradition, 108-9; "liberation economics," 37, 41, 123; and "the market," 51, 99, 132, 133, 134; mathematical co-optation of, 6, 15, 51-52; "neoliberalism," 131; present and future of, 71-77, 79; and religion, 108. *See also* Capitalism; Marxism,

Scripture Reference Index